W9-BCT-259

B & T
5 8.9

WEIMAR

By the same author

Europe Since Hitler
Russia And Germany
The Fate Of The Revolution
The Road To War
A History Of Zionism

Weimar
A Cultural History 1918-1933

Walter Laqueur

G. P. Putnam's Sons, New York

Wingate College Library

FIRST AMERICAN EDITION, 1974

Copyright © 1974 by Walter Laqueur

All rights reserved. This book, or parts thereof, must not be reproduced in any form without permission.

SBN: 399-11449-1

Library of Congress Catalog
Card Number: 74-16605
3-20-75

PRINTED IN THE UNITED STATES OF AMERICA

Contents

Illustrations will be found following page 148.

063983

063983

Acknowledgments

The pictures in this book between pages 148 and 149 are reproduced by kind permission of the following:

Archiv für Kunst und Geschichte, 1, 5, 37, 39, 48; Bauhaus-Archiv, 45, 46; Bundesarchiv Koblenz, 14, 33; Courtesy of the Busch-Reisinger Museum, Harvard University, 44; Deutsche Fotothek Dresden, 15, 16, 17, 18, 19, 21, 22, 23, 24, 31, 43, 51, 52, 55; Dresden: Graph Sammlung, 7; John Freeman, 56; Kunstmuseum, Basel, 41; International Literatuur Bureau, Hilversum, 30; National Film Archive, 35; Radio Times Hulton Picture Library, 20, 38; Gordon Robertson, 4; Wallraf-Richartz-Museum, Köln, 42; Schiller Nationalmuseum, Marbach, 25, 26, 27, 29; Süddeutscher Verlag, 6, 9, 11, 12, 34, 36, 47, 49, 50, 53, 54, 57; Ullstein Bilderdienst, 2, 3, 8, 13, 32; Wiener Library, 28.

Picture captions by Anne Garrels

Preface

This introductory survey of Weimar culture was written to stimulate interest among general readers in what was, for better or worse, the first truly modern culture. I hope I shall not be criticized for failing to accomplish something which I did not want to achieve in the first place: namely to provide a full, definitive history of Weimar culture. While the purpose of this book is modest it was not easy to write. A general survey has to cover far more ground than a specialized study. It is not too difficult (to give but one example) to discuss the German literature of the 1920s at a leisurely pace within the framework of five hundred pages. To deal with the main trends in thirty or forty pages is of necessity a *tour de force* unlikely to be appreciated; experts will have no difficulty in faulting it on various counts, whereas the uninitiated may be confused by an abundance of references to unfamiliar authors and their books. It was a risk that had to be taken.

The term 'Weimar Culture', while now generally accepted, is in some respects unsatisfactory, if only because political and cultural history seldom fully coincide in time. Expressionism was not born with the defeat of the Imperial German army, nor is there any obvious connexion between abstract painting and atonal music and the escape of the Kaiser, nor were the great scientific discoveries triggered off by Scheidemann's proclamation of the Republic. In short, 'Weimar Culture' antedates the Weimar Republic by at least a decade.

It was a fascinating period but not at all easy to come to grips with, precisely because it was so rich in content and so contradictory in character. In recent years there have been excellent monographs devoted to specific aspects of the period, such as the generational conflict which figured prominently in the early postwar years, or the literary politics of the left-wing intelligentsia, and the ideas of the right-wing critics of the Republic. But selective preoccupation with certain topics may lead to the neglect of others, and thus to a distortion of the general perspective. It would no doubt be easier for the historian if the cultural history of Weimar were identical with the plays and theories of Brecht, the creations of the Bauhaus and the articles published by the *Weltbühne*. But there were a great many other individuals and groups at work, and whether the historian likes them or not, he cannot afford to ignore them, or their ideas and activities.

The heritage of Weimar culture is an important subject in itself but it has been dealt with only in passing in the present study, which is concerned primarily with the question *wie es eigentlich gewesen ist*. The fact that Brecht is more widely performed now than all his contemporaries put together, and that Hermann Hesse has since his death found many more readers all over the world than in his lifetime, is no doubt of great significance with regard to the cultural history of the 1950s and 1960s. It is less certain that this should be our starting-point in studying the 1920s. The fact that Marlene Dietrich is remembered in 1974, while most of her contemporaries have been forgotten, does not necessarily mean that future historians of the cinema will share the prejudices and predilections of our age.

The realities of Weimar culture comprise the right as well as the left, the universities as well as the literary intelligentsia, and it would not be complete without occasional glances beyond avant-garde thought and creation. Unfortunately it is much easier to make a convincing case for approaching Weimar culture in its totality than to adhere to these principles in practice. For once one accepts the fact that not all intellectuals were on the left, that most of them, in fact, disliked the Republic, that the cultural history of the Weimar period cannot be limited to those who frequented certain cafés within a stone's throw of the *Gedächtniskirche* in Berlin, a study of Weimar culture ceases to be a well-defined concept and turns into the cultural history of the first German republic, which is a different proposition altogether. Such an approach has the advantage of conveying a more accurate picture of the *Zeitgeist* but it also means that it has to cover more ground, and that it cannot deal in adequate detail with any of the individuals, groups and disciplines which were part of that culture. There is no way of avoiding the problem of selectivity. Some of the persons and problems mentioned in a sentence or two in the present volume could be satisfactorily treated only if a whole book were devoted to them; an entire library would be needed to do justice to the various manifestations of Weimar culture.

I am indebted not for the first time to the staff of the Institute of Contemporary History and Wiener Library. I refrained from interviewing 'Old Weimarians' for the purpose of this book; anyway I have been listening to them for as long as I can remember.

London, 1973

I

Between Potsdam and Weimar

On 30 September 1918 Ludendorff and Hindenburg told the Kaiser at Supreme Headquarters at Spa that the war was lost. It was more than a century since Germany had suffered a military defeat, and its rulers were no longer familiar with the procedure to be adopted in such circumstances. Instead of bowing out in more or less dignified fashion, the Kaiser hung on, hoping that something would turn up which would make abdication unnecessary. Perhaps he preferred not to think about the future; responsibility and foresight had not been the outstanding characteristics of Wilhelm II and the courtiers surrounding him. Under his rule 'Prussianism' had become a synonym for aggressiveness and arrogance, for a society in which the military caste enjoyed the highest social prestige; while the landed aristocracy was still the ruling class although it had outlived whatever social, political and economic functions it had once possessed. It had become, in other words, an intolerable anachronism.

Once upon a time the Prussian spirit had different connotations; it stood for service, for selfless work, incorruptibility and other sterling qualities. But a whole world divided the age of von Stein, Scharnhorst and Gneisenau from the imperial braggart who had ruled Germany with the help of mediocrities for more than two decades. And yet, even in his time and despite his rule, there had been a great deal of progress; Germany before 1914 exuded confidence and optimism to a remarkable degree. Almost the only dissonant voices came from a few

Kulturpessimisten of the left and right, such as could be found in every age, as well as from a few eccentric writers and painters who predicted impending chaos and ruin, and whose inchoate mutterings were not taken seriously. Burke said of pre-revolutionary France that the unbought grace of life had gone for ever. The outstanding feature of prewar Germany was certainly not its grace of life, but it had known a sense of security such as subsequent generations were never even remotely to experience. What Stefan Zweig wrote about his native Austria applied equally to Germany. There had been in that 'world of yesterday' a state and a parliament, as well as a reliable currency based on gold; men of property could calculate without undue difficulty how much they would receive from their savings or investments in the years to come, children inherited the parental home, every family had its budget and knew how to live within its limits. It has been said that such latterday nostalgic reflections merely mirrored the sadness of an impoverished middle class. Was it not true that the great majority of the people inherited nothing, had no investments, enjoyed no security, and that a substantial part lived in dire poverty? Was it not also the age of slums, of long hours and low wages? All this is true, but it is also a fact that even if the economic position of the working classes and most of the peasantry was less than rosy, it was steadily improving; these classes too shared the general mood of optimism. It was not just weakness of character – as Lenin and Rosa Luxemburg seemed to believe – which made gradualists of the erstwhile revolutionaries who led German social democracy. On the contrary their attitude accurately reflected the mood of the rank and file. Once a small group of outcasts, they had within three decades built Germany's strongest political movement. In 1912, in the last general election before the war, their party had polled more than 70 per cent of all votes in Berlin, more than 60 per cent in Hamburg, Germany's second city. The prevailing electoral system did not give them proportional representation. Was there not every reason to assume that the reactionaries would not be able to hold out for ever against the irresistible advance of the masses? Marx, after all, had demonstrated that as the socio-economic basis changed, the legal-ideological superstructure was bound to follow suit. The belief in progress, enlightenment and reason was deeply

anchored in both the middle and the working classes. Technical innovations, such as the growing use of electricity, sym-
bolizing the victory of light over the forces of darkness, seemed
to justify their expectations. Paul Lincke, the famous light
orchestra conductor and darling of the Berlin public, had just
composed a song dealing with this very topic, which was
hummed by young and old, rich and poor. He compared the
newly invented electric bulb to a glow-worm's light, and the
verse which eventually acquired world-wide popularity ended:

Glühwürmchen, Glühwürmchen, flimmere, flimmere
Glühwürmchen, Glühwürmchen, schimmere, schimmere
Führe uns auf rechten Wegen
Führe uns dem Glück entgegen.

(Glow-worm, glow-worm, glimmer, glimmer
Glow-worm, glow-worm, shimmer, shimmer
Lead us on the right path
Lead us on to happiness.)

Happiness was the goal and, a few extremists apart, no one
believed that violence would be needed to attain it. There had
been no major war in Europe for more than four decades nor
had there been any large-scale civil disorder. Wilhelmian
Germany was certainly not a free country by West European or
American standards, but it is useful to recall from time to time
that there are degrees of oppression. It was no cruel dictatorship:
there was a constitution and there were laws which had to be
observed by rulers as well as ruled. In comparison with the
dictatorships that were to emerge in Europe after the war,
Wilhelmian Germany was a permissive country to an almost
bewildering degree. Political murders were unknown, as was
arrest and trial without due process of law. The Emperor himself was openly criticized in the press, as in the *Daily Telegraph*
affair; and if an officer assaulted a civilian, as had happened in
the little Alsatian town of Zabern, this became a *cause célèbre* all
over Germany. Workers on strike were not shot, censorship was
applied only in extreme cases of *lèse-majesté* and blasphemy, and
it is doubtful whether justice could have been flagrantly
perverted as in the Dreyfus case

Whoever chooses to ignore these facts about pre-1914 Germany is bound to be baffled by the intensity of the widespread

postwar nostalgia for the 'good old days', not just among the aristocracy, which was insignificant in numbers anyway, but among wide sections of the middle classes. If it had been a matter of 'class interest' *tout court* they would certainly have identified themselves with the liberal-bourgeois republic which had been proclaimed by the Social Democrats only with some reluctance – mainly because they were afraid of being overtaken on the left by the Spartacists. If the middle classes in their majority did not welcome the Republic, it was partly because life under the Kaiser had by no means been intolerable, and on the other hand because, having to choose between order and freedom, they would almost certainly opt for the former.

There had at one time been a fairly strong democratic tradition in Germany, but in recent generations it had grown progressively weaker. In 1918 at any rate the Republic came to Germany as a foreign importation. Parliamentary democracy was considered un-German in right-wing circles, suitable perhaps for the Americans or the French, but not for a nation which had always striven for wholeness and unity. Political parties were regarded at best as a necessary evil – evil because they expressed only part of the popular will, had a divisive effect, and restricted the operations of a strong executive without which few could envisage a state functioning. And even if it did somehow manage to muddle through, it would certainly not be able to pursue a determined, purposeful foreign policy which, according to the Bismarckian tradition, should always have primacy over domestic affairs.

The intelligentsia was by and large conservative, but even those who accepted the Republic did not feel enthusiastic. 'One serves the Republic but one does not love it', wrote the eminent historian Hans Delbrück. Thomas Mann, once a fervent believer in the justness of the war (having preached the merits of German 'culture' as against Western 'civilization'), was one of the few converts to democracy. But the only advice he could offer the middle classes and the intelligentsia was not to be obstinate, not to shy away from the term 'republic' which (he thought) was what irritated them most. ('Don't consider the Republic the domain of some sharp young Jews. Take the wind out of their sails.')

What distressed the enemies of the new political system was

not so much its name: they had no faith in parliamentarism, in the popular will. They were unhappy about the absence of a central idea and a strong authority. For the new rulers they had nothing but scorn and ridicule. It was in a way quite characteristic that the very idea of 'loving' democracy or the Republic should have been an issue at all, as if a political system was evil unless it evoked emotions of this kind. The thought itself would have struck Frenchmen and Englishmen as absurd, an exalted romantic notion. But many Germans were romantic in their attitude towards the state, and since the Republic was so unromantic, it was *mal-aimeé*.

Certain ideas had been axiomatic in Germany before 1914. These concerned the civilizing mission of the German people, the evil intentions of its rivals, the need to secure for Germany a place in the sun. Above all, there was the deep-seated belief in German military superiority. Astounding victories had been won in 1914–16 against a 'world of enemies'; the fact that the last and decisive battle had been lost was, with all its implications, impossible to accept. Hence the readiness to believe that the German armies, undefeated in battle, had been stabbed in the back by the domestic enemy. This allegation, made by among others Hindenburg, the future president of the Republic, was not just factually untrue. It was the grossest slander, for the 'home front' had for more than four years accepted without grumbling countless sacrifices simply because it had been told to do so by military leaders of indifferent quality. Nevertheless the 'stab in the back' legend was to play a central role in anti-republican propaganda during the years to come.

There were other myths concerning the 'November criminals' – the men who had signed on Germany's behalf the shameful Versailles treaty. Many were only too willing to believe in the existence of a 'hidden hand', of all-powerful forces which had brought about Germany's ruin. Millions had been killed and wounded in the war, many more had been hit by economic disaster. Such suffering gave rise to a great deal of brooding and political speculation, a search for the cause of the catastrophe. How could one explain the fact that institutions which it had been thought would exist forever had disappeared overnight without trace, and that the old masters were suddenly replaced by new men with wholly unfamiliar names? Where had they come from? What foreign interests did they serve? How could an Ebert and a Scheidemann, let alone an Eisner or a Rathenau dare to take the place once filled by Bismarck? Wide credence was given to 'documents' such as the *Protocols of the Elders of Zion*, which proved beyond any shadow of doubt that it was not the Germans who were to blame for the apocalyptic events which had occurred in their country, but foreign plotters and agents who for a long time had been at work to bring about its downfall.

The armistice was signed at Compiègne on 11 November 1918. It should have borne the signatures of Hindenburg and Ludendorff, the military leaders responsible for the defeat. Instead it was signed by Erzberger, a Catholic civilian, thus providing a convenient alibi for the high command. The new regime was off to a bad start in more senses than one: the war was over but peace had not returned. Political and social unrest, *coups d'état* and political assassinations, were to mark the next five years.

In January 1919 the extreme left staged a rising in Berlin, which was suppressed within a few days. A similar attempt in Munich in April the same year was initially more successful and lasted longer but likewise ended in defeat and bloody repression. 1920–1 were the years of the right-wing Kapp putsch and of local communist risings in the Ruhr and Central Germany. In 1922 galloping inflation set in, reaching its climax in 1923 – which was also the year of the Hitler putsch. Karl Liebknecht and Rosa Luxemburg had been killed by right-wing terrorists in January 1919, Erzberger in August 1921, Walther Rathenau, the foreign minister of the Republic, in June 1922; but these were only the best-known names in a long list of political assassinations. There were more than 2.5 million unemployed in the winter of 1923–4. The currency was stabilized early in 1924, and it was during the next five years that the Republic had its first and only respite.

The Kaiser abdicated, having been told that the loyalty of the troops could no longer be relied upon, while the sailors of the high seas fleet were in open rebellion. All over Germany authority was rapidly disintegrating. There was revolutionary ferment, but there was no revolution. The question of political succession remained wide open. Only one group knew exactly what it wanted – the radical left, which demanded a socialist republic, based on workers' and soldiers' councils. But this was the smallest group of all and its appeals for mass support fell on deaf ears. True, the Bolsheviks had also been a small minority in the summer of 1917, but the conditions for the spread of their influence had been incomparably more favourable; Berlin and Munich simply were not Petrograd and Moscow. If the communist bid for power in Germany failed, it was not just because of the absence of capable and determined leaders.

The Social Democrats, the strongest party in Germany, were the obvious candidates for the succession. But power was something they had never enjoyed and, worse, they lacked the instinct and the craving for it. Their theoreticians had written about it, to be sure, but the political leadership had long ceased to be revolutionary. They were radical democrats, they opposed the Wilhelmian establishment; but their education and experience, their whole mental make-up, had conditioned them to expect peaceful change, not revolution. 'Violence is always reactionary', declared Ebert, the future president, at a mass demonstration in Berlin in December 1918. When in doubt, the Social Democrats always chose the line of least resistance, in foreign and domestic policy alike. This is not to say that they were cowards or traitors; their freedom of manoeuvre was, in fact, much more limited than their left-wing critics would allow. Perhaps it had been a mistake to sign the Versailles treaty in the first place, thus accepting responsibility for a war which had been unleashed by the old regime. This had laid them open to charges of lack of patriotism, if not outright treason. A little less responsibility on their part would have been advisable; by refusing to sign the treaty they would probably have procured better conditions with regard to reparations, for instance. But such wisdom after the event ignores the immediate difficulties facing the country, the danger of mass starvation, of total economic breakdown, of French and Polish forces occupying additional parts of Germany. In 1918–9 there was a real danger that the German state would cease to exist. The Social Democrats would have been better statesmen had their sense of duty been less pronounced.

Equally, on the home front, it is easy to blame them for accepting the aid of right-wing military units against the extreme left. By so doing, they paved the way for the 'national-ist restoration' and made the very existence of their government in a time of crisis dependent on the goodwill of a military force which was neutral only in theory; by tradition, outlook and interest, the Reichswehr was oriented towards the right. All this is true, but it is not easy to point to an alternative. In what way could the Social Democrats have defended themselves against those who tried to overthrow them: by abducting some of their leaders and threatening to shoot them? Unlike the Spartacists, the Social Democrats had no armed units at their disposal; perhaps this was their main sin of omission. Lacking the sense for power, they failed to realize that there are moments in history when the talking has to stop and when only bayonets and machine-guns count. To blame them for having betrayed the German revolution is at best an over-simplification. Even if they had not opposed the Spartacist onslaught, the revolution would have fallen prey to the units of the old army which were still intact.

This does not absolve Ebert and Noske, Scheidemann and Wels, from the charge of failing to act decisively. During the first few months after the defeat, the right was in a state of dis-array. Just as the Social Democrats had pushed through important social legislation within a few days, they could have carried out far-reaching political reforms, such as purging the state apparatus of reactionary elements. Once they were more firmly in the saddle they could have tried to democratize the army, to make it a loyal servant of the Republic. But, afraid of acting alone, they were from the very first day almost desper-ately looking for partners to share the responsibility for running the state. The fact that the party was split was yet another source of weakness. Yet a determined effort could have been made to heal the rift with the Independents (USPD), whose ranks included those who had come to oppose the war. But there was no room between the Social Democrats and the Communists for yet another left-wing party. Within three years the USPD was to disappear from the political scene; some of its members joined the Communists, others re-entered the SPD. By that time, however, the damage had been done.

The next stage in the unhappy history of the Weimar Re-public was reached with the elections in January 1919 to the

Constituent Assembly. The Communists boycotted them because they assumed, correctly from their point of view, that they would not come out well. But for the Social Democrats, too, the results were a bitter disappointment; together with the USPD they polled only 45 per cent. Under the old (plurality) voting system which they had just abolished, the Socialists would have obtained a majority of seats in parliament. Proportional representation, while in theory the most democratic of all systems, resulted in a proliferation of parties and made stable government difficult and, towards the end of the Republic, altogether impossible. To claim that proportional representation ruined the Weimar Republic is a gross exaggeration; it is not at all certain that the Social Democrats would have been able to act boldly even with the support of a parliamentary majority. Equally, there is no doubt that proportional representation further aggravated the existing weakness and confusion. The results of the 1919 elections showed that while the great majority of the workers had voted for the Social Democrats and the Independents, the SPD had not been able to effect a breakthrough from a class to a national party. Nor were they to improve their position; their vote remained fairly stable throughout the fourteen years of the Republic, but it was never again to reach, let alone exceed, the results of 1919.

The other main pillar of the Republic was the Democratic Party, liberal and slightly left-of-centre in outlook, progressive but not too much so, in favour of reform but afraid of going too far and too fast. Everything that has been said about the SPD applies *a fortiori* to this party. Its leaders were decent people, a little timid perhaps, but firmly opposed to a dictatorship from left or right. They were neither better nor worse than the French Radical Socialists or the British Liberals, but they never exerted a similar attraction on the educated middle class. They had quite a few professors among their leading supporters and also some bankers and industrialists, but for the majority of the academics – and for the middle classes in general – the sober, matter-of-fact approach of this party was quite unacceptable. It preached understanding with France and Britain at a time when such a policy was anything but popular. The very essence of its philosophy, liberalism, was outside the mainstream of German thought. The decline of this party, which polled 16 per cent in 1918 and 1 per cent in 1932, symbolizes the decline of German democracy. Twentieth-century bourgeois parties are never militant, almost by definition; the German Democratic Party was perhaps the least militant of all.

These two forces were the only ones whose support for the Republic was unqualified. The German People's Party, while not rejecting the new state *tout court*, certainly had never wanted it; at best it was willing to give it a try. It participated in various coalition governments and had some capable leaders such as Stresemann and Schacht; electorally it fared no better than the Democrats and all but disappeared towards the end. The attitude of the Catholic Centre Party towards the new republic was ambivalent: it collaborated with the Social Democrats, but not without serious misgivings. The influence of right-wing nationalist elements was predominant in its counsels; it was bitterly opposed to the cultural and educational policy of the Social Democrats. It saw its main task in the preservation of the Christian (Catholic) values in public and private life; to such a party a 'Marxist' republic, however innocuous, was bound to be less acceptable than a monarchy which regarded religion as one of the main pillars of the state.

Up to the rise of Nazism in 1930 the traditional right found its political home in the German National People's Party. At first it suffered from the shock of the defeat and the unpopularity of the monarch, the military caste and the reactionary leaders of industry and agriculture who had constituted the backbone of the Conservative Party before 1918. In the elections for the Constituent Assembly they polled no more than 8 per cent of the total, but within the next five years, following the constant political and economic crisis, its vote almost tripled. At the other end of the political spectrum the advance of the Communists (KPD) was even more striking; having attracted a mere 400,000 voters in 1921, they received almost ten times as many by early 1924. After that date, as the postwar crisis receded, electoral support for them, as for the extreme right, decreased substantially until, towards the end of the Republic, its fortunes again changed for the better.

These were the main political forces shaping the fate of the Weimar Republic during the first ten years of its existence. National Socialism was at the time just one of many splinter-groups resulting from splits among the major parties. The Weimar Constitution put a premium on freedom and justice rather than on stability; given the specific German situation, this betrayed a lack of judgment. Those who had conceived it wanted it both to be modern and to embody the spirit of the nineteenth-century German democratic tradition; in some respects it was modelled on the American Constitution. It struck a note of compromise, not always successfully, between conflicting social, religious and regional interests. Though the SPD was the strongest party at the time, its influence on shaping the constitution and carrying out its provisions was not decisive; the nationalization of key industries and agrarian reform outlined in the constitution remained, by and large, a dead letter. The constitution was neither better nor worse than other such documents; it was certainly conceived in an admirable spirit of tolerance and compromise. It worked so badly because it was predicated on a general consensus, on the readiness to accept the new political order. But from the first, such a consensus was insufficiently developed and it grew weaker as the years passed. At a time of crisis it was bound to collapse altogether.

For the extreme left the constitution was a betrayal of radical socialist ideals, since it was not based on the idea of workers' and peasants' councils, let alone the dictatorship of the proletariat. For the extreme right it was an act of treason, an attempt to impose a system alien to the German spirit. The extreme right stood for strong, authoritarian rule with a minimum of parliamentary debate. It is one of the ironies of history that the Republic might well have survived if the Social Democrats had followed this course and adopted a firmer, more authoritarian style with some patriotic admixture while carrying out the political and social changes they had advocated all along. They should have realized that it was fruitless to strive for a full consensus and that freedom did not necessarily mean a free hand for the enemies of democracy. But they lacked the necessary toughness and inspiration; they left patriotism to the right and thought that patient work, a rational policy, free of any pathos and demagogic slogans, would sooner or later bear fruit.

They could not have been more mistaken. Theirs was an admirable approach for quieter times and for mature people who, whatever the internal conflicts, basically accepted the democratic ground-rules. Furthermore the Kaiser and the Junkers, however anachronistic their entire behaviour, however arrogant and stupid their speeches, however damaging their policies, had possessed style. The symbols of their regime were respected even by most of its critics and thus contributed towards national unity. The old state had authority; the new order conspicuously lacked it. Those who created the Weimar Republic and supported it manifestly failed to generate any enthusiasm. Again, it is not certain whether resolute and dynamic leadership would have succeeded against such heavy odds. But this is a hypothetical question, for there was no such leadership.

The parties were not the only factors to shape the political life of the Republic. During its early years the trade unions were not a force to be belittled, as the right-wing conspirators in Berlin and elsewhere found to their cost; a general strike put an end to the Kapp putsch within a few days. The trade unions could count two million members before the war; in 1920 their number had risen to almost eight million. The clerical and shop workers, who had their own associations, also became much more powerful. But the German trade unions no longer exerted a great deal of influence on their members. Much water had flown down the Rhine and the Elbe since the early, heroic, illegal days. Their leaders were decent, honourable men, devoted to the cause of workers and employees; in ordinary circumstances they would not have dreamt of using the power of the unions to influence the political struggle. Routine work over many years had transformed them into little bureaucrats who were lost at a time of crisis. The grave economic situation undermined their position as mass unemployment further reduced the power of their organizations.

Outside the trade unions it was difficult to find substantial support for the Republic. The Churches were officially neutral in the political struggle. The Protestants, though more numerous, had far less cohesion than the Catholics, who exerted much more influence on their flock through a great many social and cultural associations. It had been traditional church policy to be on good terms with the powers that be, but there was not the slightest doubt that the monarchy had been much more to their liking, quite apart from the fact that it had also been so much stronger and more awe-inspiring than the Republic. They would never have dared to attack the Emperor and his ministers in the way they felt free to criticize the leaders of the Republic. The political outlook of most church leaders was conditioned by their social background and their upbringing. True, there were a few Social Democratic sympathizers among Protestant churchmen, and the Catholic Church at one stage excommunicated the Nazi leaders. But the overwhelming majority of both priests and lay leaders in the two churches were politically conservative and regarded the Republic as an unsatisfactory form of political organization.

When the Social Democrats came to power they made a few new appointments affecting the senior ranks of the state bureaucracy; by and large they left it untouched. The bureaucracy on its part served the new masters without going out of its way to support the democratic regime. Its role was important, for while minister followed minister, often in rapid succession, the permanent officials remained; and in the absence of firm control they had wide freedom of action. Some of them were in fact, if not in name, shaping the policy of their respective departments. The state bureaucracy had a reputation for competence and incorruptibility which was not undeserved. It also had a way of doing things which, to put it mildly, did not make it universally popular. The arrogance of the old regime had been infectious and had worked its way downwards. The bureaucracy represented the state; the idea that it also owed a duty to the public was considered outlandish. There was some change in the climate after 1918, but progress was agonizingly slow. The bureaucracy was not so much anti-democratic as a-democratic. The great majority was willing to do its duty to any master; it accepted the Republic as it later accepted the Nazis. On the whole the Republic had the cooperation of the bureaucrats, and it would have been unrealistic to expect more.

There were some important exceptions. The behaviour of many judges was simply outrageous. It was not just that extremists of the right could, quite literally, get away with murder, whereas those of the left had to face the full severity of the law. Even the leaders of the Republic, moderate men by any standard, could not hope for a fair trial however grievously

Wingate College Library

they had been libelled. Instead of appointing democratic judges who could be trusted to honour the constitution, the Social Democrats out of misplaced respect for the independence of the judiciary did not dare to touch this bastion of the reactionary forces. Thus the Republic was undermined from within and comfort provided for its enemies.

When asked by the Social Democratic leaders whether the Reichswehr was reliable so far as the Republic was concerned, von Seeckt, its commander, used to answer: 'This I do not know, but it certainly obeys me.' Within the Reichswehr there were various shades of opinion. Some officers were openly hostile to the Republic, whereas others were willing to co-operate, albeit without enthusiasm, on condition that there was no civilian interference in military affairs and that they obtained all the financial and political support they needed. Most members of the new German army were by no means active supporters of Nazism; only towards the end of the Weimar period did some of them fully identify themselves with the Hitler movement. But by its whole tradition and outlook, the Reichswehr was anything but a pillar of the Republic. The captains, majors and colonels of the old Imperial army were its commanders; they were imbued with a spirit of militant nationalism and they found the leaders of the Republic wanting in this respect. On the other hand, the Social Democrats' attitude towards the professional army was one of suspicion. As they were indebted to the Reichswehr for its help in the early days of the Republic, they did not dare to reform it by manning key positions with republican officers. Where, anyway, would such officers have been found? It would have taken a long time to train a military counter-establishment; it would have faced violent opposition and the Social Democrats shied away from any head-on collision. They had no clear concept of how to run the army. Some of them were inclined towards pacifism; others, probably the majority, would have preferred an army run more or less on the lines of a militia. But this was clearly impractical in view of the development of modern warfare. Thus the Reichswehr remained the power in the background, the great political question-mark at a time of crisis, tolerating the Republic but unwilling to defend it against its internal enemies.

The Weimar police force was more loyal to the new state. In many cases it was commanded by Social Democrats who had no inhibitions about its reform. The police corps was traditionally more 'proletarian' in character, its officer corps much less exclusive, for a career in the police force had not been deemed an occupation suitable for gentlemen. Such loyalty to the Republic did not, of course, prevent the police from serving with equal zeal the Nazis, who took it over lock, stock and barrel, having ousted the Social Democratic appointees. As in other democratic regimes, the political police was not powerful and thus not in a position to counteract the activities of the Republic's enemies.

During the early days of the Republic the Free Corps was a factor of some political importance. Subsequently, its role was to some extent taken over by the veterans' organizations and the paramilitary formations of the big political parties. The Free Corps was composed of remnants of the old army, some young idealists, some criminal elements and, above all, young officers who could not find suitable civilian employment. They proclaimed that they would save Germany, though in fact most of their energies were devoted to combating the internal enemy (the left) rather than the external one (mainly the Poles). The veterans' organizations, such as the Stahlhelm, constituted the reserve army of the right. They were unalterably opposed to everything the Republic stood for, and the 'stab in the back' theory found its most fervent supporters in their ranks. The reception which had been accorded to the returning officers and NCOs had not been forgotten: they had been chased through the streets and spat at, and their epaulettes had been torn off. For a while many of them had been compelled to hide. The Free Corps was disbanded by 1921–2, whereas the paramilitary organizations, above all the SA, the Nazi stormtroopers, gathered strength only a decade later.

In strictly military terms the paramilitary organizations did not represent a serious threat, but the psychological impact was tremendous. The torchlight processions, the rallies, the mass parades with sometimes hundreds of thousands of participants, seemed to presage the arrival of an irresistible force and thus the beginning of a new era. The republican forces never succeeded in arousing similar enthusiasm among the younger generation.

Their leaders maintained that Germany would neither be awakened nor saved by marching columns, by demagogic speeches, by ruthless attacks on political opponents. Such sensible advice was unfortunately quite out of touch with the mood of an activist younger generation, instinctively longing for a *Führer* (not, to be fair to them, necessarily the one who ultimately emerged). This generation preferred drums to speeches and parades to long and inconclusive discussions; eventually it decided that the elected leaders were incapable of coping with the crisis.

These developments reached their climax during the last years of the Republic, but the underlying mood had existed well before. It was reflected in, for example, the development of the German youth movement, the *Wandervögel* and the *Bünde*, and their political offshoots such as the *Tat* circle and the Young German Order (*Jungdo*). These minority elitist groups, limited almost entirely to middle-class youth, were a specifically German phenomenon which had no parallel in other countries. The youth movement had its origins in the prewar period, and was distinguished by a great deal of romantic and cloudy idealism. Politically these bodies were naive, uncommitted to any of the existing parties, and ultimately an easy prey to demagogic leaders. As the crisis deepened, they began to make radical social demands; but theirs was an unthinking, aimless radicalism which could with equal ease turn left or right or lead nowhere at all. The common denominator was contempt for 'the system' with its vested interests, cliques and party caucuses. They talked a great deal about 'responsibility' and 'duty', and the longing for a great leader deepened. For the raucous jingoism of beer-hall parties they had nothing but contempt. They saw the prospects for a better Germany not in terms of political action; the new Reich of which they talked was, like Stefan George's, not of this world. They saw it as their task to educate a new elite to cultivate a new, inward love for the fatherland and the *Volk*. The Republic was certainly not their spiritual home and most of them eventually accepted Nazism without serious qualms, even though the advent of Hitler meant the dissolution of the youth movement.

In their overwhelming majority, the German educated classes gravitated towards the right. The Weimar Republic certainly did not correspond to their idea of a well-run, effective state commanding the loyalty of its citizens. There were exceptions; a substantial number of educated Catholics supported the Centre Party, and the Jews, rejected by the right as alien elements detrimental to the German spirit, gravitated towards the democratic parties or further left. But they were a small minority, and while some of them had leading positions in the mass media, they had no political influence. On the contrary, the presence of some Jews in key positions provided a convenient target for anti-semitic attacks. The universities were one of the main strongholds of the anti-democratic forces during the Weimar era. The nationalist ideology had been deeply rooted among students and teachers alike, and the shock of defeat was therefore all the more acutely felt in these circles. Immediately after the war there was a great deal of talk about 'revolution', albeit in a vague and abstract way, and about a new and more just social order, but two years later this mood of confusion and contrition had already disappeared, and Ernst Troeltsch and other observers noted a new upsurge of the right. It was symbolic, in more ways than one, that the president of the German Republic was told by the rector of Berlin University that he would not be welcome to address the students, and the Republic took this insult, like so many others, lying down. (Berlin, incidentally, was by no means the most reactionary of German universities.) Initially the right-wing militants were a minority but they met with hardly any resistance. Towards the end of the decade, their influence grew by leaps and bounds and the Nazis emerged as the strongest party in the universities well before they did so in the country at large. Their political activities included violent attacks on pacifist, socialist and Jewish professors; the attitude of the authorities was one of studious non-intervention.

The number of students grew rapidly (from 80,000 in 1925 to 126,000 in 1931) and their chances of finding suitable employment worsened as the economic situation deteriorated. The image of the well-to-do student engaged in duelling and other more harmless pastimes, such as falling in love with the daughter of his Heidelberg landlady – the subject of countless operettas and films – was far removed from the harsh realities of German student life. Economic factors were admittedly not the only ones, and often not the decisive ones, underlying the radicalization of university life. Nor was it a foregone conclusion that material deprivation and the loss of hope would necessarily drive these students towards the extreme right. But given the general climate of the Weimar Republic and the fact that the extreme left had so little attraction for these circles, it is not difficult to understand why the students found a radical movement of the right more congenial.

The directors of industry and the managers of the big banks rarely appeared in the limelight, but they played a not unimportant role in the history of the Weimar Republic. Harry Graf Kessler, in a lecture at Williamstown, Massachusetts, in 1923, characterized them as follows:

> These German captains of industry are rarely the owners of their works; often nothing but their leading technicians. Many of them have risen from the ranks and have never become, even after long and successful careers, true capitalists. With a jealousy and harshness which sometimes borders on fanaticism, their eyes are centred on the big factory which they have nursed into greatness, and to which they have devoted their lives. Some of them, even at the height of their careers, look more like trade union officials or well-to-do laborers than like millionaires. They do not play golf! They do not even care much for money, looking on it but as a sort of concentrated fuel with which to set new furnaces ablaze.*

The picture was slightly overdrawn. It is true that Stinnes, for example, who emerged after the war as Germany's leading industrialist (his empire crumbled soon after his death in 1924) was not a man of extravagant tastes. But there was also Ottmar Strauss of Cologne, a *bon vivant* second to none, not to mention a whole host of *nouveaux riches* (*Raffkes*), whose style of life and ostentatious spending provided an inexhaustible source of inspiration for journalists and cartoonists.

Among the industrialists there were extreme authoritarians and rightists such as Kirdorf, whereas others, such as Bosch, had a more developed social conscience and showed an active interest in the wellbeing of their employees. A few industrialists, such as Rathenau (of the big electrical concern AEG), Cuno

*Count Harry Kessler, *Germany and Europe*, New Haven, 1923.

(on loan from a big North German shipping company) and Helfferich, director of the Deutsche Bank, took a prominent part in politics. But most of them had no political ambitions, and even their interest in politics was strictly limited. That they were opposed to any form of nationalization goes without saying, and they tried to counteract, not without success, the growing influence of the trade unions. As the economic depression deepened, they insisted on reducing and, whenever possible, stopping social benefits because, they claimed, the country could not afford it. They represented a powerful lobby on some issues but quite frequently failed to agree among themselves on the policies to be advocated; there were marked conflicts of interest between the various branches of the economy. The big landowners had played an important role under the monarchy but they did not recover their influence in the Republic. It was only towards the end of the 1920s that they emerged again as a political pressure-group of some consequence, demanding a protectionist policy and government subsidies.

Wilhelmian Germany had been governed more or less autocratically by a clearly defined elite; it was far more difficult to define with any degree of accuracy the identity of the new republican establishment. Some sections of the old elite had survived, but they had to share power with new forces. Political power was far more widely spread. There was a fragile and complicated balance of power with frequent changes and fluctuations, and public opinion played a much greater role than in the old Reich. The new establishment ruled a country which was in some respects quite different from prewar Germany. It was smaller and poorer, having lost under the provisions of the Versailles treaty 13 per cent of its territory and almost 10 per cent of its population as well as all its colonies. In economic terms the losses were even more substantial; 26 per cent of Germany's coal production and 75 per cent of its iron ore. German heavy industry, which had been the backbone of the country's stormy economic development during the preceding decades, thus found itself severely weakened in comparison with its competitors in world markets. The country had also lost all its big merchant ships, half of the smaller ones, one quarter of its fishing fleet, one fifth of its river fleet, 5,000 locomotives and 150,000 railway wagons. Consequently, in the words of the economic historian Gustav Stolper,

> More foodstuffs had to be imported; minerals hitherto mined in Germany had to be purchased abroad; exports of other raw materials had to be curtailed. The loss of the merchant fleet deprived the country of the foreign exchange paid by other countries for the fleet's services. The loss of capital invested abroad cut down the influx of profit and interest payments.

To these losses should be added the other debts incurred as a result of financing the war.

In addition, the Allies now demanded reparations as compensation for the damage caused by German aggression. These demands were psychologically only too understandable, yet elementary prudence should have taught the allied statesmen not to expect too much from an impoverished country on top of what they had already seized. But such sober considerations were unpopular so soon after a victory which had been gained at great sacrifice; John Maynard Keynes was one of the few exceptions, but his voice did not count for much at the time. And so it was decided that Germany was to pay 132 billion marks, an altogether unrealistic sum, which was subsequently (in 1930) reduced to 37 billion. The payments, both in cash and in kind, were to continue up to 1988. In fact Germany stopped paying during the Great Depression and the whole scheme was discontinued *de jure* after Hitler became chancellor. The Allies were only too willing to concede to the Nazis what they had refused to the statesmen of the Republic. Altogether, reparations constitute a sorry chapter in postwar history. The sums paid and the deliveries made by Germany under this scheme were relatively small, and it is by no means certain that Britain and France drew any real benefit from them. The political damage, on the other hand, was substantial. The right-wing backlash which eventually brought about the downfall of the Republic drew much of its inspiration from the 'chains of Versailles', which had to be broken if Germany was ever to rise again. The loss of the colonies would have been quickly forgotten, the loss of Alsace-Lorraine and parts of eastern Germany might have been accepted by the majority in the course of time. But the idea that the grandchildren of those alive in the 1920s would still have to pay tribute to the victors of 1918 was totally unacceptable The demagogues had a field day and the democratic leaders who pursued a policy of 'fulfilment' (*Erfüllungspolitik*) were gradually discredited.

The reparations issue quite apart, Germany's postwar economy faced an uphill struggle, and even the experts were at a loss as to how to cope with its problems. There is no denying that the currency situation was handled with almost incredible ineptitude; the total collapse of the mark could certainly have been prevented. But the surprising thing was not the breakdown of the German economy during the five years after the war but the fact that it recovered after 1923.

The story of the collapse has often been told and analysed. The essential facts are briefly as follows: when war broke out in 1914 the official exchange rate was $1 = 4.20 M. During the war the value of the dollar doubled and by November 1921 it stood at 270 M. After that date the decline of the mark continued with short interruptions; in 1923 the fever turned into delirium and by mid-November the official value of one dollar was no less than 4,200,000,000,000 M. Then the currency was stabilized, literally overnight and altogether successfully. It was a psychological issue rather than an economic problem, for once the public reached the conclusion that a further decline was impossible, a new currency was bound to succeed irrespective of whether there existed any cover for it.

The inflation period and the Great Depression are two of the major milestones in the social history of the Weimar Republic, but they are equally important in its political and cultural history. They affected everyone living in Germany at the time, his mood, his outlook on the future, whether he had enough to eat, whether he could afford to pay his rent and buy coal to heat his home. The war had been fought in distant parts, only able-bodied men of a certain age had shared the *Fronterlebnis*, the experience of fighting. But the *Inflationserlebnis* was common to all; it made a few clever manipulators very rich overnight, brought modest prosperity to a small section of the population – namely those who could acquire real estate or other property which would not lose its value. But for every one who made a profit there were hundreds who were ruined; the middle classes who had invested their funds in state loans, shares accounts and such like, the pensioners and the working classes, suffered from the steep decline in the real value of their income. True, in some respects the inflation acted as a great leveller – but a leveller of misery. While a senior government official had earned about seven times as much as an unskilled worker before the war, he now received, after tax, only 1.8 times as much. However, since the real income of the unskilled workers had also fallen since 1914, both groups were up in arms against the government, which they held responsible for their plight. The government was also blamed for its inactivity vis-à-vis the manipulators and the black-marketeers who suddenly dominated the social scene and whose speculations aroused tremendous resentment. Fat, ostentatious, vulgar, smoking enormous cigars, driving around in a luxurious car, he was depicted in a thousand cartoons. One of the most famous showed Raffke in front of the ruins of the Colosseum in Rome: 'Don't build if you don't have the money.' But most of the comment, verbal and pictorial, from George Grosz to the extreme right, was less amiable.

The shock of the inflation was profound and not all its political repercussions were felt immediately. Some of the impact was temporarily softened as a result of the economic revival which set in following the stabilization of the currency and which for five or six years caused a far-reaching change in the whole climate. By the end of the 1920s important sectors of the national economy, above all the chemical, electrical, and machine-tool industries, had been modernized and were again able to compete successfully on world markets. The merchant fleet had been replaced and German exports were a third higher than before the war. The rebuilding of German cities got under way again after almost a decade of neglect, and around them hundreds of new suburbs came into being which were a model of their kind and attracted a stream of admiring foreign visitors.

This economic recovery was made possible by the existence of a skilled labour force unique in Europe and by the adoption of modern (American) production methods; 'rationalization' became the great slogan of the 1920s. Some leading firms amalgamated and the giant concerns which came into being – such as I.G. Farben in the chemical field and Vereinigte Stahlwerke in heavy industry – were able to operate more efficiently than the smaller units of an earlier era. Above all the expansion was the result of the influx of foreign capital, first and foremost from America. It has been estimated that between the end of the inflation and the beginning of the Great Depression foreigners invested some twenty-five billion marks in Germany. During that same period Germany made reparation payments valued at ten billion and invested another ten billion abroad. The decisive factors were that confidence in Germany had been restored, that money was again available, and this was sufficient to give a tremendous impetus to the economy. Although the middle classes had lost much of their property, incomes began to rise again, the unemployed disappeared from the streets, and the shops were full. Great new fortunes were amassed in industry, and at the other end of the scale real wages of metal and building workers doubled between 1924 and 1928. Yet behind this appearance of prosperity and restrained optimism Germany's economic situation was still precarious, largely because of the lack of capital and the resulting dependence on foreign loans. The state became the nation's leading investment banker since the private banks did not have sufficient means to finance the needs of the national economy. The German *Wirtschaftswunder* of the 1920s was undercapitalized, resting to a large extent on short-term loans from abroad; subsequent events were to show that this was a perilously narrow and uncertain base.

This then in broadest outline was the political and economic background to the developments on the cultural scene. But any such account leaves a great many basic questions unanswered: How did Germans live at the time? In what essential respects did conditions in Germany differ from those prevailing elsewhere in Europe or in the United States? What was the mood, the taste, what were the hopes and fears of the citizens of Middletown, Germany? No account of Germany in the 1920s which fails to deal however briefly with these aspects would be complete. But these are the most difficult questions of all and they often defy the historian's ingenuity. Comparative statistics are available for the output of steel, coal and agriculture, but how is one to assess the socio-cultural environment, the quality of life, the *Zeitgeist*? These are intangibles, and any description must be based on impressions rather than measurement. Furthermore, generalization is made more difficult by the fact that Germany was in many respects much less homogeneous in character than most foreigners assumed. True, there were no national minorities, or hardly any; but there were a great many other divisive factors quite apart from social class and political orientation. This applies to the differences between big cities and countryside, between the agricultural east and the industrial west, between mainly Protestant North Germany and the region south of the Main which was predominantly Catholic. Germans in north and south, in west and east, differed in character, in temperament, in cultural tradition; they spoke widely diverging dialects. A Bavarian certainly found it much easier to understand an Austrian than a visitor from Northern Germany talking *Plattdeutsch*. There still were strong particularist movements, there was a feeling that the south and the west had been exploited for too long by the underdeveloped Prussian, Protestant north. There was a great deal of instinctive antagonism towards Berlin, political and cultural. The position of Paris and London as the respective capitals of their countries was beyond dispute, regardless of political outlook and cultural orientation. Many Germans, on the other hand, felt very strongly that Berlin did not represent the real Germany. It was a dynamic city populated by a neurasthenic generation (to quote Eduard Spranger), a city of social conscience and extreme individualism, a centre which attracted the most productive and creative forces but also, very often, the far-out, the sick, the failures, the lunatic fringe. It had a sizable Jewish community which made a strong impact on the city's cultural life; in this respect it bore a certain resemblance to New York. But Berlin's leadership was not undisputed; some would even claim that it was no longer part of the real Germany.

What then was the 'real' Germany? Germany, including the Saar, had in 1925 some sixty-three million inhabitants. It was an industrialized country; the number of those employed in industry and agriculture had been about equal around the turn of the century, but by the late 1920s industry employed almost twice as many people. The number of those employed in trade and transport had risen even faster. But, with the exception of

Berlin, urbanization had not kept pace. The capital had one million inhabitants in 1880; in the 1920s it passed the four million mark. At the same time 36 per cent of the population still lived in small rural communities of fewer than 2,000 inhabitants, and only 27 per cent in big cities of more than 100,000. Thus the overwhelming majority of Germans was located in villages or in small and medium-sized towns. This is a fact of vital interest for the student of politics, for it helps to explain an apparent paradox: namely that Hitler came to power despite his comparatively weak showing in the big cities. Germany's ten biggest cities at the time were Berlin, Hamburg (with a little more than a million inhabitants), followed by Cologne, Munich, Leipzig, Dresden, Essen, Breslau, Frankfurt and Düsseldorf. All these cities had Social Democratic-Centre majorities, or, as in the case of Cologne and Munich, left-Centre-Catholic majorities. The Nazi Party never attracted more than a third of Berlin's voters, not even on the very eve of Hitler's accession to power. Their showing in Hamburg was even weaker and the situation in most other big cities not radically different.

Clearly it is difficult to discuss any aspects of the Weimar Republic for any length of time without bringing in politics. Physically, postwar Germany was hardly different from the pre-war Reich; the great battles of the war had been fought in France, Belgium and Russia, while the homeland remained un-scathed. Parts of Germany were of unrivalled scenic beauty but not many foreigners thought of it as a tourist centre. They came to study at German universities, which still had a great reput-ation; they went to Berlin and the Ruhr to examine German technology and industrial expertise; but Germany was not among the countries visited for enjoyment. (The attraction of Berlin for some young foreign intellectuals was a special case.) It was a solid country, one of the most orderly in the world, permeated by the work ethic and accustomed to discipline. There was always a great deal of activity, purposeful or not – it was not an ideal place to rest or relax. Leisure, too, was highly organized; there were countless *Vereine* devoted to shooting, bowls, gardening, beekeeping, rabbit-breeding, the study of Esperanto and countless other pursuits. Prewar Germany had innumerable societies but it had no society. The old aristocracy met the lesser nobility and the captains of industry and banking only with reluctance; it ignored those who were not of blue blood and was only dimly aware of the existence of artists and intellectuals. Small-town society consisted in its higher reaches of senior government officials, small factory owners, high-school teachers, physicians, local bank managers, lawyers and perhaps some religious dignitaries. It was an atomized society despite the constant talk about community spirit and *Volksgemeinschaft*.

Prewar Germany for all its undoubted achievements and sterling qualities was on the whole a rather boring country. This no doubt was one of the reasons why so many people far removed from militarism and without strong feelings about the French, the British or the Russians, nevertheless welcomed the outbreak of war in 1914. It seemed a blast of fresh air after decades of suffocation. Weimar Germany, whichever way one looked at it, was anything but boring; for the first time in its modern history it even exerted a strange fascination on foreigners. The very fact that the Germans had lost the war, that German society had been uprooted, that conflicts and antagonisms had replaced order and discipline, made the country far less predictable. Many of the old taboos had disappeared; there was much greater openness towards new ideas. But at the same time the upholders of the old order and its values had by no means disappeared. The clash between tradition and modernism continued with a vengeance, and since Germany was at one and the same time the home of the most modern, avant-garde trends and the most violent reaction against them, it naturally became the most interesting country in Europe. 'It is hard now, nearly thirty years later, to explain even to myself the kind of attraction which Germany exerted on young men of my generation at Oxford', Goronwy Rees wrote in retrospect. Ilya Ehrenburg, a restless roving European reporter with no predilection for Germany, stated flatly in 1928: 'There is no doubt that Germany has become the most interesting country of Europe.' Unlike Mr Isherwood and his friends, Ehrenburg was not primarily interested in Berlin, with its radical politics and literature, its avant-garde theatre and its sexual freedom. He pointed to Stuttgart as an example, comparing it with a city of comparable size in France, Bordeaux. There was no doubt in his mind that Stuttgart came out on top from such a comparison. It had a number of newspapers, many museums and art galleries, several theatres and a large concert hall. The new architecture was American in the best sense, with white glass cubist complexes, full of light; Gropius and Le Corbusier and their pupils had been at work. Ehrenburg found that in some essential respects the Germans had changed: they had not become richer, but they had learnt for the first time how to spend money. Janos Flesch, one of Berlin's fashionable physicians (his patients included Albert Einstein) waxed lyrical when looking back on Berlin: it was *Kosmopolis*, a truly international city. Trying to define the general mood he quoted that curious German Renaissance knight Ulrich von Hutten: *Es ist eine Lust zu leben* (Bliss is it to be alive). Berlin, wrote the playwright Carl Zuckmayer, was worth 'more than a mass – it tasted of the future'. Alfons Goldschmidt, a left-wing critic, saw the capital through more jaundiced eyes: a grey city, full of noise and dust, shabby, a symphony of dissonances. 'Here no one laughs, no one is gay.' He could have reached similar conclusions about London and Paris by observing the passengers in an early morning commuter train. But he was far more enthusiastic about other German cities: Hamburg, for instance, 'a much quieter place with beautiful roads along the Elbe'. Even in the smaller towns, despite the gradual standardization with its vulgar, monotonous chain-stores and cinemas, he found some redeeming features; they had either preserved or created something of their own.

Before 1914 it had been the custom for gifted young people to escape to Berlin from the stifling provincialism of Goerlitz and Pasewalk. So many young Rastignacs, they wanted to meet like-minded people, to make a fortune or to become famous, to write the great play or novel the world was waiting for. But as it turned out not that many great plays and novels were written at the tables of the Café Josty and the Romanische Café. There was a tendency towards clannishness among Berlin intellectuals; they ignored the rest of Germany and countered the attacks against Berlin with sneering references to the backwoodsmen (*das platte, allzu platte Land*). In fact there were quite a number of major cultural centres outside Berlin. There was nothing provincial about the *Frankfurter Zeitung* or the Munich theatres or the Dresden

Opera under Fritz Busch, where Richard Strauss's *Arabella* and *Die ägyptische Helena* were first performed. The Hamburg Jungfernsteg, the Kaiserstrasse in Frankfurt, the Schweidnitzerstrasse in Breslau, the Bruehl in Dresden, could stand comparison with any of the major Berlin avenues. In France and Britain musical life was almost entirely concentrated in the capital; in Germany on the other hand, Dresden and Leipzig, Hamburg and Cologne, Breslau and Munich competed, often successfully, with the capital. Nor were the plastic arts and their appreciation restricted to Berlin; the Warburg Institute was located in Hamburg, the Bauhaus in Weimar and later in Dessau, Paul Klee taught in Düsseldorf, Max Beckmann in Frankfurt, Otto Dix and before him Kokoschka in Dresden, which boasted one of the finest galleries in the world.

There is no denying that Berlin had the finest stage in the world at the time, and precisely for that reason it is instructive to recall where some of the outstanding plays of the age were first presented: Georg Kaiser's *Die Bürger von Calais* was first performed in Frankfurt, so was his *Gas* and Carl Sternheim's *1913*, as well as Walter Hasenclever's *Antigone*; Reinhard Goering's *Seeschlacht* in Dresden; Fritz von Unruh's trilogy *Ein Geschlecht* again in Frankfurt; Ernst Toller's *Masse Mensch* in Nuremberg, his *Hinkemann* in Leipzig; Arnolt Bronnen's *Vatermord* in Frankfurt; Brecht's *Trommeln in der Nacht* and *Im Dickicht der Städte* in Munich, his *Baal* in Leipzig, while his *Mann ist Mann* was first performed in Darmstadt and Düsseldorf on the same evening. It is a revealing list and bears witness to a great deal of enterprise on the part of local theatres and their directors, and a desire to keep up with new works and ideas. It is unlikely that a new French or English play by a leading writer would have had premieres in Lille or Liverpool.

An intellectual map of Germany in the 1920s would register a remarkable degree of polycentrism. In Frankfurt Karl Mannheim the sociologist was teaching as well as Paul Tillich, the theologian, and Wertheimer, one of the founders of the school of Gestalt psychology. Felix Weil provided the money for what was later to be known as the *marxisant* Frankfurt School of philosophy and sociology. Among the leading figures in Hamburg were Ernst Cassirer the philosopher, Erwin Panofsky the art historian, William Stern the psychologist, Otto Stern, Nobel Prizewinner in physical chemistry – all of them men of world renown. Leading philosophers, sociologists and jurists such as Jaspers, Heidegger, Alfred Weber and Radbruch were teaching in the small university towns of Heidelberg, Freiburg and Marburg (where young Erich Auerbach got his first appointment). Everyone agreed that Göttingen, with Courant, Hilbert and Weyl, Minkowski, Landau and Max Born, was the mecca of mathematicians; their students included Johnny von Neumann, Oppenheimer and Szilard, Edward Teller and Victor Weisskopf, Peierls, Bethge and Wigner.

It would be as easy as it would be tedious to enumerate all the leading spirits of the age who did not hang up their hats in the capital. Reference, however cursory, should therefore be made to the specific character of these cultural centres and the tension between them and Berlin. Leipzig and Breslau were stolid, sober cities; cities of work rather than high culture. But in the world of book publishing Leipzig held a place of paramount importance, and the Breslau stage and opera were well known jumping-off points for Berlin; the number of actors and singers, theatre producers and conductors, who made the jump is legion. Before the war Munich had been a cultural centre in many respects superior to Berlin; drinking a cup of coffee in the Café Luitpold or Stefanie, one would meet within an hour almost everyone who was anyone among the leading painters of both the older and the younger generation, not to mention a great many writers and composers. Munich had lost out to Berlin even before 1914 because it was not sufficiently open to the new trends; it had never liked Naturalism, embraced Impressionism only half-heartedly and was not really interested in the Post-Impressionist fashion, even though it was the birthplace of the Blaue Reiter. Thomas Mann in an essay on 'Munich as a Cultural Centre' (1927) listed some of the reasons for the city's decline: Once there had been a climate of humanism, of tolerant individualism, of humour and youth, an artistic atmosphere which presented a conscious and deliberate contrast to misanthropic Berlin; prewar Munich stood for democracy against Prussian feudalism and militarism. This Munich ceased to exist after the war; in the early 1920s the city became a stronghold of all the reactionary forces. The atmosphere was no longer congenial to a flowering of the arts – it was in some respects anti-cultural. They said, *Mir san gesund* (We are in good health), and meant that philistinism had triumphed. But even if Munich was no longer the rival cultural capital, it still counted among its residents Thomas and Heinrich Mann, Feuchtwanger, and for a while Brecht, Wolfskehl and Karl Vossler, Pfitzner and Halbe; *Simplicissimus*, Germany's foremost satirical periodical, was published there; it had excellent theatres, an opera and museums, not to forget Karl Valentin, the great comic actor. Munich's decline was relative; depressing when compared with the prewar state of affairs, it was less abject when compared with contemporary Marseilles or Birmingham and their standing as cultural centres. German culture, in brief, was not restricted to a square mile or two in the west of Berlin.

If it is difficult to generalize about the German *Intelligenz* before 1914, it is almost impossible to do so for the period after the First World War. For within the German intelligentsia there were various groups representing totally different attitudes, policies, points of view, political and unpolitical, left and right, and some who defied classification altogether. The limelight shifted from time to time. The liberal intelligentsia had set the tone roughly speaking up to the 1860s and were followed by the national liberals, who held the position up to the end of the war, whereas the left-liberal intelligentsia predominated during the 1920s. But none of these ever had the scene all to itself; various factions coexisted in time without speaking the same language. The liberal Berlin intellectuals tended to overrate their impact on the country at large. Kurt Tucholsky, for one, had no such illusions. In 'Berlin und die Provinz', an essay he wrote in 1928, well before the right-wing revival, he said that the reputation of the great democratic newspapers and the libertarian associations bore no relation to their real power; the other side was 'silently omnipresent', it was much more cunning and far less scrupulous. It is doubtful whether this conflict can be reduced to the simple juxtaposition of Berlin versus the provinces, or of the clash between avant-garde and philistine. German writers, including Thomas Mann and other leading spirits of the age, tended to attribute too much significance to *Bildung*; it dawned on them only gradually that illiterate people could be humanists and democrats by instinct whereas highly educated men could advocate cannibalistic ideologies and even become commanders of SS *Einsatzgruppen*.

Most Germans, it has been noted, did not live in big cities, and there is no denying that the small-town atmosphere had changed less than the Berlin climate. Quite frequently it had changed for the worse because the civic spirit, the *Bürgergeist*, the solidarity which had been one of the great virtues of these intimate communities, had weakened or disappeared altogether. But social change had by no means bypassed the small town. Fashions changed and so, more gradually, did people's physique. It is instructive to look at old family scrapbooks and photograph collections or illustrated weeklies of the prewar period. The formality and the conventions of that era manifested themselves in heavy suits and waistcoats, in plus fours, braces and heavy boots. The change in women's fashions was even more striking; the rich flowery hats became cherished relics to be used at fancy-dress balls. The corset gradually disappeared, the hemline rose until, in 1926, the knee was reached. Bobbed hair (with fringe) appeared and swimming costumes changed out of recognition. Young ladies of all classes made a determined if not always successful effort to have a figure like Diana, in contrast to their mothers' generation for whom Juno had been the ideal. The Republic had given women the right to vote; at the same time something akin to a social revolution had taken place. Under the Kaiser it had been unusual for women to follow any definite profession; working-class girls went into a factory or were shop assistants, a middle-class girl's place was at home, reading novels, playing the piano or doing embroidery, while waiting to be married off; only a handful went to university. In this respect little had changed in centuries. The war gave a powerful impetus to women's emancipation; by the 1920s some eleven million of them were working full time. They conquered the offices; after 1918 there were hardly any male typists or secretaries. *De facto* equality of the sexes was a long way off, there was no equal pay for women and in the professions such as law and medicine there was still a great deal of resistance to their entry. But equally there was no doubt that important changes had taken place which were to affect family life as well as sexual mores. Women were no longer ignored by the politicians, and they represented a labour force without which the economy could no longer operate.

It is difficult to define the impact of these changes on women, for they had paradoxical effects: some became harder, almost masculine; others more feminine and sexy. Women welcomed the disappearance of the old taboos and at the same time regretted it. Half vamp and half Gretchen, they smoked cigarettes and drank hard liquor – and wept as they read the new editions of sentimental love stories which their mothers and grandmothers had so much enjoyed. They gave their votes more often than not to the anti-republican parties rather than those to which they owed their new rights. They liked to dance; after 1918 Germany experienced a veritable dance fever in every form and shape: Beauty (i.e. nude) dances, Charleston, shimmy, tango, all had their day, while Mary Wigman, Anna Pavlova and Josephine Baker conquered Berlin. They admired the stars of the theatre, the opera, and above all the film. And there were of course a great many to whom none of these generalizations applied.

These trends were not of course exclusively German; all Western countries were affected by them to a greater or lesser extent. The same applies to the growing importance of technology, to the increasing popularity of sport and to other aspects of mass culture. Some called it disapprovingly the Americanization of German life. Pulses quickened, the quiet, introspective atmosphere of the prewar world had gone forever, newspapers carried such titles as *Tempo*. The 1920s were an impatient, restless age: its critics complained about the feverish atmosphere which was driving people to loss of control and ultimately insanity: *Die Zeit fährt Auto und kein Mensch kann lenken*, wrote Erich Kästner in one of his poems. (There had been fewer than 100,000 private cars in Germany when the war ended; a decade later there were 1.2 million.) Most of the evils of modernity had originated in the United States. True, American hotels were better and so were the railways, as a contributor to the *Deutsche Rundschau* noted in August 1927; one day, flights across the Atlantic would be a matter of routine. But who wanted to travel that fast? America stood for technical progress, but it also symbolized in many eyes the absence of culture, soulless materialism, the new barbarism.

Such criticism was more frequent among the right than in left-wing circles. The German progressives, like the Italian Futurists, in some ways admired American technical progress. Mayakovsky wrote an Ode to Chicago; so did Bert Brecht who had never been there. George Grosz, Brecht and their friends were fascinated by the exploits of American boxers from Bob Fitzsimmons to Jack Dempsey. America meant violence and freedom and the avant-garde was fascinated by both. John Heartfield, the inventor of photomontage, had adopted what he thought was an American name; during the war years both he and Grosz made a show of speaking English in public. The American way of life also had its critics on the left; some expressed horror at the effects of mass culture, of the anonymity of life in big cities. They were afraid of a kind of progress which they thought would inevitably lead to a technocratic dictatorship (Kaiser's *Gas I* and *Gas II*), and ultimately to wholesale destruction (Toller's *Masse Mensch*).

Meanwhile German scientists and technicians were in the forefront of progress. To the mass of people the inflatable airships (*Graf Zeppelin*) symbolized German technical achievement. These dirigibles had first appeared before 1914; an attempt to use them in the war had been less than successful because they were extremely vulnerable to enemy artillery. But in 1924 a new *Zeppelin* (LZ 126) flew non-stop from Friedrichshafen in southern Germany to Lakehurst in New York in 81 hours and 17 minutes; its captain and crew got a tickertape welcome. Another, bigger *Zeppelin* (LZ 127) flew around the world in 1929 and over the North Pole in 1931. Seen in retrospect the whole venture was a false start because air traffic did not develop in the direction first envisaged by Count Zeppelin, a former cavalry officer. The same applied to Do (for Dornier) X, a giant flying-boat with six propellers and twelve engines which could carry up to 169 persons. But what really counted in this age of experimentation; was the immediate psychological impact, which was tremendous, providing balm to the wounded German national consciousness, all the more perhaps because the Versailles treaty had virtually banned the development of a German aircraft industry. Germany could still outproduce and outconstruct the rest of the world. The ambition of German technicians was to produce the fastest vehicles. The

Bremen, a new 50,000-ton liner, won the 'Blue Ribbon' for the fastest crossing of the Atlantic on its maiden voyage in 1928. The same year Opel built the first rocket automobile, which accelerated from 0 to 100 km in exactly eight seconds. Germany also had some of the fastest and most reliable railways. At 23.00 hours on the night of 8 March 1929 the radio station at Berlin-Witzleben put out a television programme, scenes from a current movie called *Weekend*, showing girls in bathing suits. The pictures were received all over town and there was high praise for their quality.

The 1920s witnessed a great expansion of sport. Gymnastics had been invented by the Germans; football of course had been played before the war, and so had tennis, but boxing had been forbidden and a special police permit was needed for athletic competitions. Only after the war did sport become really popular; Paul Samson-Koerner (about whom Brecht wanted to write a play) and later Max Schmeling, who was world heavyweight champion in 1930, were national heroes. Hundreds of thousands, if not millions, flocked on Sunday to soccer matches. Throughout the week there were six-day cycle races to watch; in summer there was swimming, sailing and boating, while in the winter skiing became the popular sport – some forty years before it conquered America. The intelligentsia, as so often, was divided. Some wrote with dismay about these soulless activities, the chase after irrelevant records, the sad spectacle of a hundred thousand onlookers rooting for the champion. Siegfried Kracauer saw it as a danger to working-class (and white-collar) militancy. Frank Thiess, writing in 1928 on 'Intellectuals and Sport', said on the other hand that he would always send pale, bespectacled boys to a good sports teacher if it turned out that they were reading Paul Claudel as well as Heinrich Mann. But he also said that sport should have a content and a spiritual purpose; whereas Brecht opposed any endeavour to make sport a 'cultural value': 'I am in favour of sport precisely because it is unhealthy (i.e. risky), uncivilized (i.e. not acceptable to the establishment). It is an end in itself.'

A socio-cultural history of the 1920s is a mosaic consisting of an endless number of stones, large and small. It consisted of knickerbockers (even Thomas Mann wore them), mass tourism, the growth of department-stores, the death-mask of *l'Inconnue de la Seine*, the hit songs of the period, occultism, nudism, the immense impact of radio and the cinema. A detailed account would have to deal with the appearance of the five-o'clock tea and the long weekend; it would have to cover gangsterism and the corruption scandals – puny by international standards but given great publicity by the mass media. Needless to say it is quite impossible to bring all these aspects of the 1920s under a common denominator. They were as much part of the *Zeitgeist* as the Bauhaus, *The Magic Mountain*, Professor Heidegger and Dr Caligari.

The mood of the time was subject to marked changes and these in turn were connected with the political and economic history of the Republic. The optimism of prewar Germany was smothered under the horrors and deprivations of the war and the shock of defeat. For a brief moment there was a fresh upsurge at the end of the war; some believed with the writer René Schickele that a new world had been born in November 1918, that mankind had at long last been liberated. Schickele wrote that 9 November 1918 had been the most beautiful day in his life: 'I was in heaven. I thought never again would I be alone, never again would I despair of myself or of others. For the first time I felt secure . . . the new world was wide open.' But these high hopes did not last and the despair that followed was all the deeper. The immediate postwar period, with its political upheavals and economic crises, eroded whatever belief in a revival still existed; there was a growing sense of rapidly approaching doom, of *finis Germaniae*. These were the years of *The Decline of the West*, of Karl Kraus's *The Last Days of Mankind*, of George Grosz's *Ecce Homo* and of many apocalyptic poems and plays. The vision of impending catastrophe was most fully and most relentlessly expressed in the films of that period: *Dr Caligari*, Fritz Lang's *The Weary Death* and *Dr Mabuse, the Gambler*, and above all in Murnau's *Nosferatu*, with the very fitting subtitle 'A Symphony of Terror', and *Faust*. Was not Germany that very town threatened by the figure of Mephistopheles?

After 1923 the preoccupation with death and perdition gave way to a feeling that mankind, after all, had been given another respite. There was cautious optimism; things were looking up. *Es geht wieder aufwärts* was the reaction of the politicians and the man in the street; the intellectuals were more sceptical and decided to retreat from politics for the duration. So far as they were concerned the acute terror was replaced by a vague feeling of malaise, the conviction that things were not as they should be.

That the extreme right was unhappy about cultural developments goes without saying. Just as they hated the new state, so they loathed its culture. They were repeating in a number of variations what a Berlin police prefect had said after watching an early Gerhart Hauptmann play: 'The whole trend ought to be liquidated.' For them the manifestations of the new spirit were a betrayal of the national values and the German tradition, were degeneracy, *Kulturbolschewismus*. Nor were the centre and the left much happier about the prevailing state of affairs. In 1929 George Steinhausen, a worthy academician, published an ambitious history of German culture, the last pages of which were devoted to the latest developments. He saw a great deal of shade and virtually no light. The new technological-capitalist-materialist civilization had brought in its wake a general cultural decline. The new era of the mass spirit, of activity for activity's sake, was basically anti-cultural; it laid waste heart and soul. In one camp Steinhausen saw nothing but collectivism (and other isms), and in the other an exaggerated inclination towards irrationalism and an excessive stress on the 'German idea'. The destruction of the old gods could have been excused had the new age given birth to other values of true greatness. But in fact, apart from sport and technical progress, it had produced nothing of the sort. *Kulturpessimismus* is a universal disease; its ecology has been insufficiently studied, but there is reason to believe that it was more deeprooted and more widespread in Germany than in most other countries. Seen in retrospect, the Republic was culturally less sterile than the Empire; it may not have been one of the greatest of ages but it was certainly a creative one, giving birth to many new ideas and impulses. Yet this is not how many contemporaries saw it; they regarded it as a period of cultural decay and moral bankruptcy.

The fin-de-siècle mood was aggravated by liberal guilt-feelings, as revealed in the famous Krantz trial in 1927. A number of high-school students and their girl-friends had been sleeping around; there was jealousy, and it ended in a double suicide. This led to the trial of a member of the group in which the accused was eventually acquitted. Save for the unfortunate death of two young people, the whole affair was one of utter banality. However the lawyer defending Krantz played with great virtuosity on the guilt-feelings of the older generation. The general tenor of his plea was that everything could be put down to the guilt of society, everything was rotten, everything had to change. The liberal and left-wing press almost without exception accepted this cue for breast-beating and answered, Amen. Right-wing and clerical circles, needless to say, asserted that the affair confirmed that Weimar society was rotten to the core. In fact no society, however perfect, would have been able to prevent young people from engaging in sexual promiscuity, to forestall jealousy and suicide; no one had ever argued that 'society' was responsible for the sad fate of young Werther. But some liberals in the 1920s were only too ready to accept blame. Such masochism was not without its dangers, for it undermined society and made it difficult to defend the Republic against the calumnies of determined and unscrupulous enemies.

The pessimism of the left-wing intelligentsia was only natural; it saw its vocation, by definition, in opposing the status quo. The Republic fell short of their expectations in many respects; the Social Democrats were irresolute, always ready to make corrupt compromises with political forces to their right. Weimar justice was reactionary, abortion was illegal, as was homosexuality, the Reichswehr engaged in all kinds of illegal activities, and anyone who dared to write about them invited trouble. The old nationalist, militarist, aggressively Pan-German spirit was by no means dead. There were, in other words, a great many worthy causes to be sponsored, but this alone does not explain the venom with which some spokesmen of the extreme left attacked the Republic and all it stood for as something that was rotten through and through and not worth defending. A French intellectual of the left, however deeply opposed to official policies, would have drawn the line somewhere; he would not have said, as some of the Germans did: 'this country is not my country.'

It has been said in retrospect that some of these anti-patriots felt in their bones what was going to happen a decade later. Explanations on these lines may have some validity with regard to individual writers such as Joseph Roth, who was anything but a revolutionary; he had lost his home as the result of the war and his work is full of dark forebodings, anticipating the fate of the émigré. But this was an exception; in the 1920s there was nothing inevitable about the advent of barbarism – it was no more than a possibility. Yet quite a few intellectuals maintained that Germany could no longer be saved. Ironically, their pessimism was at the time no more than a small cloud on the political horizon. It was the product of a vague malaise, a dissatisfaction with the general state of affairs. Their doubts and discontent made the intellectuals of the left blind to the achievements of their age; they would have been most surprised had they been told that only a few decades later Weimar Germany would be the subject of a cult, and that students of history would find it of much greater interest than Britain and France in the 1920s. Far from basking in the sun of success they were building their counter-utopia more often than not in France, for it was in Paris that they saw the fulfilment of their dreams. Walter Benjamin, a master of the German language, suddenly announced in the 1920s to one of his friends that he could no longer write in German, and wrote to him in French, a language in which he expressed himself not without difficulty. Heinrich Mann was the foremost pioneer of modern German Francophilia. What attracted him above all was the fact that French intellectuals played a far greater role than the Germans in the fate of their nation, had the people on their side, constituted a real power. Even Thomas Mann, who during the war had attacked his brother so bitterly for his pro-French aberrations, admitted in later years that it was a fact beyond dispute that the role of French writers as leaders and teachers of their nation was incomparably more important than that of their German confreres.

The idealization of things French was most pronounced in the case of Kurt Tucholsky. This great mocker was moved by Paris to near ecstasy: in Paris men were more polite, nicer, even the reactionaries had *esprit*, and wrote excellent French; the women were pretty and charming. In Paris one got up in the morning in a good mood; whistling a merry tune, one left one's house:

Wie schön ist es hier zu leben; ohne diese Gesichter die keine sind;
ohne Krach und Krakeel – ohne den staubigen Berliner Sommerwind.

Zehn Jahre zu spät. Und doch darf ich nicht klagen. Es tut so wohl auch einmal Ja zu sagen.
(How nice it is to live here, without these faceless faces without noise and brawls, without the dusty Berlin summer wind. Ten years too late – and yet I must not complain. It is so good to say 'yes' for once.)

Later Tucholsky was to become a little more critical, but basically his attitude never changed. In another poem ('Park Monceau') several years later he wrote:

Hier ist es hübsch. Hier kann ich ruhig träumen. Hier bin ich Mensch – und nicht nur Zivilist.
(It is nice here and quietly I can dream. Here I am a human being – and not a mere civilian.)

This curious love-affair was based on a double misunderstanding, for neither was Germany a cultural desert nor Paris that much of an oasis. French sophistication often went no deeper than the famous Viennese charm. The French intellectual establishment was by no means wholly admirable, and as for the real France, the future émigrés were fated to know it much better in the 1930s; their education was to be completed in the internment camps of Gurs and Vernet.

It is useful to remember, however, that once the German situation had become more stable the number of intellectuals who really expected cosmic catastrophes was comparatively small. In retrospect it is easy to understand why. The downfall of the Republic was by no means a foregone conclusion; it is tempting but unhistorical to magnify the element of inevitability. The anti-republican forces had scored between 30 and 40 per cent in all elections since 1920, but in the elections of 1928, after four years of peace and prosperity, their share of the total was lower than ever before. German democracy was not yet firmly rooted, but the same had been true for many years of the French Third Republic after the defeat of 1870–1. Anti-semitism in France around the turn of the century had been more pronounced than in Germany but it had not in the end become a factor of decisive political importance. There was a great deal of philistinism in postwar Germany; although exaggerated, the lamentations of the intellectuals were not necessarily all wrong. But was the situation elsewhere, whether in France or Britain or the United States, that much different? By 1928 German democracy had survived several major shocks and there was no cogent reason to assume that it would succumb to the next crisis. The turning-point came only in 1930 when the effects of the Great Depression were felt and when the coalition of democratic forces fell apart. It was then, but only then, that the writing on the wall had to be taken in deadly earnest.

2
The Left-Wing Intellectuals

The attempt to classify the intelligentsia on political lines is fraught with dangers. Cultural life is not parliamentary; most of the issues debated are not political, and votes are not usually given according to party affiliation. The cultural avant-garde, to give but one example, is by no means identical in composition with the advocates of political revolution. But given the polarization of German politics in the 1920s, it is virtually impossible to comment on the intelligentsia as such. In no other country were the internal conflicts more bitter, the distance between the various factions greater than in Germany. If from time to time the battle was suspended, it was not because all passion was spent, but because the two sides were no longer speaking the same language. A Barbusse or Romain Rolland had incomparably more in common with a Maurice Barrès than a German intellectual of the left with Carl Schmitt or Ernst Jünger. The French writers were heirs to the same cultural tradition, they had been to the same schools, read, more or less, the same books, went to see the same plays, were preoccupied with the same moral, political and social issues. They would attack each other savagely as traitors and a disgrace to mankind, but, if pressed hard, they would admit that the opponent belonged to France too (as General de Gaulle once said of Sartre). It is unlikely that a French intellectual of the right would have claimed that he and his friends had a monopoly of *esprit* or fine prose.

In Germany, on the other hand, the right was firmly convinced that the left was anti-patriotic and thus not part of the

German people, while the left claimed that the right was stupid and barbaric. The only common ground was the indisputable fact that both were unhappy, though for different reasons, with the Republican order and the existing state of affairs in general. The right maintained that, given the Versailles *Diktat*, the pacifism of the left was high treason; the left claimed that the militarism of the right was bound to lead to a new world war. There was not the slightest willingness to take each other's point of view seriously, let alone to compromise. Ernst Bloch might as well have written in Hebrew so far as the nationalists were concerned. The left, in so far as it was at all aware that there were intellectuals outside its own camp, regarded their outpourings as mere gibberish on which no sensible man would waste much time. For was it not a well known fact that an intellectual, by definition, had to be a man of the left?

The German right regarded the left-wing intelligentsia as a noxious element; the Marxist-liberal-Jewish intellectuals were more dangerous than gangsters, for ordinary criminals were merely engaged in offences against property, and occasionally violence against persons, whereas the left-wing intellectuals were helping to bring about the spiritual murder of an entire nation. There were degrees in the intensity of these sentiments; the more moderate intellectuals of the right were grudgingly willing to put up with Thomas Mann and Max Reinhardt, but certainly not with Tucholsky, Brecht or Piscator. The extreme right-wingers demanded the total eradication of all un-German, anti-patriotic influences. It bears repeating that this deep antagonism prevailed not only during the immediate postwar crisis, and again during the years of depression; an abyss divided left and right even during the years of relative calm, when political issues were not particularly prominent. The way of thinking of the two camps, their mode of expression, their whole mental make-up, were different. Just as a man of the right would not dream of attending a performance of a Krenek opera, not to mention one of the plays staged by Piscator, a left-wing intellectual would take no interest in right-wing literature about the war. Each camp had its own newspapers, literature, theatre, music, cinema; it was perfectly possible to live without ever meeting representatives of the other side. If the cartographers of ancient times had marked *terra incognita* with inscriptions such as *Hic sunt leones*, each side believed that outside its own camp there were only skunks and asses.

Having established the fact that there was not one German intelligentsia but two or more, it is only fair to add that both left and right were hopelessly split into countless factions and groups, almost constantly engaged in internecine quarrels. The phenomenon is not novel, nor specifically German. Thus, an attempt to sketch a profile of the left-wing and the right-wing intellectuals can produce, at best, only an approximation not a true likeness, an ideal type or an identikit picture which may make it easier to understand a complex and elusive phenomenon even though the outlines are inevitably blurred.

The left intelligentsia consisted of several thousand radical journalists, writers and artists, some professional men and women such as physicians and lawyers, young people of no specific profession who had studied philosophy or German literature – and later settled in Berlin, and morely rarely in Munich or Frankfurt – who could not or would not enter academic life. Frequently they had no visible source of income other than some financial support from home. Sometimes they were active in politics, more often they were just fellow-travellers. They were participants in the great debates on the principles of modern art, capital punishment, trial marriage, Charlie Chaplin and other such subjects conducted in books, periodicals and above all in conversation in the avant-garde coffee houses. For the most part their background was middle-class; there was a handful of aristocrats among them and about as many men and women of working-class origin. The strong Jewish element was unmistakable, though a Zionist or a religious believer would hardly have considered them 'good Jews'. Many artists would be found in their ranks; they assumed that the political avant-garde and the cultural avant-garde were pursuing the same general ends and were thus bound to be natural allies. However, this was mere wishful thinking; the interest of the Social Democrats in things cultural was – as we shall show – strictly limited, and the Communists switched after a few years of experimentation to a cultural policy which was anything but revolutionary in inspiration.

The left-wing intellectuals rejected the Weimar Republic above all because it was so different from their early dreams.

They resented the survival of the old bureaucracy which had been taken over essentially intact, of a judiciary meting out blatantly biased political justice, a Reichswehr which, though small in number, constituted a sinister and powerful force. The fact that there were backstage dealings between the Reichswehr and the Red Army did not worry the Communists but was a matter of great concern to the independent left. The left campaigned without notable success for penal reform, for the abolition of capital punishment and greater sexual freedom (they wanted to do away with paragraphs 175 and 218 of the penal code, dealing with homosexuality and abortion respectively). In this struggle they faced not only the opposition of the right but the resistance of the influential Catholic Centre Party as well; for the Social Democrats and the Communists these were at best marginal issues and they were not willing to invest much effort in fighting for reform. The left-wing leaders assumed, probably correctly, that in so far as the working class cared about these problems it was instinctively against change.

The left intellectuals realized that the conflict between social democracy and communism was one of the main sources of weakness of the left and appealed in countless proclamations and manifestoes for left-wing unity. But the division was deep; the Social Democrats never forgave the Communists the attempt in 1919 to overthrow a government headed by socialists by means of armed rebellion. For the Communists, on the other hand, Ebert, Noske, Scheidemann and their comrades were the gravediggers of German socialism, more dangerous than the Nazis. The gulf was unbridgeable, and the left intellectuals in the end added to the fragmentation by joining various splinter-groups standing between social democracy and communism. Most of them were pacifists and this, too, increased their isolation. For since the Versailles treaty had reduced the German army to a small standing force of 100,000 men (while forbidding an air force or tanks), no political party was willing to make anti-militarism a major political issue. The right was traditionally in favour of a strong army; the Communists regarded pacifism as a petty-bourgeois aberration. The left-wing intelligentsia stood for close cooperation with Germany's neighbours and in particular with France, historically the arch-enemy of the Reich. But this was even less popular than pacifism among

the public at large, for friendship with France was possible only
on the basis of the Versailles treaty, the great abomination for
all German patriots. Versailles was tantamount to national
oppression, to robbing Germany of part of its territory, to ex-
ploiting the German people for generations to come. It was
denounced not only by the right but also by Lenin and the
Communists as a *Diktat* imposed by the imperialist robbers. To
try to persuade the German people, as the left-wing intellectuals
did, that it was rough justice, punishment for the aggressive war
which Germany had launched in 1914, was a hopeless under-
taking. The Democrats and the Social Democrats pursued the
policy of 'fulfilment' but as a matter of *Realpolitik*, not because
they thought Versailles was a just peace or that Germany had
been solely responsible for the outbreak of war.

Whichever way one looked at it, the left found itself in complete isolation, sponsoring worthy, humane and progressive
causes which unfortunately no one else was willing to back. This
feeling of isolation bred extremism and irresponsibility among
the unaligned left; their attacks on the prevailing order became
progressively shriller, their criticism more and more destructive.
Tucholsky, the most brilliant and most fertile German satirist
since Heine, wrote that since 1913 he had become one of those
'who think that the German spirit was poisoned almost beyond
recovery, who did not believe in an improvement, who regarded
German democracy as a facade and a lie'. In 1931 he published
a copiously illustrated volume of short notes and essays:
Deutschland, Deutschland über alles, a broadside against the
Reichswehr, the Church, the judiciary (formerly the people of
Dichter und Denker – poets and thinkers, the Germans had become a nation of *Richter und Henker* – judges and executioners),
the beer-drinking students, Hindenburg, the Social Democratic
commanders of the Prussian police, Stresemann, trade union
secretaries and almost everyone else in a position of authority.
It was an all-out attack, not just on the German philistine, his
customs, the way he arranged his home and educated his children, but on the German way of life in general, a denunciation
not merely of militarism but of national defence as such ('There
is no secret of the German army I would not hand over readily
to a foreign power', Tucholsky wrote). He ridiculed not just the
veterans' associations with their chauvinistic slogans and

parades, but derided systematically and with mordant wit each and every manifestation of patriotism. All this, needless to say, was grist to the mill of the extreme right. It did not make a single militarist repent but it strengthened a great many people in their belief that left-wing intellectuals were traitors, or at best totally irresponsible people who should not be taken seriously. The impression that emerged from Tucholsky's book was that everything German was *a priori* bad and stupid (*Deutsch is dof* as he once said) and had to be eradicated. In an article on 'The Face of a German' Tucholsky depicted the average German more or less as George Grosz had done in his cartoons; a rather thick-set head, a none-too-high forehead, cold, small eyes, a nose ever ready to lower itself into a mug of beer, a disagreeable toothbrush moustache. It was a caricature of Weimar Germany, part of it true, much of it distorted, all in questionable taste and serving no useful purpose. For what could the poor Germans do about their looks, their small eyes and low foreheads? The picture in Tucholsky's book which scandalized people most at the time was a photomontage, 'Animals look at you', showing eight somewhat sheepish and rather ugly gentlemen, aged sixty-five or over, most of them in military uniform. It was a pathetic sight, but there was nothing particularly animal or evil about them, given the unfortunate fact that men usually look more handsome and virile at thirty than at seventy and that babies are more likely to smile than retired generals. If Tucholsky wanted to imply that the German army and police needed better-looking officers, the Nazis a few years later provided them in the figure of Heydrich and other young men of striking appearance.

Tucholsky's book was a caricature but it deserves to be taken seriously because it reflects so well some of the basic weaknesses of the writers of the left who were doubly homeless. Strangers in their native country, they were unable to identify themselves with either of the two big socialist parties. Whether the target was Adolf Hitler or some unfortunate Social Democratic minister, it was all the same to them. Tucholsky and his friends thought that the German judge of the day was the most evil of characters and German prisons the most inhumane; it took Freisler and Auschwitz to modify their views. They imagined that Stresemann and the Social Democrats were the most reactionary politicians in the world; only a few years later they had to face Hitler, Goebbels and Göring. When Brüning was chancellor they sincerely believed that fascism was already ruling Germany or at any rate that the situation was so bad it could not possibly deteriorate any further – until the horrors of the Third Reich overtook them. The crowning irony was that the period was in fact one of unprecedented political and cultural freedom in Germany. Not, to be sure, in absolute terms; from time to time a writer, artist or journalist would be sued for blasphemy or treason; neither the German judge nor the commanders of the Reichswehr believed in democracy, and there were many cases of gross disloyalty vis-à-vis the Republic. But by depicting them as the ultimate in barbarism and depravity the intellectuals of the left overshot the target and defeated their own purpose; for who would believe that German judges were more reactionary than British judges in the 1920s, or that the French generals were greater admirers of social democracy than their German counterparts?

The despair of the German left-wing intellectuals dated back to 1919. They had persuaded themselves at the end of the war that the new state would be ruled by them (*die Geistigen*) and administered according to their ideals. But the intellectuals had neither divisions nor weapons; they even lacked a trade union able to defend their own material interests with the necessary vigour. They had never been among the privileged, and no one thought of asking them to join the new establishment. They might not have joined anyway for they intensely disliked the leading Social Democrats' whole life-style and culture, their dullness and their jokes (if any). The majority of the leading figures of the SPD were of working-class origin. Ebert had been a saddler, Severing a locksmith, Scheidemann a printer, Noske a basketmaker, Wels an upholsterer. Intellectually they were self-made men; they had been to party schools, had read Marx and Engels and Kautsky; some of them had been active in workers' cultural associations, reading-circles and peoples' theatre groups (*Volksbühnen*). They had not always been conservative. When, back in the 1890s, their party had discussed modern art, Ebert had taken issue with old Wilhelm Liebknecht who, like all men of his generation (including the Russian revolutionaries), had been reared in the idealistic tradition of

Schiller, whom they quoted on every occasion. Ebert had defended Gerhart Hauptmann against Liebknecht, in whose eyes the new Naturalist plays with their anti-heroes were both ugly and anti-revolutionary. Liebknecht certainly underrated the impact of a play like *Die Weber* even though his instinct so far as the politics of the Naturalist authors were concerned was not far wrong; few of them remained socialist sympathizers. But if the iconoclasts of the 1890s found their defenders in the socialist movement, there was no sympathy for the Expressionist revolution of 1910, for abstract painting and atonal music; on this issue there was full agreement between revisionists and revolutionaries such as Rosa Luxemburg and Lenin. The new art, as they saw it, had no message for the working class; it was of no help and comfort in its struggle.

German social democracy traditionally had not much respect for intellectuals; they were useful as editors of party newspapers, and occasionally as speakers, even though they usually had difficulty in finding the right approach for a proletarian audience. It ought to be remembered that the SPD was at the time a working-class party lacking any real desire to broaden its class basis. In any other capacity the intellectuals were found wanting: they were unwilling to do the *Kleinarbeit*, the essential daily chores of party life on which the movement depended. Such routine work was of no interest to them; instead (as the party leaders saw it) they were forever pressing utopian demands divorced from reality or pursuing campaigns which were of no obvious concern to the working class. The socialist party worker was almost exclusively concerned with the current tasks facing him; the intellectual was obsessed with the future, as often as not the distant future. For this and other deficiencies – such as lack of political judgment and tactical ability – intellectuals were not made to feel at home in the party.

The intellectuals on their part, while eager to serve the cause of socialism, were antagonized by what they regarded as the 'petty-bourgeois aspirations' of the working-class militants. One of them (Henrik de Man) has described the process of gradual disillusionment: like other intellectuals who had joined the socialist movement, he felt inferior to the masses because of his non-proletarian origins. For years he tried to obliterate all those features which had made him different from the masses, but eventually he came to realize that most of his proletarian comrades, including those in leading positions, were deep down far more bourgeois in outlook than he himself: 'I would have been able to put up with barbarian, but not with semi-educated petty-bourgeois elements.' De Man ended his chequered career as a renegade, but this does not necessarily invalidate his testimony. Gustav Landauer, a revolutionary (albeit of the non-Marxist persuasion) second to none, who died a martyr to the cause, reached with much regret and sadness the same conclusion: the proletarian had a deep and powerful inclination towards philistinism, *Spiessertum*. Whatever the Marxists contemptuously said about the character, life-style and cultural tastes of the petty-bourgeois, Landauer maintained, applied equally to the worker. Many left-wing intellectuals shared this opinion, though they preferred to keep it to themselves.

As the Social Democratic leaders saw it, the intellectuals were essentially bohemians preoccupied with problems which were of little interest for the working class. Such people were best held at arm's length; they would be more use to the party as fellow-travellers than as members. The fact that quite a few intellectuals were lax in their sexual mores and attached great importance to sexual reform did not endear them to the average party leader or militant whose standards were essentially old-fashioned. The anti-intellectual prejudice was more pronounced in German social democracy than among the French, the Italian or the Austrian socialists, among whom intellectuals were frequently found in leading positions, perhaps because, as was said, German social democracy was more truly working-class. It is difficult to think of a Jaurès, a Léon Blum or an Otto Bauer as a leader of the German Social Democrats. True, some SPD leaders were not of proletarian background Hilferding for instance, or Breitscheid – but neither belonged to the inner circle at the top. It is also true that the part played by intellectuals in the leadership slowly grew; by 1930 one in five among the party leaders had had higher education. But a university degree did not necessarily imply sympathy with the aspirations of the literary intelligentsia, nor did the cultural avant-garde look on Hilferding or on Breitscheid as one of themselves.

If the left-wing intellectuals felt inferior vis-à-vis the leaders of the pre-1914 working-class party, they had only contempt for the men who stood at the helm of the SPD after the war. These were, in their view, petty bureaucrats who cared neither about socialism nor about cultural values. They had no greatness, no revolutionary fervour; above all they had no style. As the intellectuals saw it, the party functionaries felt at ease only with kindred spirits: in shirtsleeves, drinking beer, at the card table or playing nine-pins – a typical German *Vereinsmeier* and philistine, not a Robespierre or a Garibaldi to whom they could look up. For them the Eberts, Scheidemanns and Wels were not just unrevolutionary types, they utterly lacked any trace of charisma. As Gustav Mayer, the historian of German socialism, wrote in his autobiography, these were little people, petty-bourgeois pedants of limited intellectual scope: 'I admit that there was scarcely a single figure in the entire leadership of the SPD who, measured by strict standards, aroused within me any profound ethical respect and admiration.'

This negative image of the socialist was certainly exaggerated, but what matters in this context is not so much historical truth, which was a little more complicated, but how the intellectuals perceived it. It is certainly true that after Bebel German social democracy did not produce any figure of more than average calibre, and this at a time when the magnitude of the challenges facing the party demanded superior leadership. In 1918 Kautsky was just an aged theoretician, Bernstein a marginal figure isolated from the mainstream, Rosa Luxemburg an outsider. The SPD leaders during the Weimar era were men of loyalty and integrity, staunchly democratic in orientation. But there is no denying that they were uninspiring, incapable of generating enthusiasm. The intellectuals might have accepted a strong authoritarian figure riding roughshod over inner-party democracy. They had no respect for the weak, irresolute men who stood at the head of the party once inspired by Marx and Lassalle and led by Liebknecht and Bebel. Thus intellectuals were inclined to join the Social Democrats, if at all, only with great reservations. More frequently than not they found their way to various uninfluential left-wing splinter-groups, or to factions to the right of the official party line, such as the circle of the *Sozialistische Monatshefte*.

The difficulties the intellectuals experienced within the Communist Party were of a different character. In its early years the KPD leadership consisted predominantly of intellectuals. Paul Levi, a Jewish lawyer who drove a Studebaker, liked modern literature and went to Switzerland for skiing holidays, was the most influential figure during the early years; with all his gifts he was an unlikely leader of a proletarian party. Among the charges brought against him after he had been expelled, the claim that he had been 'distant from the masses' figured prominently. Gradually, the key positions in the party passed from Levi, Reuter, Scholem, Katz and Ruth Fischer to men of impeccable proletarian origin such as Thälmann. This had the double advantage of making the party more attractive to the masses and its leaders easier for the Comintern to manipulate. The cultural activities of the Communist Party were dominated (with one notable exception) by intellectuals of bourgeois background. These left-wing Maria Magdalenas, the bohemians of 1910, had chosen the path of virtue: Johannes R. Becher, perhaps the most prominent among them, presents the case of an eccentric poet becoming an exemplary propagandist for the party line. The Malik publishing house had been set up to promote the Dada movement, but within a few years it became the most influential distribution centre of left-wing and Soviet literature in Germany. Its directors were the brothers Wieland Herzfelde and John Heartfield. The list of Expressionists, *Wandervögel* and young aesthetes who joined the KPD at one time or another is a long one; the one who became most widely known in later years was Georg Lukács, the Hungarian exile who had however been very much at home in the German cultural milieu even before 1918. He remained an unconventional figure even after his conversion, and thus came under fire early on for insufficiently mastering the thought of Marx and Lenin, for belittling the élan of the working class and attributing exaggerated revolutionary potential to the intelligentsia. The real trouble with Lukács, needless to say, was not that he had failed to understand Lenin; he understood him only too well and expressed disagreement at a time when it was still possible to do so without fatal consequences. The one truly proletarian figure in these circles was Willi Münzenberg, not an intellectual himself but a cultural impressario of genius, instrumental in establishing countless newspapers, magazines, film companies, cultural associations. An erstwhile associate of Lenin in Switzerland, Münzenberg was the first to grasp the importance of the popular-front technique in the cultural field, of establishing a periphery of fellow-travellers around the party. Like so many others he was eventually expelled as a dangerous deviationist; the circumstances of his death in France in 1940 have not been cleared up to this day.

During the years of 'relative stabilization' the attitude of the left-wing intelligentsia towards the Communist Party was one of friendly but somewhat distant support, limited in the main to signing manifestoes on behalf of Communist militants facing bourgeois justice, in defence of the Soviet Union (which was, for no good reason, thought to be in danger of military attack from France of all countries), petitions on behalf of Tom Mooney, Sacco and Vanzetti, and Communists persecuted in the Balkans, in China and Japan. The Communists on their part were disinclined to draw bourgeois elements any closer into the party since this would have been in contradiction to their policy of 'proletarianization of the leading cadres'. The situation changed somewhat after 1929 in the wake of the economic crisis and the rise of Nazism. Some intellectuals now wanted to identify themselves more closely with the KPD; unfortunately, it was precisely during this period that the Comintern was in a strongly sectarian mood and did its utmost to antagonize the would-be supporters. This was the time when *Linkskurve*, the leading Communist literary journal, was founded. The man behind it was Andor Gabor, a Hungarian émigré who in contrast to Lukács tried to carry out party instructions to the letter – to encourage and promote a truly proletarian literature which had to be politically relevant, a weapon in the class struggle. But such a literature, as Gabor saw it, could be created only by writers of proletarian origin; bourgeois intellectuals would only contaminate it. From the iron rule of proletarian origin Gabor excepted only himself and, probably with some reluctance, Becher, his co-editor. He pursued his assignment with such enthusiasm that even latterday Communist historians have found fault with his excess of zeal. To appreciate the higher lunacy of those days *Linkskurve* has to be read. It is difficult to convey in measured language the full flavour of its style and its cultural level. Suffice it to say that it devoted most of its pages not to the struggle against Nazism, nor even to combating 'social fascism' (social democracy), but to attacks on writers and artists who were only too eager to collaborate with the Communists: Henri Barbusse, Upton Sinclair, Romain Rolland. In Germany Piscator and Ossietzky were attacked, as were Döblin, Toller, Remarque and Kästner. From Heinrich Mann, *Linkskurve* wrote, 'the world of progress can no longer expect anything'; Tucholsky was derided as a fashionable snob, the Bauhaus denounced as a group of formerly radical petty-bourgeois elements seeking an escape from reality – this at the very time when the Bauhaus was headed by a Communist, Hannes Meyer. But then Meyer, *horribile dictu*, had accepted a commission for a building for the German trade unions . . . Ehrenburg was dismissed as a nihilist, Klee and Kandinsky were described as 'darlings of the bourgeoisie'. Alfred Rosenberg, the chief Nazi cultural propagandist, would not have found much to quarrel with in the black-list of *Linkskurve*.

As the Weimar period neared its end the Communists made some halfhearted attempts to be less sectarian in their approach to the left-wing intellectuals. But there could be no basic change in Communist tactics, since the leitmotif of the overall Comintern 'third period strategy' was that the masses were growing more radical and the struggle against the traitorous 'social fascists' had to be intensified. Given the fact that the Communists made themselves as uncooperative as possible, that these years witnessed the emergence of Stalinism in Russia (and the total subordination of the KPD to Moscow), given also the appearance of a new, and not very attractive, set of *apparatchiki* who took over the party leadership, it is surprising that Communists found any support at all among the intelligentsia. But such was the fascination of a militant party for the intellectuals that despite all the handicaps it attracted far more of them, especially among the younger generation, than did the Social Democrats.

The intellectual sympathizers of 1930, to be sure, were acting without the benefit of hindsight: Stalin was not yet the Stalin of the purges, few German intellectuals knew what was really happening inside Russia. Developments in Soviet cultural policy were largely unknown in these circles, still fascinated by that earlier period which had produced *Battleship Potemkin*, the militant poetry of Mayakovsky, Constructivist art and the revolutionary theatre. They saw a new society in the making, without exploitation and the indignities of capitalist civilization, in which a new and higher type of human being was being born. History itself seemed to be a fellow-traveller, Arthur Koestler wrote, and communism appeared as a logical extension of the progressive-humanist trend in Western history, the fulfilment of the Judeo-Christian tradition, of liberalism and the ideals of the French Revolution. Hedda Massing, not an intellectual herself but a member of a Berlin Communist circle in the 1920s, later wrote about her friends:

> We were all very poor during these years. And we were very happy. We had little to eat and very few clothes, we did not go to the movies or theatre for lack of money, and our apartments were bare and miserable. But we were elated and gay, young idealists, part of a growing movement. We belonged to a party which had gained recognition, we edged our way into public life in Germany. We were joined by many gifted people from all walks of life.

Above all the Communist Party was a dynamic movement, its members had a sense of mission, of riding the crest of the wave of the future, very much in contrast to the Social Democrats who were in a kind of permanent stupor, a decline from which there could be no recovery. The left-intellectuals were sometimes acutely unhappy about the follies of Communist policies, but since the party was in a state of siege with Hitler as the only apparent alternative in the struggle for power in Germany, they would usually find extenuating circumstances to defend the 'party line' against its critics.

In later years many of them were to leave the party or cease to be fellow-travellers; even a Piscator or a George Grosz, whose savage cartoons had been one of the most effective weapons in the political struggle during the early 1920s, would find refuge from Nazism in America rather than Russia. There they would meet Brecht, Feuchtwanger and other apologists for Stalinism who, as the moment of truth came, sensibly enough preferred Roosevelt to Stalin, and California to Siberia. A few would remain faithful to the party and they would be suitably rewarded by becoming ministers, deputy ministers or at least heads of academies. But this looks ahead to a later period; during the 1920s the Communist Party in Germany still seemed a revolutionary movement, a progressive force. For this reason it had considerable attraction for part of the intelligentsia.

In absolute terms the number of people involved was small, even if we add to the known Communists those who joined the party but were advised to keep the fact secret. The KPD wanted to be known as a working-class party; moreover its leaders felt that the intellectuals could be of more help to the cause from outside. Fellow-travellers had greater freedom of action, which also suited the intellectuals because they were not subject to strict party discipline. For in the final analysis there were too many bones of contention which made close cooperation with the Communists very difficult for most intellectuals, however sympathetic to the cause. Mention has been made of their instinctive pacifism, which was unacceptable to the KPD. They gravitated towards Paris, whereas the Communist mecca was in the east. The Communist leaders whom the left-intellectuals came to know struck them either as honest but stupid (such as Pieck and Thälmann), or as devious and too clever by half (such as Heinz Neumann or Ulbricht). There was certainly no Lenin or Trotsky among them, not even a Bukharin or a Radek. Nor did the intrigues and frequent changes at the top inspire confidence. True, the Communists talked about working-class unity but they did nothing to make it possible; towards the very end of the Weimar Republic they stressed the need for an anti-fascist front but in fact continued to attack social democracy with undiminished vigour. All this was bound to create misgivings among the left-intellectuals who, with all their eagerness to find a political home, could not in most cases embrace communism with the necessary unquestioning, uncritical enthusiasm of the true believer.

Reluctantly, they accepted the fact that they were bound to remain homeless, politically ineffective. Some devoted their efforts to pacifist activities, others to sexual and penal reform. Yet others, seeing no scope for political activity, turned to theoretical studies, to philosophical or sociological research. In some ways they were well equipped for this task, for many of them had had the benefit of a good philosophical training. But this also meant that they could not take Lenin's philosophical writings quite seriously, let alone those of his epigones. They were not really political philosophers, although their dialogues proceeded on a high level of abstraction in the tradition of classic German philosophy; they were far more interested in cultural problems in the widest sense. Lenin's strength had been the conviction that theory and practice were (or, at any rate, should be) one and indivisible. There was no obvious connexion between political practice and the new German ideology developed in Berlin and Frankfurt in the 1920s.

The German left-wing philosophers realized, quite correctly, that Marxism had to be brought up to date and made applicable to Western Europe. They thought, to put it bluntly, that Leninist ideology was partly irrelevant, partly too primitive for Central and Western Europe. This much was common to Lukács and Korsch, to Bloch and the Frankfurt School, even though they differed in many other respects. They were not Leninists and subscribed without hesitation to what Lukács had written in 1918: 'Politics is simply the means; the end is culture.'

Georg Lukács, a Hungarian with a special interest in aesthetics and Hegelian philosophy who had studied in Heidelberg before 1914, was the most influential thinker of this group of Western Marxists. Towards the end of the First World War he became a Communist, acting as commissar for education and culture in the Belà Kun government of 1919. After its downfall he emigrated first to Vienna and later to Germany, where he remained until 1933. Lukács's fame as a political thinker rests on his *History and Class Consciousness*, published in 1923. Soon after its appearance he dissociated himself, partly under duress, from the views expressed in the book, but this does not diminish the significance of a work which was to become one of the modern classics of heretical Marxist literature. Lukács's basic idea was simple: he rejected what he regarded as the vulgar and primitive philosophical views of Engels (*Dialectics of Nature*) and Lenin (the representationist theory of knowledge). These he saw as relics of nineteenth-century positivism and scientism, of the ideology of Kautsky and the Second International. Communist philosophy had to be purged of these un-Marxist (and certainly un-Hegelian) influences.

Lukács had turned to communism in the last resort not because the laws of natural science were pointing in that direction, nor because it was the most rational mode of production, but because it seemed the only road to a new, higher stage of civilization. In this stage, man's alienation would be overcome, the laws of historical materialism would no longer apply, Engels's famous 'leap from the realm of necessity to the realm of freedom' would become reality. Ten years later Marx's early philosophical fragments, with their heavy emphasis on alienation, were rediscovered and published; Lukács could have drawn a great deal of comfort from their publication had he persevered in his youthful indiscretion. But in the meantime he had retreated, having been severely condemned by Lenin, and after even more bitter attacks by lesser Russian interpreters of Marxism. It was quite intolerable that a Western Marxist should dismiss Soviet philosophy in such a high-handed way; the Russian party had triumphed in the struggle for power, and for that reason if for no other it was entitled to respect in the theoretical field as well. Clearly it would not have been able to seize power on the basis of a deficient theory.

The core of Lukács's argument was even more embarrassing. He claimed that the working class by itself was incapable of developing a consistent revolutionary theory, that it was not really aware of its class interests and therefore needed to be led by a small, elitist, strictly disciplined vanguard party, composed largely of intellectuals. This party would not emerge from the working class but would come into existence, and remain, as an autonomous body. If necessary it would even have to oppose the working class, since it had the deeper understanding of the course of history which the proletariat lacked. This small, fanatically devoted group of people would have to renounce their individual liberty; they would have to engage in any tactics, legal or illegal, moral or immoral, likely to promote the cause of communism. They would be ready, if necessary, to enter into alliances (albeit of a temporary character) with any party or group, however remote from Marxism, if this would promote the cause.

Lukács's work was denounced by the Communist leadership despite the fact that he had only taken further certain of Lenin's ideas about the inability of the masses to move beyond a trade union mentality without the help of a party of professional revolutionaries. If Lukács had erred in overshooting the mark in his exegesis of Leninist theory, his book was certainly no overstatement as a comment on Bolshevik practice under Lenin and, *a fortiori*, after his death. Basically the leading Bolsheviks had to agree with him, but their attitude to power politics resembled their approach to sex: one could do certain things but it was tactless and politically unwise to write about them openly. A mass movement could not admit that there were several levels of truth, one for the initiated, another for the rank-and-file, and a third for the masses. Since Lukács was a prominent party member and not an uncommitted intellectual, he had to choose between recantation and expulsion. He chose to stay in the party and for three decades refrained from commenting on politics. Instead he published essays on literature in which he praised the classics and damned the moderns, unlike the Western Marxists who took a more favourable view of the latest cultural trends. Admittedly he was not greatly impressed by Soviet literature either. In his later writings he showed himself somewhat less dogmatic than the official party line but never again strayed very far from the established canons of Marxism-Leninism. He retained a certain following in the West because, unlike the Russians, he could express himself in Western philosophical terms. But the original, independent approach which had distinguished his early works had vanished – or could no longer be expressed. After many ups and downs in his personal fortunes he died in Budapest in 1971, more widely admired and read in the West than in the East. A few years before, *History and Class Consciousness* had been reprinted in the West with a new preface by Lukács putting the book that had made him famous into 'proper political perspective'.

The year *History and Class Consciousness* appeared also saw the publication of Karl Korsch's *Marxism and Philosophy*, another milestone in the history of Western Marxism. Korsch was one of the leaders of the KPD at the time but he resisted the general trend of mechanically copying the Soviet experience both on theoretical and practical grounds. Like Lukács, he had a sound philosophical training; he claimed that it had been a mistake to transform Marx's theory of social revolution into a social philosophy. Marxism was not a philosophy, its task was not to explain all the riddles of the universe. Philosophy was not dead, as the *Vulgärmarxisten* were asserting, law and morality were not outdated metaphysics. Marxism was the heir of philosophy, not a new, all-embracing *Weltanschauung*. Abstract as these arguments sounded, the dispute concerned politics as well as doctrine. The philosophical discussion of 1923 was, as Korsch wrote several years later, only a weak echo of the political and tactical disputes inside the world Communist movement; it took the form of a dispute about the Leninist interpretation of Marx and Engels 'which had already been formally canonized in Russia, and, on the other hand, what were alleged to be views that deviated from the canon in the direction of idealism; of Kant's critical epistemology and Hegel's idealist dialectic'.

Korsch and other Western Marxists, most of them German, were unwilling to accept Lenin's approach to philosophy, which struck them as crude if not altogether unphilosophical. Lenin, as they saw it, had always approached philosophy with one overriding concern – its practical use for the revolutionary struggle. In other words he was concerned primarily with the question whether materialism was useful, not whether it was true. Thus Lenin's materialist philosophy

> becomes a kind of supreme judicial authority for evaluating the findings of individual sciences past, present and future. This materialist 'political domination' covers all the sciences, whether of nature or society, as well as all other cultural developments in literature, drama, the plastic arts and so on; and Lenin's epigones have taken it to the most absurd lengths. This has resulted in a specific kind of ideological dictatorship which oscillates between revolutionary progress and the blackest reaction. (*The Problem of Marxism and Philosophy.*)

When these lines were written in 1929–30 Korsch was no longer a member of the KPD, but the full consequences of the canonization of Leninism as a philosophy were only beginning to emerge.

Lukács and Korsch were the most Marxist of the pro-tagonists of a Western Marxism; others, less orthodox in approach or less interested in theory, took their ideological misgivings less seriously. For Brecht, who had been taught the essentials of Marxism by Korsch, this was an exciting experience in his development as a playwright, and since he was always more interested in the theatre than in theory it was much easier for him to continue working with the party. Even more remote from politics was another unexpected convert to Marxism, the essayist Walter Benjamin. A man of encyclopedic knowledge and original ideas, perhaps the greatest literary critic of his age, he did not find a place in the academic hierarchy because his studies were too unconventional and daring. A man of cosmopolitan intellect, Benjamin was equally at home in French literature, and his studies of the Baroque age, of Goethe and of the 'Work of Art in the Age of Mechanical Reproduction', were works of great profundity and excellence. In the words of Hannah Arendt, Benjamin was the most peculiar Marxist ever produced by a movement which had more than its share of oddities. His literary idols were Goethe, Proust, Péguy, Kafka and . . . Brecht, who, he thought, was a poet of rare intellectual power. He was 'essentially a metaphysician, pure and simple, attracted by subjects which had little or no bearing on metaphysics' (Gershom Scholem).

Having discovered Marxism Benjamin set about the practice of 'reductionism' (i.e. explaining the cultural superstructure by direct reference to the economic basis) in a way which would have made a *Vulgärmarxist* blush. He struggled all his life with the Jewish question on a metaphysical level and then from one day to the next was bowled over by the book of a primitive Communist hack precisely because he was impressed by its reductionism, its explanation of Judaism and Jewish history exclusively by reference to economic motives and trends. The works of the great metaphysician Benjamin were, for obvious reasons, never published in the Soviet Union; during his lifetime (he committed suicide in Vichy France in 1940) interest in them was limited to a small circle of admirers. But his writings were rediscovered in the 1960s and his place in the parnassus of Western Marxism is now assured.

Ernst Bloch, a friend of Benjamin – the two had met in Switzerland during the First World War – was yet another independent radical thinker who became one of the patron saints of Western Marxism. Difficult to classify – part writer, part philosopher, part prophet – his fame, unlike that of some of his colleagues, has not spread outside Germany because he is virtually untranslatable. The style of his books, beginning with *Geist der Utopie* up to the three-volume *Das Prinzip Hoffnung*, is a curious mixture of expressionist style and Old Testament pathos interspersed with Marxist terminology. They reveal the author as a man of formidable erudition but not of equal clarity of thought, a moralist engaging from time to time in abject genuflections before Soviet society and Stalin, the great leader and thinker. He was under no compulsion to do so; unlike Lukács he never lived in the Soviet Union. Like Benjamin he was a genuinely naive man, never exposed to political realities, a political philosopher devoid of political instinct. Whereas Korsch the Marxist had to leave the party in the relatively liberal 1920s, Bloch could teach philosophy in East Germany throughout the Stalin era and up to the late 1950s, despite the fact that his philosophy, but for the use of some jargon, was basically un-Marxist. While paying lip-service to historical materialism, Bloch is the most faithful heir of German idealist philosophy among Western Marxists. At the centre of his philosophy figures man, his hopes, dreams and aspirations which alone give meaning and content to the world. The future of man and of mankind is by no means predestined. He can choose. The decision has not yet been made, there is no certainty, only hope. Thus the Promethean, Faustian element of *die Tat*, the act, is reintroduced into Marxism; little remains of the forces of production and next to nothing of dialectical materialism *à la* Engels and Lenin.

Why did the Communists tolerate for so long a philosophy quite alien to their own, whereas in other cases offenders were expelled for the slightest deviation? Part of the answer has already been given: Bloch's metaphysics is difficult to understand whereas the thrust of his comments on current affairs is quite clear: praise of the Soviet Union; attacks on American imperialism. Furthermore, Bloch's philosophy is basically optimistic; in contrast to other contemporary 'bourgeois' philosophers he believed in progress; if his work was not Marxist it was at least 'bourgeois-progressive'. And lastly, in contrast to what some of Bloch's disciples thought of his philosophy, it was not really a 'major revolutionary force'; its appeal was strictly limited by the abstruse language, the lack of systematic thought and the many internal inconsistencies. It was often invoked with awe, but seldom studied and even less frequently adopted.

The main centre of unorthodox Marxism in the later years of the Weimar Republic was the Frankfurt Institute for Social Research (Institut für Sozialforschung). Founded in 1923 with a donation from a local millionaire with left-wing sympathies, it was headed first by Carl Grünberg and later by Max Horkheimer. Some of its leading members were (not without reservations) members of the Communist Party, but for tactical reasons did not advertise the fact. Others belonged to smaller left-wing factions or were radical Social Democrats, or simply unattached left-wingers. The publications of the Institute in Frankfurt, and *a fortiori* later on in Paris and New York, eschewed obvious propaganda and Marxist-Leninist terminology; even the word Marxism was only rarely used. The Frankfurt School (the name under which it has entered history) was mainly interested in theory, not in the practice of the class struggle. A discussion of the 'critical theory' for which it became famous is beyond the compass of this study, if only because before 1933 this theory existed only in rudimentary form; it was fully developed and formulated only in the years of emigration. Furthermore the 'critical theory' was basically the work of two men, Horkheimer and Adorno, whereas the other members of this circle either developed theories of their own (such as Marcuse and Fromm, who in some essential points differed from Horkheimer and Adorno) or had interests in fields other than philosophy: Grossmann was a fairly orthodox Marxist economist, Walter Benjamin and Leo Löwenthal wrote on literature, Siegfried Kracauer on sociology and on the cinema, Otto Kirchheimer on law, Franz Neumann on political science. Most of them remained Marxists of sorts, but their subsequent intellectual development usually carried them far beyond their original point of departure.

In so far as the Frankfurt School had a common denominator it was some kind of Marxist humanism based on the Enlightenment and the left-Hegelian tradition; Marx's *Paris Manuscripts*, discovered in the early 1930s, strongly reinforced the preoccupation with the problem of alienation. This common approach included a belief in reason and freedom, a rejection of positivism, as well as the uncritical faith in progress and the naive materialism which were typical features of 'scientific socialism'. Lastly, psychoanalysis had a lasting impact on most members of the school, and this too brought them into conflict with the official Marxist theory of the day, both Kautskyan and Leninist. The concern of the Frankfurt School was with 'man as the sole creator-subject of the social world'; it was not limited to the Marxist socio-economic infrastructure. For Marx labour had been the central factor in his theory, man's means of self-realization; science and technology were the tools for rational self-expression in work. For the Frankfurt School, with the exception of some orthodox Marxists, science was 'reification' and thus alienation, i.e. an oppressive factor. In their view culture was more than a mere function of labour, subordinate to it. They maintained that the victory of socialism would not necessarily bring about the de-alienation of man, it would not free man from the tyranny of economic forces, it would not inevitably make him 'entirely human'. This explains the growing interest of the Frankfurt School in anthropology, the study of man, rather than of economic forces. As they realized that their quest for a totally free society, free of constraints, was unlikely ever to be realized, their erstwhile confidence was gradually tempered by scepticism; in theory man could be free, but it was doubtful whether this was a practical possibility. But these doubts, too, belong to a later period.

During the Weimar era the members of the Frankfurt School were mainly preoccupied with the critique of contemporary culture from a left-wing position. While they differed in essential respects from the right-wing *Kulturkritiker* (the stress on reason), their starting-point was not wholly dissimilar. The esoteric language they used made their whole endeavour intelligible only to a small circle of like-minded people. This, incidentally, applied to most of the writings of the German neo-Marxists; the German language has an inbuilt tendency towards vagueness and lack of precision, and the Frankfurt School, to put it mildly, made no effort to overcome this drawback. When Walter Benjamin submitted one of his main works to a university to obtain the *venia legendi*, the professors returned it to him because they literally did not understand a single word. But in comparison to Adorno, Benjamin's writings were almost a model of clarity. The use of a private language limited the influence of the Frankfurt circle, but it was also a safeguard in turbulent times. None of the members of the circle was arrested when the Nazis came to power. The non-political Bauhaus or the non-Marxist *Weltbühne* attracted their ire, but no one bothered about reification and its opponents.

The basic weakness of the Frankfurt School was not, however, linguistic; it was the lack of connexion between its philosophy and its politics. They were, as we said, more interested in socialist theory than in practice, but they could not ignore politics altogether. They had to take cognizance of Stalinism and of fascism. Stalinism could be explained, up to a point, as a regrettable aberration, the attempt to build socialism in a backward country with unsuitable and insufficient means, the result also of the failure of the European proletariat to come to the help of the Russian Revolution. But unless one believed that future developments would somehow act as a corrective, the Soviet experience opened the door to serious doubts: what if the Russian Communists imposed their rule (and incidentally also their philosophy) on the left-wing movement in the West? What if the Communist revolution was to be successful only in backward countries in conditions similar to, or worse, than those in the Russia of 1917? What if it should appear that the historical destiny of Marxism, far from being one of universal liberation, was simply that of an ersatz capitalism, modernizing society in underdeveloped countries? Of these questions the Frankfurt Schoolmen could be only dimly aware in the 1930s. But there was another far more burning issue, that of fascism, and in this respect, too, the standard Marxist explanation could not satisfy them. They regarded fascism as the political mani-festation of the same metaphysical, relativist, irrational forces they encountered as their main enemy on the philosophical level. They accepted the fact that economic factors and class interests were involved, but they also detected other factors such as the authoritarian personality, which played a central role in the victory of fascist movements. These studies were to be the main preoccupation of some members of the School during the years of exile. With the return of Horkheimer and Adorno to Germany after the Second World War, the Frankfurt School experienced a striking but shortlived revival; and in the United States, too, it found new disciples. These more recent developments belong, however, to the legacy of Weimar; in 1932 the prediction that Herbert Marcuse would one day provide ideological inspiration to a generation of American students would have appeared about as likely as the forecast that Willy Brandt would one day be Chancellor of West Germany.

The left-wing thinkers mentioned so far are those whose fame has outlasted the Weimar period. But fame is frequently a matter of accident; there would have been no Marcuse revival had he emigrated to Moscow or Istanbul. There were other interpreters of socialist thought who are now forgotten but who were at the time more prominent than those mentioned hitherto. Some of them were revisionists, such as Henrik de Man, whose diagnosis of fascism was in some respects far more astute than that of the radical left; he emphasized for instance the importance of the nationalist element in fascism and the significance of symbols which Marxism had usually underrated – always to its detriment. Neo-Kantians, like Leonard Nelson and Siegfried Marck, tried to provide a new theoretical basis for the socialist movement; Arthur Rosenberg, a former Communist Reichstag deputy, reconsidered recent German history from an unorthodox Marxist point of view. Economists such as Fritz Sternberg and Henryk Grossmann undertook research into the character of contemporary capitalist economy, Sternberg following a lead given by Rosa Luxemburg, according to which capitalism had to expand in what would now be defined as the Third World if it was to accumulate surplus value. The era of imperialism and of capitalist expansion had provided a 'close season' for the proletariat in the developed capitalist world, thus promoting the growth of a labour aristocracy and reformism. But as imperialism had expanded virtually all over the world, the close season was coming to an end, and a new revolutionary wave was rising. This interpretation differed somewhat from the one provided by Hilferding, Kautsky and Lenin in as much as it postulated a catastrophe but not necessarily the victory of socialism. For capitalism in decline could as well lead to the ruin of civilization, to barbarism – a possibility which had already occurred to Marx sixty years earlier.

With all their ideological sophistication and their general readiness to expect the worst, most left-intellectuals were baffled by the rise of Nazism and were at a loss to provide a satisfactory explanation. During the early years it was their conviction that Nazism, being so unintellectual a phenomenon, was hardly worthy of serious study. But by 1930 at the latest it should have been clear that the study of a movement which threatened their country, their very existence, was an assignment of great urgency and importance. Nevertheless one looks in vain for any serious attempt in the writings of the intellectuals of the older generation, or of the young men and women (as, for instance, Erich Fromm and Hannah Arendt) who in later years were to devote so much time and energy to the interpretation of this very topic. Admittedly, it would not have made the slightest difference if they had done so; even the most realistic analysis would not have slowed down the momentum of the mass movement which was about to conquer Germany – and then, as one of its songs said, 'the whole world'. But the helplessness of the intellectuals vis-à-vis Nazism on the level of theoretical interpretation was a striking manifestation of an innate weakness which demands further investigation. It was closely connected with the attitude of left-intellectuals to politics in general and the question of commitment, and this takes us back to some of the issues already discussed in passing.

The problem of commitment existed from the first to the last day of the Republic, though it was most acutely felt in the early and the late years of Weimar. The editor of the *Tagebuch* wrote in 1927 that 'for us collaboration with a political party is foreign and unthinkable', but that was a particularly calm year; in 1919 or 1932 he would probably have reacted differently. In the early Weimar days there was a marked willingness to collaborate with the new order on the part of the intellectuals, based no doubt largely on their belief in the leading role of the man of letters. Together with 'the people' they would carry out the revolution which would bring the 'wave of love' that would 'open the hearts of men'. They really did expect the transfer of power to the intellectuals. In Munich in 1918 one of them, Kurt Eisner, proclaimed the Bavarian Soviet Republic; he was a Social Democrat newspaper editor who opposed the war and had joined the Independent Socialists (USPD). Other leading figures of the revolutionary movement in Bavaria were the writers Ernst Toller and Erich Mühsam and the essayist and translator of Shakespeare, Gustav Landauer, half anarchist, half Proudhonist. The sad fate of the Bavarian Soviet Republic is well known; its intellectual leaders fared no better. Eisner and Landauer were assassinated, Toller and Mühsam imprisoned. This to all intents and purposes was the end of the intervention of intellectuals in South German politics. In Berlin the political activists among the intelligentsia were spared Eisner's and Landauer's fate, but only because they were totally ineffective and thus attracted hardly any attention. The attempts to 'organize the intelligentsia', the declared programme of *Die Aktion* and of Kurt Hiller's Council of Intellectual Workers, aimed at the impossible, for who had ever been able to organize intellectuals for effective concerted action? The historian Lujo Brentano, who for a short while headed one of the branches of the council, later wrote that presiding over its meetings was like chairing a gathering of anarchists: an apt remark because instinctively they were, of course, all anarchists. The then editor of the *Weltbühne* withdrew after a short while from the Council of Intellectual Workers because he thought the group was childish and confused; it rejected democracy, advocating a dual dictatorship – the economic dictatorship of the workers and the dictatorship of the intellectuals against 'the tyranny of the *ungeistige* majority'. Kurt Hiller was the moving spirit behind this and similar groups; he believed in logocracy, the power of the word. According to this doctrine not all intellectuals were among the chosen, but only the men of the word among them, the literati. Toller objected that intellectuals were not endowed with some higher faculty of judgment, but his arguments failed to impress Hiller who continued to extol the mission of an intellectual aristocracy summoned to spread *Geist* among the masses.

Hiller was admittedly an extreme case, but the assumption that the intellectuals should play a leading part in the politics of the Republic was by no means confined to him. If the *Tagebuch* in 1919 suggested Gerhart Hauptmann as president of the Republic, the *Weltbühne* in 1932 advocated the candidacy of Heinrich Mann; when this did not materialize they settled for Thälmann, the Communist leader. So far as the intellectuals were concerned it was either all or nothing. Coalition politics, the sharing of power, would only mean compromise and thus corruption. They had no real concept of the realities of political life; reality, as Gottfried Benn once wrote, was a capitalist concept – the spirit recognized no reality. 1848 had been the revolution of the intellectuals, of professors, students and workers; it had been prepared by lawyers, carried out by artists and led by novelists and poets, as Proudhon wrote at the time. Why, they asked, should 1918 be different? Perhaps they were not wanted, and in that case they might as well opt out of politics altogether. A minority joined the extreme left, a very few later moved to fascism, but the great majority retreated into an unpolitical, essentially negative neutrality towards the Republic. With *this* Republic they had nothing in common.

The negative attitude of vocal sections of the intelligentsia was reflected in the line taken by the *Weltbühne*, the most influential journal of the non-partisan left intelligentsia. Founded before the First World War as a journal devoted mainly to the theatre and related arts (*Die Schaubühne*), it became in the 1920s under Hellmuth von Gerlach and Carl von Ossietzky largely political in character. Its star writer was Kurt Tucholsky; using several pseudonyms, he provided every week biting little sketches to the delight of his left-wing admirers and the fury of the reactionaries. Every good cause was espoused by the *Weltbühne* – pacifism, sexual reform, penal reform, working-class unity. It attacked chauvinism, militarism, the old bureaucracy; it published startling revelations about the Free Corps, the Black Reichswehr and the attempts to rearm Germany in contravention of the Versailles treaty. Tucholsky in his brilliant essays tried to 'sweep away with an iron broom all that is rotten in Germany. We will get nowhere if we wrap our heads in a black-white-red rag and whisper anxiously "later my good fellow, later" . . . No, we want it now!'

These attacks were supremely well written and delivered with great passion. They were also directed indiscriminately against left and right, against friend and foe alike. A few examples should suffice: *Die Weltbühne* was second to none in its desire for reconciliation and friendship with France, and it published countless appeals to this end over the years. Yet at the same time it made vitriolic attacks on Stresemann and the German Foreign Ministry, which was pursuing this policy though it was extremely unpopular at the time. According to the *Weltbühne* the 'Stresemann type' was more dangerous than the Stahlhelm, the revanchist military organization of the extreme right. To provide another illustration: the *Weltbühne* attacked the Social Democratic leaders not just for their political mistakes, which were many, but for their personal shortcomings, their lack of *savoir-vivre*, their gaffes, the fact that they did not have the benefit of a university education. 'There was an element of nasty snobbery in all this and a rather cheap delight', Gordon Craig writes, in exposing the personal and intellectual inadequacies of people like the Reichstag President Paul Löbe, who was in his own way doing rather more than Tucholsky to fight the rising tide of National Socialism.

Even on the issue of fascism the attitude of some *Weltbühne* writers was not entirely above suspicion. In 1926 Mussolini was no longer a newcomer on the political scene; two years after the murder of Matteotti there should have been no illusions about the character of fascism. But the attitude of quite a few left intellectuals was by no means one of outright opposition. Kurt Hiller wrote an admiring essay in *Die Weltbühne* about the *Kraftkerl* Mussolini. Tucholsky commented in the same journal: 'There are two powers in Europe which have achieved what they wanted: Fascism and the Russians. The decisive factor in their victories was their courageous intransigence.' On another occasion he wrote about fascism in France: 'this is above all an intellectual [*geistig*] affair, which has nothing whatever in common with the German rowdies.' He was impressed by their quest for new values and approved of their rejection of parliamentary democracy. The same year Ernst Bloch and Walter Benjamin wrote essays in the same journal about 'Italy and Porosity' which managed to survey the Italian scene without once mentioning the fact that fascism was in power in Italy. The *Weltbühne* attitude to Nazism was of course totally negative, but in trying to explain the roots of the phenomenon the journal was wrong much of the time. There was an unfortunate tendency (writes Istvan Deak) to present the Nazis as a bunch of psychopaths who could not win lasting popular support and would soon be repudiated by the masses. The Nazis were mere puppets of the conservatives and, of course, of heavy industry. Hitler, the *Weltbühne* editor wrote, was Hugenberg's Golem, who would never be permitted to pursue an independent policy. If Hitler's policies were no longer to suit the interests of those who had provided the money, the Nazi movement would disappear as suddenly and mysteriously as it had mushroomed and would be replaced by a more reliable party.

The 1930 elections, in which the Nazis emerged as the second largest party, induced the *Weltbühne* to blame the Social Democrats for having concentrated their attacks on Hitler and Co. instead of launching their main assault against Brüning and the Catholic Centre Party. In 1932 it accepted the Communist thesis that fascism (personified by Brüning) was already in power; hence it seemed only logical to suggest that it would not be a bad thing if the Nazis were given power. Unable to cope with the many problems facing them, they would soon lose their popularity and destroy themselves by mismanagement. The idea that there was perhaps after all a certain qualitative difference between Nazism and bourgeois democracy even in its existing, severely curtailed, form was not accepted by Ossietzky. In his own case and in that of some of his friends, it happened to be the difference between life and death.

It is, of course, not quite fair to concentrate on mistakes committed by left-intellectuals as if these had been leaders of political parties. It was a time in which few political observers were consistently right; and it is easy to think of even more outrageous examples of misjudgment outside Germany – of Shaw's and Wells's attitude to Mussolini in the 1920s, and of the admiration of Stalin by so many Western intellectuals in the 1930s. It may well be true that (in the words of his biographer Harold Poor) Tucholsky's negativism and despair were partly at least a pose, that in the early years at any rate he predicted disaster while hoping for and half-believing in salvation. The motives of the *Weltbühne* writers were generous, their hearts were in the right place; they were, as we said, in the forefront of the battle for every good cause; their great weakness was that they were 'indiscriminate in their selection of targets and immoderate in their expenditure of ammunition' (Gordon Craig). The negative attitude and the withdrawal into sectarianism was in all probability only a reaction to their sense of impotence. Tucholsky was quite aware that even the most biting satire could not change political realities. In 1931 he wrote that his work apparently had made no impact: 'I write and write – and what effect does it have on the conduct of the country?' The answer was all too obvious. His dilemma was that of all left-wing intellectuals: whatever they did or refrained from doing was of no public interest except to provide grist to the mills of Goebbels and Alfred Rosenberg. The struggle proceeded in the streets, the political assemblies, the beer-halls, the party head-quarters – anywhere but the places frequented by the intel-lectuals.

They were not the conscience of the nation, and no one looked to them for moral or political guidance. When Cherny-shevsky wrote that novels, essays and poetry 'have a far greater significance for us Russians than they have in any other country', he was only stating a well-known fact. In France, too, as the Dreyfus Affair had shown, intellectuals played an important part in public life and on occasion decisively influenced the course of events. Heinrich Mann, writing before the First World War, looked with admiration and envy to Paris: 'They had it easy, the *littérateurs* of France, who resisted established power, from Rousseau to Zola – they had the people on their side, they had soldiers.' In Germany, *Macht* and *Geist* were poles apart, and this was never more glaringly obvious than at a time of crisis. True, even Heinrich Mann had not given up hope: 'The use of power which is not filled with goodness and kindness will not last', he wrote in *Der Untertan*. Twenty years later Alfred Döblin, at the depths of the economic depression, expressed similar hopes in his *Wissen und Verändern*. But the intellectuals remained outsiders, facing overwhelming odds with the tide running against them. Thus the whole issue of their responsibility must be seen in true perspective. It was after all Hitler, not Tucholsky, who buried the Weimar Republic. Even if the left intellectuals had been less embittered about the fact that their noble dream had not been realized in Weimar, even if their perspective had not been dictated by utopian visions and moral absolutes, even if they had all rallied to the defence of the Republic, the outcome would most probably have been the same. The political parties through which they should have worked would still have rejected them. A hundred years of German history could not be undone in so short a time; it would have taken a major miracle to propel them into a position of real influence. Powerless as they were, they had to watch the unfolding tragedy from the sidelines, commentators, not actors in the events which were to shape their fate and that of the nation for many years.

It was not at the time considered good form in their milieu to discuss the fact that a great many among them were Jews, or at any rate of Jewish origin. So far as the public at large was concerned this was not exactly a secret, and the antisemitic critics made the most of it. They referred to Jewish Marxism, Jewish degenerate art, the Jewish *Weltbühne*. Most German Jews were neither intellectuals nor radicals; indeed there were far more Jewish tailors than writers and journalists; politically, German Jewry was left-of-centre but did not gravitate to the extreme left. There was a handful of Jews among the leaders of the Social Democrats and up to 10 per cent of the SPD deputies were of Jewish extraction, but it is difficult to think of any prominent figure among them after 1920. There were many Jews among the leading Communists during the early years of the Republic, but their numbers too dwindled rapidly as the party underwent proletarianization and Stalinization; among the one hundred KPD deputies elected to the Reichstag in November 1932 there was not a single Jew. What is perhaps even more significant, among the five hundred Communist candidates who contested those elections there was not a single Jew either. The small left-sectarian groups such as the SAP (which split away from the SPD in the early 1930s), the various factions which seceded (or were expelled) from the Communist Party for left or right-wing deviations, such as the KPO or the Nelson Bund (ISK), were heavily Jewish, but they were insignificant politically and did not attract the limelight.

Antisemitic propaganda claimed that Weimar was a *Judenrepublik*; this was true to the extent that Jews did indeed play a bigger role than in Wilhelmian Germany, when they had been kept out of public office. The 1919 revolution opened to them political careers which had not existed before. For a few months the activities of Eisner and Rosa Luxemburg (who regarded her Jewishness as a mere accident of birth) were given wide publicity, but after 1920 only one Jew, Walther Rathenau, attained a position of prominence, and he too did not exactly make frequent use of his Jewishness. Rathenau was anything but a man of the extreme left, but this hardly mattered to the right-wing terrorists who killed him in 1922. There were many Jews in publishing and in the theatre; most of the contributors to the *Weltbühne* and the *Tagebuch* were of Jewish origin. They were well represented in most fields of learning, literature and the arts; almost all of them were highly assimilated and thought of themselves as Germans. This was even more characteristic of those on the extreme left, of whom many had formally disavowed any connexion with the Jewish community. They maintained that Jewish problems were of no particular interest to them, but what mattered in the last resort was, of course, not how they saw themselves but what others thought of them. In a letter written after 1933 Tucholsky bitterly noted that officially he had renounced Judaism many years before but that he had come to realize that this had been an impossible endeavour.

The attraction of the left for the Jews is an interesting and complex phenomenon, but it is not specifically German. Briefly, they gravitated towards the left because it was the party of reason, progress and freedom which had helped them to attain equal rights. The right, on the other hand, was to varying degrees antisemitic because it regarded the Jew as an alien element in the body politic. This attitude had been a basic fact of political life throughout the nineteenth century and it did not change during the first third of the twentieth.

Without the Jews there would have been no 'Weimar culture' – to this extent the claims of the antisemites, who detested that culture, were justified. They were in the forefront of every new, daring, revolutionary movement. They were prominent among Expressionist poets, among the novelists of the 1920s, among the theatrical producers and, for a while, among the leading figures in the cinema. They owned the leading liberal newspapers such as the *Berliner Tageblatt*, the *Vossische Zeitung* and the *Frankfurter Zeitung*, and many editors were Jews too. Many leading liberal and avant-garde publishing houses were in Jewish hands (S. Fischer, Kurt Wolff, the Cassirers, Georg Bondi, Erich Reiss, the Malik Verlag). Many leading theatre critics were Jews, and they dominated light entertainment.

This German-Jewish cultural symbiosis had few if any enthusiastic supporters among the Germans and a great many enemies who would have gladly done without Marx, Freud and

Einstein, let alone Tucholsky, the Jewish film-makers and theatre critics. Many had been aware of the problem well before the First World War. In March 1913 a young Jewish writer named Moritz Goldstein had published an article entitled 'German-Jewish Parnassus' in the fortnightly *Kunstwart* which created something of a minor scandal, provoked many letters to the editor and was discussed for a long time in the German press. Briefly, Goldstein argued that the Jews were directing the culture of a people which denied them both the right and the capacity to do so. The newspapers in the capital were about to become a Jewish monopoly; almost all directors of the Berlin theatres were Jews; so were many actors. Musical life without the Jews was almost unthinkable, and the study of German literature was also to a large extent in Jewish hands. Everyone knew it, only the Jews pretended it was not worthy of notice; for what mattered, they claimed, were their achievements, their cultural and humanistic activities. This, said Goldstein, was a dangerous fallacy, for 'the others do not feel that we are Germans'. They could show the others that they were not inferior but was it not naive to assume that this would in any way diminish their dislike and hostility? There was a basic anomaly in the Jewish situation. The liberal Jewish intellectuals were good Europeans, but they were also split personalities, divorced from the people among whom they were living. They could make a great contribution to science, for science knew no national frontiers, but in literature and the arts (and, he should have added, in the political sphere) any major initiative had to have popular and national roots. From Homer to Tolstoy all the really great works had their origin in the native soil, the homeland, the people. And this 'rootedness' the Jews lacked, despite all their intellectual and emotional efforts.

Among those who answered Goldstein was the poet Ernst Lissauer, who during the First World War won notoriety in connexion with his 'Hate England' hymn. He bitterly opposed any attempt to restore a ghetto on German soil or a 'Palestinian enclave'; on the contrary, the process of assimilation was to be carried to its successful conclusion. If so many Jewish intellectuals were radicals and had no feeling for the German national spirit, this was no doubt because they were still discriminated against in so many ways. But once those barriers fell, they too would be fully integrated into the mainstream of German life.

Ten years later a republic had been installed, and Jewish intellectuals were no longer hampered in their professional careers; they became professors, government officials, even cabinet ministers. But this did not bring about a diminution of antisemitism. Jakob Wassermann was one of the most 'German' writers of that age, yet even he, writing shortly after the war, reached deeply pessimistic conclusions about the cultural symbiosis:

> Vain to seek obscurity. They say: the coward – he is creeping into hiding, driven by his evil conscience. Vain to go among them and offer them one's hand. They say: Why does he take such liberties with his Jewish obtrusiveness? Vain to keep faith with them as a comrade in arms or a fellow-citizen. They say: he is Proteus, he can assume any shape or form. Vain to help them strip off the chains of slavery. They say: no doubt he found it profitable. Vain to counteract the poison.

Arnold Schoenberg, who had been converted, found, as he wrote to Kandinsky in 1923, that 'I am neither a German, nor a European, not even perhaps a human being, but a Jew'.

Schoenberg continued to compose, Wassermann to publish his bestselling novels, and even Moritz Goldstein did not emigrate to Palestine but became literary editor of a leading Berlin newspaper. But it is also true that these three and many others eventually had to leave Germany and that the symbiosis came to an end in an even more gruesome way than anyone had expected. It is easy to show that Goldstein's thesis was exaggerated: the number of Jews teaching German literature, for instance, was not large, and it is also true that Jewish writers had more German than Jewish readers. Jewish writers were hypersensitive, as Thomas Mann once observed to Wassermann. Kafka in a letter to his friend Max Brod commented on the impossibility of writing in German, the use of the German language being the 'overt or covert . . . usurpation of an alien property, which had not been acquired but stolen, (relatively) quickly picked up, and which remains someone else's property even if not a single linguistic mistake can be pointed out'. Franz

Werfel shared these misgivings, at least in regard to Kafka; no one beyond Teschen-Bodenbach would ever understand him, he once said. He could hardly have been more mistaken, as the spread of Kafka's posthumous fame has shown.

There existed, in short, a very real Jewish problem. A majority of educated Germans believed that Jews had acquired too much influence in the cultural life of their country. Some would have preferred to eliminate them altogether. The situation in Germany (and Austria) differed from that in Britain and France; there were very few Jewish intellectuals at the time in Britain; and while their number was more substantial in France, the French intelligentsia was far more sure of itself than the German – the slogan of 'Jewish domination' of French cultural life was never taken quite seriously.

According to the German antisemites the Jewish intellectual was cosmopolitan, rootless, destructive in his criticism, lacking creativity, forever denigrating the supreme values of the German spirit, which he was unable to understand. This was of course a caricature, based on a kernel of truth which was distorted out of all proportion. True enough, Jewish writers (with some exceptions) tended more than their non-Jewish colleagues to emphasize in their works the universal human element, to play down the specific, the national. Beyond this general observation it would be difficult to find a common denominator. But antisemitism was an instinctive attitude; the Jew was considered an alien even if it was difficult to define the specific character of his alienness; no amount of reasoning would eradicate this feeling. Goldstein realized that it was futile to

> show the absurdity of our adversaries' arguments and prove that their enmity is unfounded. What would be gained? That their hatred is genuine. When all calumnies have been refuted, all distortions rectified, all false notions about us rejected, antipathy will remain as something irrefutable. Anyone who does not realize this is beyond help.

It hardly mattered that Jews were not equally strongly represented in all branches of Weimar culture; the flowering of the visual arts proceeded largely without Jewish participation, and there were not many Jewish philosophers and sociologists.

For in the last resort it is quite true that what made Weimar culture *sui generis* is unthinkable without the Jews. Given the strength of antisemitic feeling at the time, the isolation of the left intelligentsia was a foregone conclusion. The Jews gave greatness to this culture and at the same time helped to limit its appeal and make it politically impotent.

If the German-Jewish cultural symbiosis was highly prob- lematical, a catastrophe was not a foregone conclusion. There could have been gradual change; Weimar culture had anyway reached an impasse well before Hitler came to power. But for the economic crisis and its political repercussions the liberal- left-Jewish public would have continued reading the *Tagebuch*, the *Weltbühne* and the *Literarische Welt*, whereas the others would have stuck to the *Deutsche Rundschau, Deutsches Volkstum, Die Tat* and the *Kunstwart*. The groups would have coexisted, not necessarily peacefully, just as coteries of different political and cultural orientation coexisted in other countries. It could have happened, but it was not to be.

Stefan George told one of his disciples in 1933 that since the expulsion of the Jews from Spain, there had been no disaster comparable to what was about to happen in Germany: 'That was the end of Spain. This will be the end of Germany.' Strictly speaking it was not the end of Germany, not even of German culture; writers continued to publish their novels, composers had their symphonies performed, Otto Hahn split the atom, Domagk and Spemann received Nobel Prizes for medicine, Butenandt for chemistry. But the most interesting period in German cultural history did indeed come to an end. Germany was not to recover from the loss and the world has not witnessed an era of similar creativity.

3
Thunder from the Right

Both left and right-wing intellectuals in the Weimar Republic had, in theory, the choice between several parties, and both were, in the last resort, politically homeless. Just as the left-wing intelligentsia was anything but monolithic, so right-wing ideologists ranged from those advocating terrorist measures to moderates expressing vague discomfort at the way things were going in the Republic. There was reluctance to accept the new order even among moderates. Hans Delbrück, who accepted Weimar – much to the disgust of many of his colleagues – maintained that he could not participate in celebrating its anniversary, for 'the Republic was still too young to ask for respect'. What German professor would have refused to pay respect to the Reich in 1872 on the ground that it had come into existence only one year earlier? At the other extreme there were the wild men of the right, a motley crowd: rabid anti-semites, nihilists, charlatans and true believers, arch-conservatives and 'Bolsheviks of the Right', paranoiacs and desperadoes, uprooted men who may have chosen politics rather than gangsterism because it seemed to offer greater rewards.

It is not easy to think of any common denominator that would cover the whole range of the right wing; certainly many of them were not 'conservatives' in the traditional sense, for what was there to conserve? They were united in their opposition to the Republic and of course to 'Weimar culture', which they thought an abomination. All of them were in favour of a strong authoritarian state; but some thought that the *Volk* would have to be regenerated and the race 'purified' first, while others preached aggressive nationalism without identifying its specific features. Most right-wing thinkers would have rejected the 'intellectual' label, for an intellectual, by definition, was a man of the left; the term had been used in France around the turn of the century by the right as a derogatory term to denote their left-wing enemies. Intellectualism was arid, negative, rationalist; an intellectual lacked intuition, faith, feeling, respect for all that is sacred. In Nazi parlance the term was invariably used as an expression of contempt or ridicule. But however much they resented the label, most right-wing ideologists were, of course, intellectuals of sorts, including Goebbels and Rosenberg.

If the right-wing critics of Weimar agreed on the symptoms of the disease, there was no unanimity about when it had started and whether it was at all curable. The majority believed that Germany's spiritual decline had not started in November 1918; they saw its origins in the last third of the past century. The tocsin had first been sounded several decades earlier against the growth of soulless materialism, the unfettered progress of capitalist culture, the ascendancy of Berlin – the un-German metropolis – the brutality, emptiness and *Entseelung* ('alienation' in current parlance) of the age. The works of Lagarde, Langbehn, Lienhardt and others less well known had been read by thousands, and the legacy of *Kulturpessimismus* was again invoked after 1918.

The emptiness of the Wilhelmian era had been as acutely felt by the young idealists of the right as by their contemporaries on the left, but they had reacted in a different way. Neither right nor left had advocated violent political action before 1914; to bring about this change a major earthquake was needed. The right, like the left, had reacted by advocating cultural remedies: a change in life-style, a return to old values, a more simple and natural life. Hence the call for a *völkische Kultur* – as against cosmopolitan civilization. *Kultur*, as the right saw it, was rooted in the people, had a soul; whereas *Zivilisation* was soulless, external, artificial.

The pre-1914 seers had warned against the dangers of decay, but only a minority had listened to them. Germany was prosperous and outwardly at the height of its power. But the parades, the pomp and circumstance had just been a varnish covering the putrefaction underneath, and after the defeat it became apparent just how pervasive the decay had been. Wherever a German patriot looked he found little to comfort him: the national values were openly undermined and turned into ridicule: pacifist novels abounded; the manly values were dragged into the dirt; on the stage, incest, pederasty or at the very least marital infidelity were glorified. Berlin had taken over from Paris as the world capital of lasciviousness and obscenity.. Illustrated magazines featured naked dancers and international gangsters, frequently shown in company with each other; the cinema corrupted the young generation by glamourizing sadism and rape, with prostitutes and their protectors as the main heroes. It seemed as if only the criminal, the ugly, the blasphemous, was of any interest to modern art. The rest was low or at best middle-brow culture suitable for entertaining philistines. All over Germany the literati were in command, enemies of order, profiteers of chaos. Like tubercular bacilli they affected all weak cells in the body politic. Rootless themselves, they were bitterly attacking any manifestation of healthy patriotism. They had no shame or modesty, they were the apostles of sensationalism, forever in search of new trends and fashions, however worthless. Their stranglehold had to be broken to make a cultural recovery possible.

This, broadly speaking, was the Weimar cultural scene as seen by the right-wing intellectual. He most certainly overrated the number and the influence of his enemies: for every pacifist novel there were two that were militarist in inspiration; for every attack on the old order, there were several directed against the new state. But our patriot was in no mood to engage in quantitative analysis; so far as he was concerned it was an outrage that a Tucholsky or a George Grosz could find any outlet for his traitorous and blasphemous effusions. While arguing that he represented the great majority, the right-wing intellectual felt himself acutely isolated. The enemy, on the other hand, was omnipresent; he dominated the scene, his voice was the only one to be heard. A few weeks after Hitler had come to power Friedrich Hussong, one of the most implacable enemies of the left-wing intelligentsia, summarized this resentment in a book significantly entitled *Kurfürstendamm*:

A miracle has taken place. They are no longer here. . . .
They claimed they were the German *Geist*, German culture,
the German present and future. They represented Germany
to the world, they spoke in its name. . . . Everything else was
mistaken, inferior, regrettable kitsch, odious philistinism. . . .
They always sat in the front row. They awarded knighthoods
of the spirit and of Europeanism. What they did not permit
did not exist. . . . They 'made' themselves and others. Whoever served them was sure to succeed. He appeared on their
stages, wrote in their journals, was advertised all over the
world; his commodity was recommended whether it was
cheese or relativity, powder or *Zeittheater*, patent medicines or
human rights, democracy or bolshevism, propaganda for
abortion or against the legal system, rotten Negro music or
dancing in the nude. In brief, there was never a more shame-
less dictatorship than that of the democratic intelligentsia
and the *Zivilisationsliteraten*.

Underlying the denunciation of Weimar culture was the
assumption that the process of cultural decay and moral disintegration was by no means accidental. It was concerted and
centrally planned: a deliberate conspiracy by world Jewry to
undermine everything that was still healthy in Germany so that
the country could never again recover and rise to greatness. If,
according to Alfred Rosenberg, Bolshevism was the revolt of
the racially inferior elements against the old (Aryan) elites,
Kulturbolschewismus was its equivalent in the cultural sphere.
Against paranoia – one of the consequences of the defeat –
rational arguments could make no headway. Nor would right-
wing intellectuals be impressed by the idea that Germany in the
1920s was facing a crisis of modernity which was worldwide in
character. They ignored the fact that the cinema, the loosening
of family ties and sexual mores, were characteristic of other
countries too, or that anti-militarism was as widespread in
France and Britain as in Germany. The nationalist ideologues
were in no mood for such comparisons; they compared Berlin
not with London, Paris or New York but with what Germany
had once been and with what, in their view, it should be
again.

In their extreme form these views were admittedly confined

to the lunatic fringe, but in a somewhat less crude and sweeping fashion the dissatisfaction with the existing state of affairs was shared by large sections of the middle classes. Thus Gustav Stresemann, not a wild man of the extreme right but a moderate *par excellence*, foreign minister and pillar of the establishment, bitterly complained in a speech to students in 1926 that the 'intellectual [*geistige*] gentry' had been proletarianized. They were no longer the foundation on which the state had been built. For centuries the family, with its closely-knit ties and its ambitions, had functioned as a germ cell; it had provided the recruits for the government, the officer corps and the clergy in Prussia and Germany. This class had been educated to serve but they were no longer needed. Was it a matter of surprise that they quarrelled with God and their fate? That they refused to accept a moral order that made beggars of those who had done their duty, whereas men devoid of scruples rose to influence, power and wealth?

The new anti-militarism with its satirical poems and cartoons was anathema not only to the ex-officers but to much wider circles. It affected the many families which mourned fathers and husbands, brothers and sons. There were millions of them and it could easily be predicted how they would react to the cartoons of George Grosz and the poems of Tucholsky. For if the anti-militarists were right, all the sacrifices had been made on behalf of a worthless cause. But as the nationalists saw it, Germany had been encircled by a world of enemies who envied its progress and would not allow the Germans to gain that 'place in the sun' which was rightfully theirs by virtue of their efficiency and their cultural achievements. Having defeated Germany because its domestic front did not hold, its enemies had perpetuated in the Versailles treaty the lie of Germany's war guilt. The treaty was denounced for its inequities not only by the German right but by many liberals in the West and by the Bolsheviks, yet this did not make the German right any more friendly towards liberalism or communism.

There was more than enough ammunition even if one disregarded foreign affairs. As already mentioned, the right saw one of the main causes of the cultural and moral decay in the loosening of family ties. Right-wing attitudes towards women's emancipation had always been, at best, ambiguous. The function of woman was to be wife and mother, and the emergence of a new social system in which many women went out to work (and even liked it) seemed unnatural. For this order created a new type of modern emancipated woman, with the film star, the sportswoman and the woman of the demi-monde as its idols. Before the war, one right-wing spokesman wrote, there had been real ladies but *eheu fugaces . . .*

The new elite was based neither on culture nor on a social ethos but on money and fashion. Before the war there had been a genuine society and true social life (*Geselligkeit*); after 1918 there was dancing, and the great chase after various, mostly dubious, kinds of entertainment. Germany's great cities had become provincial without however regaining the quiet, calm, small-town atmosphere of intimacy and friendliness.

According to the right-wing prophets of doom, monogamy was on the way out and trial marriage (or worse) was practised. Divorces more than doubled between 1913 and 1930 and adultery was openly extolled in countless films, novels and hit songs. All this was bound to have a terrible effect on the young generation. It was one of the constant complaints of the right that there was little if any idealism left among the young; boys and girls grew up in an all-pervasive climate of materialism and cynicism. They read thrillers and pornographic literature, and juvenile delinquency was increasing at an alarming rate. Partly this was the fault of the parents, partly of teachers, who had been infected by liberal and Marxist ideas, advocating an education without ideals, without discipline, without national aim and purpose.

The *Kulturpessimisten* were equally unhappy about the new financial and economic elite. In the nineteenth century the national economy had made spectacular progress because German inventors had perfected technology, because able artisans had slowly worked themselves up, often from the most modest beginnings, because workers had been diligent and efficient. 'Made in Germany' had been a synonym for excellence. But more recently the economy too had been depersonalized: family firms had been bought up by big anonymous concerns and trusts, the creative industrialist had been replaced by the financial speculator, the royal merchant by the black-marketeer. Everything now centred on profit and money. The old work ethic had vanished, labour had become drudgery, it no longer gave satisfaction.

The right-wing intellectuals were ready to admit that to a certain extent these dismal developments had been inevitable; they were the outcome of industrialization and capitalism. Since they had no alternative to capitalism and had no idea how a modern society could be run without industry, their critique was necessarily vague. But, as the right saw it, the situation had been aggravated by Jewish speculators and manipulators who had streamed into Germany from the east; their activities were tolerated and sometimes abetted by the new state, leading members of which benefited from the spread of corruption. The cases of Sklarek, Barmat and Kutisker attracted much publicity, even though these men were small fry indeed in comparison with the great profiteers of the inflation such as Stinnes. But Stinnes was of Aryan birth, he was a German patriot, and he also happened to control many newspapers. In right-wing circles, to give another example, there was much indignation that the actor Max Pallenberg and his wife, the actress Fritzi Massary, had allegedly earned 400,000 marks (about 100,000 dollars) in a single month. Thyssen made more money and so did Kirdorf, but these captains of industry did not have the misfortune of being Jewish.

The man of the right suffered from a major moral-cultural hangover during the postwar period. Delbrück once published an entertaining essay entitled 'The Good Old Days' in which he conclusively showed that since time immemorial pessimists had always proclaimed that the age of the fathers and grandfathers had been in every respect vastly superior to their own, especially in its moral climate. In fact, this was by no means true, certainly in so far as these things could be measured. It was claimed, for instance, that the crime rate (and alcoholism) had shown an alarming increase since before the war, but the statistics simply did not bear this out. But the men of the right needed no statistics; they knew in their bones that something was radically wrong. They knew that forces were at work to destroy time-honoured beliefs and traditions. Modernism, as they saw it, was all-pervasive and yet difficult to define. It was the negation of the old Romantic world-view and of German idealism, it was the antithesis to all that had made Germany

great in the past, it was Brecht and Weill against Goethe and
Beethoven, not to mention Hölderlin and Spitzweg. The new
trend was in stark contrast to German *Innerlichkeit*, wholesome-
ness, organic growth, rootedness. Modernism stood for the sickness of the soul, for the loss of equilibrium, for alienation and
dehumanization. Seen in this context, both mammon (capitalism) and collectivism (mass culture plus communism) were
manifestations of modernism. Many an educated German felt
uncomfortable vis-à-vis these trends which, he suspected, were
about to destroy his world; he wanted to combat the forces of
evil and he was groping for alternatives.

The right maintained that as a first step German art and
literature would have to be purged of their domination by
alien influences. While often rejecting racialism in its cruder
form, it argued that not all literature written in German was
necessarily German literature. Whether the work of a Jewish
writer was good or bad, interesting or boring, was immaterial in
this context; more often than not it did not belong to German
literature. The German public had to be re-educated to re-
discover its own cultural heritage, to appreciate the work of the
'quiet ones' (the *Stillen im Lande*): those who, unaffected by
fashionable trends, far from the hustle and bustle of Berlin
literary coffee houses and artistic salons, pursued their vocation
irrespective of awards, public recognition and financial success.
What the Berlin cultural impresarios contemptuously dismissed
as 'provincialism' was in actual fact rootedness, idealism, the
aristocracy of the spirit. These were the men and women who
were upholding cultural standards when culture was threatened
by *Kulturbolschewismus*.

But what was *Kulturbolschewismus*? The thinkers of the right
had only the haziest ideas on the subject; most of them grotes-
quely misjudged Communist cultural policies, assuming in all
earnest that Dada, Brecht's refrain *Erst kommt das Fressen, dann
kommt die Moral*, or Walter Mehring's *Merchant of Berlin* represented the aesthetic theory and the moral philosophy of
Marxism-Leninism. They failed to understand that the Communist attitude towards the bohême was at bottom not much
different from their own; that Communist cultural policy in the
Soviet Union, after a short experimental interlude, changed
course, putting the emphasis on heroic, positive values; that so

far as their attitude to 'unhealthy modernism' was concerned, the right and the Stalinists were brothers beneath their skins. All this should have been clear by 1931–2 at the latest, but the right-wing intellectuals failed to see it; perhaps they did not want to take cognizance of it because it did not fit in with their concept of *Kulturbolschewismus*.

Among those groping for an alternative way of life, the youth movement ought to be mentioned. It had come into being well before the outbreak of the First World War, a neo-Romantic reform movement, apotheosizing the group rather than the individual, an expression of a fresh awakening to life. As we shall see, the Blaue Reiter artists and the *Jugendbewegung* had this in common: they confronted the anaemic intellectualism of a civilization self-consciously preening itself, while threatened with suffocation in the materialism of a utilitarian faith in progress, in the belief in a new world which, to them (to quote Nietzsche), 'still seemed abundant in beauty, strangeness, doubt, horror and divinity'. They did try spontaneously, if often awkwardly, to alter the human condition at a time when philosophers and sociologists were writing about the 'alienation of man', the 'atomization of society', the diminishing of human contact; when the anonymity and impersonality of modern life, a loss of vitality in individuals and a growing social torpor were already themes of contemporary cultural and social criticism. But all attempts to prolong the youth movement into later life were unsuccessful. The movement shared an adolescent experience, it inculcated certain values and interests in its members, some definite character-ideals and the love of nature; but as the boys and girls grew up these were superseded by other interests, impressions, friendships and loyalties.

Beyond the youth movement there was a multitude of sects and cults, more political, more faddish and less interesting. There was full agreement among them that the war had been inevitable and that Versailles was a national disgrace. They were anti-liberal, anti-parliamentary, anti-democratic and, to varying degrees, antisemitic. Rejecting the class struggle, they called for a strong leader. Over and above acceptance of these basic tenets they were engaged in permanent internal quarrels on a great variety of subjects. The monarchists wanted the Kaiser back, or at least one of his sons. Others maintained that the Kaiser had behaved ignominiously in 1918. Ludendorff and his wife sponsored an anti-masonic campaign and a new religion. The *Völkische* (in contrast to the monarchists) maintained that the defeat and the rule of the 'November criminals' were the legitimate outcome of the rot that had set in under the monarchy as the result of putting all the emphasis on the nation – and of neglecting the *Volk*, the purity of the race, blood and soil. Some rightists favoured a conservative military dictatorship; others combined extreme nationalist slogans with revolutionary demands. If the left had its Dada and other cultural and political splinter-groups, the right was equally fragmented. While Dada did not take itself too seriously, the right-wing sectarians were profoundly convinced, like some sixteenth-century alchemists or astrologers, that they had discovered the philosopher's stone. Some of them combined racialism with spiritualism, others with occultism, yet others with various number games or sun worship.

The more extreme elements among them opposed modern civilization *tout court*, including radio and cinema, advertising and dance music, weekends and motorcycles. All these were manifestations of the soulless new civilization, enhancing man's alienation from nature and from his fellow man. Some of these advocates of the simple life joined forces to settle on the land in small communities. But such ventures involved them in endless contradictions. For a return to the soil, however praiseworthy, would hardly provide the industrial basis which Germany needed to become a strong military power again. To give another example: nudism, according to German right-wing thought, was an abomination, and the dances of Josephine Baker, the toast of Berlin in the 1920s, were a frequent target in their literature; yet 'Nordic' nudism had not a few adepts. According to the gospel of the right the sanctity of family life was one of the preconditions for the moral recovery of the German people and they castigated the 'system' for loosening the ties of family. Yet among the *Völkische* sects there were also some advocates of polygamy, such as Willibald Hentschel and the Artam Bund. Hentschel regarded the current state of the Aryan race as alarming, hence his conclusion that, to quote George Mosse, only a crash breeding programme could recover lost ground and halt the degeneration: 'Constant production, constant propagation of the race was imperative, and the breeding capabilities of Aryan men and women must be used to the full.' Hentschel also anticipated some of the ideas of a later generation of school abolitionists: the children of Mittgart, as the new settlements were to be called, were not to breathe the dust of soul-destroying schools up to the age of sixteen.

The Nazis played no significant part in the internal debates of the right-wing intelligentsia until about 1930. Some of their ideas were propagated in periodicals specializing in extreme antisemitism, such as Fritzsch's *Der Hammer*. The literary historian Adolf Bartels, another fellow-traveller, waged relentless war against Jews and pseudo-Jews in German literature; Alfred Rosenberg published his collected essays from the *Völkische Beobachter* (*Der Sumpf*, 1930); and in 1927 the *Deutsche Kunstkorrespondenz* (later *Deutscher Kunstbericht*) was launched to wage all-out war against *Kulturbolschewismus* in the plastic arts. But Rosenberg was the only active Nazi among them, and he was not an intellectual heavyweight. A Baltic German by origin, he had joined the Hitler movement early on, a true believer, a fanatical antisemite and a massive bore, utterly lacking force, sparkle or humour. For the German intelligentsia he was not quite *salonfähig*; the fact that the Nazis made him their chief intellectual shows that there was no abundance of talent in their ranks. His technique as a writer was simple and frequently not without effect. He published excerpts from Tucholsky or Kästner, from Ernst Glaeser or Walter Mehring, with just a sentence to the effect that these indecencies and blasphemies were typical of the spirit of the criminals who were ruling Germany. He assumed, rightly no doubt, that his readers would find the texts so outrageous that no further comment was necessary. Goebbels was far more gifted than Rosenberg but he wanted to appeal to the masses not to the intelligentsia, assuming, correctly as it later appeared, that once the Nazis were a mass movement the nationalist intelligentsia would join it anyway. The Nazis had a far more astute grasp of the realities of power than the other right-wing leaders; they did not think highly of intellectuals as allies in the political struggle, and they made no great efforts to win them over.

Disagreements among the German right concerned political as well as cultural subjects. There were those who were deeply impressed by the achievements of Italian fascism and thought that the Italian national revival could teach Germany a lesson in its hour of distress. Others took a dimmer view of Mussolini, partly because the new Italian regime was trampling under foot the national rights of Germans (in South Tyrol), partly because the Italians were obviously not 'Nordic' and thus racially inferior to the Germans.

Some right-wing intellectuals were so disappointed by the cowardice and egotism of the German bourgeois that they tended to write him off as an ally in their struggle against the 'system'. Hence the call for a 'conservative revolution', a 'revolution from the right', and occasional massive attacks on the traditional right. Others took a more tolerant view. The Catholic Centre Party, they argued, was basically patriotic in inspiration, and the same applied to most middle-class organizations. Whoever did not belong to the left was a potential ally; the patriots simply did not know their own strength. This was certainly true so far as sheer numbers were concerned, and also publicity outlets. If the left had the *Weltbühne* and the *Tagebuch* and a few other magazines at their disposal, the forces of light had the *Preussische Jahrbücher* and the *Süddeutsche Monatshefte*, the *Türmer*, *Kunstwart* and *Ring*, *Die Tat* and *Deutsches Volkstum*, not to mention influential Catholic periodicals (such as *Hochland*, *Stimmen der Zeit*, *Das Neue Reich*, *Gral*), which also did their part in the struggle against *Kulturbolschewismus*. Moreover, most German publishing houses were by no means dominated by the left, nor were the majority of the daily newspapers (from the *Kölnische Zeitung* to the *Deutsche Allgemeine Zeitung* in Berlin, the *Hamburger Nachrichten*, the Munich and Leipzig *Neueste Nachrichten*).

The allegations about the stranglehold of the Jewish-left-liberal clique belonged largely to the realm of fantasy; the idea that an honest, gifted patriot had no chance to make himself heard was simply not true. The trouble was that the right did not have a great deal of talent in its ranks; in fact, the political leaders of the right did not think very highly of their own intellectuals. Hitler borrowed a good many ideas from the *völkisch* sectarians; there is very little of his own in Nazi ideology; all the basic ideas had been well known even before the war. But at the same time Hitler referred only with contempt to the thinkers of the right, monarchists and racialists alike. The right-wing ideologists reflected the intellectual climate of the 1920s fairly accurately and to a certain extent helped to shape it, but they were in their way as uninfluential as the intellectuals of the left. So far as the parties of the right were concerned, they were not much in demand; intellectuals, however patriotic, were socially not quite acceptable in a conservative world still dominated by Junkers, generals and captains of industry. They were quite out of place among the new Nazi elite. They would be invited as a curiosity, they might be given some financial assistance, but no Spengler or Moeller van den Bruck, no Ernst Jünger or Carl Schmitt, was needed to explain what was wrong with Weimar. They would be praised as staunch patriots, their books would be published, bought and sometimes even read, but no one would dream of consulting them whenever political questions of importance were concerned.

The attitude of the Nazis towards the right-wing ideologists was even more negative than that of the conservatives, partly because they had a Führer who was omniscient and could not acknowledge a debt to other thinkers or seers, but also because the thinkers of the right usually deviated on one or more important points from official Nazi doctrine: some of them were nationalists of the old school, others regarded antisemitism as a marginal issue, and most of them were not sufficiently respectful vis-à-vis Nazism as a movement with cultural ambitions. By denigrating the intellect and attacking rationalism, the thinkers of the right had undermined their own position. For once it had been established that the life force, blood, myth, the will to power were the central forces, and that it was pointless to subject them to critical analysis, it followed that intellectual interpreters were no longer needed. Everyone could feel these things, one exegesis was as good as another, everybody was his own ideologist – and the Führer the ultimate arbiter.

If the intellectuals of the right had little political influence, they still made a substantial contribution to the general climate of opinion and for this reason their views are of more than academic interest. Among them Oswald Spengler was the most widely known. His magnum opus *The Decline of the West* was conceived originally in 1911 as a critique of German foreign policy, a warning against the blind folly, the criminal and suicidal optimism prevailing in the late Wilhelmian era. By the time the first volume was finished it had turned into something altogether different: a new cyclical philosophy of history, a morphology of culture, a commentary on the present state of mankind and a prognosis – *the* philosophy of the future, in Spengler's own words. Spengler had asserted that there had been eight fully fledged cultures – meaning those attaining maturity and lasting each for about a millennium. He found that they had all been subject to certain laws governing their rise and decline. Spengler's thesis about Apollonian, Magian and Faustian man was rejected by most historians who, with a few notable exceptions, were not even willing to discuss his work seriously as a contribution to scholarship. But the general reader was dazzled by what appeared to be the tremendous erudition, the broad sweep and the unshakeable certainty of the writer. Above all, his comments on recent history were impressive and provocative. With the nineteenth century the decline of the West had set in; the age of materialism, uncertainty and formlessness. Imperialism had opened the door to centuries of perpetual warfare and to the new Caesars who would eventually take over. This in turn would lead to a new primitivism and mysticism (or religiosity). That Spengler was a man of obvious talent even his critics did not dispute; it was less obvious what this edifice, all the errors of fact quite apart, had to do with the writing of history. It certainly combined ingenious ideas and expressed a mood which appealed for a variety of reasons to many contemporaries. But in the final analysis Spengler's approach was unhistorical; he had simply picked and chosen from the sources what he wanted to find. He had invoked Clio in vain; as poetry his visions would have been unassailable; as an academic work equipped with all the outward apparatus of scholarship it was no better than the work of any other learned and industrious charlatan.

Spengler's magnum opus had been written in anticipation of a German victory, in which case it would in all probability have been ignored. It was precisely the defeat which made it topical and appealing. Coupled with a political pamphlet published in 1920, *Preussentum und Sozialismus*, it provided a Guide to the Perplexed. As a French historian wrote after Spengler's death:

In the twenties Spengler offered the wares that at the time were in most demand: A certain pathos, a determined anti-intellectualism, a heroic notion of destiny, anti-aestheticism, the thrill of the mere human being before the majesty, the broad majesty, of History. . . . This is what gave Spengler his success: Not the success of an analytical and deductive historian, but the success of a prophet, of a magician, of a visionary, perfectly adapted to the needs of a troubled Germany. (Lucien Febvre – quoted by H. Stuart Hughes)

The Republic of Weimar, needless to say, was rejected by Spengler – it was not a state but a business enterprise; it had no authority, no lasting message. Earlier than other right-wing thinkers, Spengler realized that old-style monarchism had no future in Germany, although, as he once put it, Friedrich Wilhelm I (not Karl Marx) had been the first conscious socialist. Socialism was a matter of upbringing; every genuine German was a worker, while the average Frenchman was middle-class in his outlook. Thus Prussianism and socialism were essentially the same thing; according to the Prussian ethic, the king was the first servant of the state. Spengler suggested that the elite of the working class and the most farsighted conservatives should join forces against the common enemy – liberalism and capitalism – to create a truly democratic and socialist Prussian state. He advised the Social Democrats to take as their model Bebel, a man of action and an authoritarian who was in favour of military discipline, rather than Marx, a Jewish moralist, deeply rooted in the world of liberalism, who had mistakenly believed that economics were more important than politics. Marxism, as Spengler saw it, was simply the capitalism of the working class. To survive, Germany needed not the indiscriminate nationalization of the means of production but an effective (Prussian) technique of administration and the slow transformation of the worker into a cog in an immense industrial machine. Much as Spengler disliked mass democracy, and much as he regretted the eclipse of the aristocracy, he realized that the age ahead belonged, at least temporarily, to the masses. (He was not quite consistent in his predictions; on other occasions he announced that Germany was far more likely to produce a new Caesar than a new Goethe.) His message to the conservatives was thus simple: they had to adapt themselves to the mass age, to democratic rules. Like Hofmannsthal, Thomas Mann and Moeller van den Bruck, he was one of the main proponents of that nebulous slogan, the 'conservative revolution'. Eventually, the message was taken up not by the traditional right wing, unable to jump over its own shadow, but by Adolf Hitler, quite independently of Spengler's writings.

Spengler viewed National Socialism with misgiving even though he paid his respects to the 'mighty phenomenon' of the national revolution, which constituted a considerable advance in comparison with the state of Weimar. But he did not accept the theory of Aryan blood and the *völkisch* myth, which were in his view reprehensible – part Romantic fantasy, part relics of nineteenth-century Darwinist positivism. The Nazis, he maintained, had produced a great deal of sound and fury; they had intoxicated the younger generation. Whether they were capable of the hard, patient work which would lead to future victories was by no means certain: 'Enthusiasm is a dangerous burden on the road to politics.' Hitler, 'a heroic tenor – not a hero', was, in Spengler's view, not a man of the same stature as Mussolini. Hitler, he suspected, would exacerbate the tension between the various European nations and this would open the door to the real danger, the onslaught of the non-white peoples. These, together with Russia, threatened Faustian (Western) culture, and a disunited West would be incapable of meeting this threat. The Nazis on their part, while recognizing Spengler's merits as a detractor of Weimar and all it stood for, attacked him for what they considered his misguided views, his determinism and pessimism. If he wrote that the Nazis raved like mendicant friars, they replied that he had an ice-cold contempt for the people, was hypnotized by his own intellectual constructions and blinded by his prejudices. This charge was true only in part, for although Spengler always stressed the element of inescapable destiny (he says at the end of *The Decline of the West*: *nolentem fata trahunt, volentem ducunt.*) he did not in fact accept with equanimity the prospect of decline; all his political writings were devoted to finding ways and means of escaping this fate.

As a symptom of the *Zeitgeist*, articulating the general malaise, Spengler's work is of great interest, even though his

suggestions were of limited use to the German right. He propagated elitism and an authoritarian regime, hardly a great
innovation in right-wing doctrine. He understood the necessity
of making certain concessions to the masses. But he was quite
incapable of developing a right-wing populist programme
which could have appealed to the masses, for with all the
grandiose visions encompassing many cultures, millennia and
continents, essentially he remained a nineteenth-century conservative. The socialism he envisaged was private enterprise
('based on the old Teutonic desire for power and for plunder')
without strikes or pressure-groups in which the state (represented by efficient and incorruptible bureaucrats) would act as
the ultimate arbiter. It may be unfair to blame Spengler for the
vagueness of his notions on domestic policy, for he was, of
course, far more interested in foreign affairs. Foreign policy was
fate (*Schicksal*), domestic affairs a necessary evil. Spengler was
widely read at the time, probably as much among the liberal
middle class as among the right; unlike other German right-
wing thinkers he even had a certain revival after the Second
World War. But his political impact, as we have said, was
insignificant. The Nazis did not need him, and he did not
identify with them; when the 'national revolution' came he
failed to recognize his own children, as one Nazi put it.

One day in 1920 Spengler was invited by the June Club to
hold a debate with Moeller van den Bruck. The June Club was
an exclusive political debating society in the German capital.
Founded shortly after the war, its political spectrum reached
from the democratic centre to the far right, with the emphasis
however on neo-conservatism. At no time did it have more than
a few hundred members, but since most editors of national
journals of opinion and also some leading politicians belonged
to it, its real importance was greater than mere numbers would
suggest. Moeller was one of the stars of the club, in some ways
the right-wing intellectual *par excellence*. Born into a well-to-do
family, he dropped out of high school, married at twenty-one,
was divorced soon after and devoted his time to editing and
translating modern literature (including Baudelaire, Barbey
d'Aurévilly, Thomas de Quincey). His literary magnum opus
was the editing and translation of Dostoevsky's collected works
(in twenty-two volumes) between 1905 and 1914. Living in

virtual seclusion and suffering from various neurotic complaints, he moved to Paris at the age of twenty-six to escape being drafted into the German army. So far his biography reads like that of a typical 'decadent' *littérateur*; a *bohémien*, a cosmopolitan rather than a German nationalist, a drifter lacking political interest. But then, all of a sudden, he discovered the 'Prussian style' through a study of architecture and provided a vivid, if idealized and overdrawn, picture of the culture of Prussianism, with its precision, sobriety and lack of romanticism.

Between the outbreak of war and his death (Moeller committed suicide in 1925) he wrote a great deal on politics; the titles of his two main books, *The Right of Young Peoples* and *The Third Reich*, indicate the general direction of his thought. The conflict between old (Britain, France) and young peoples (Germany, Russia and America) was the key to the world war and to the subsequent disaster. The revolution had been a major disappointment but it could still be made a success if only the conservatives would take it over.

Moeller's orientation towards Russia was spiritual rather than political in character; he did not know what to make of the Soviet Union and wavered between the idea of setting up Germany as a bulwark against Bolshevism, and attacking the extreme anti-communists such as Ludendorff who wanted to pursue an interventionist policy in collaboration with the Allies. Germany's place, he maintained, was on the side of the young peoples. *The Third Reich* was if possible even more vague, and as a political programme of no use whatsoever because Moeller neatly evaded clear answers to the pressing problems facing Germany. He attacked traditional conservatism both for having been liberalistic almost from the beginning and for having been reactionary in character. But it did not emerge from his writings what form the new purified conservatism was to take. Like Spengler, he suggested that the conservatives should borrow heavily from socialism to create a new, German socialism. The German working class, rooted in the liberal and internationalist theories of the nineteenth century, had failed to understand that only an imperialist policy would provide an answer both to the national and the social problems facing the German nation. But how could such a doctrine be squared with the anti-imperialist ideas of the *Right of Young Peoples*? Such contradictions and inconsistencies were typical of Moeller's muddled thoughts; when pressed hard he would answer, 'We have to be strong enough to live in contradictions.'

Moeller could not make up his mind whether German socialism was to be a planned, state-controlled economy, or based on capitalist principles. Like Spengler he was fascinated by foreign politics and found social issues boring; the invocation of socialism was little more than a bow to the *Zeitgeist*. Moeller is remembered mainly for the catchphrase about the Third Reich (the book was originally to be called 'The Third Party' or 'The Third Viewpoint'). Clinging to the magic number of three, which had intrigued thinkers from Joachim of Fiora to Hegel, he solemnly announced that the third party was the party of continuity in German history, the party of all Germans who wanted to preserve Germany for the German people, the party to end all parties. Its protagonists were the men ready to fight for the final Reich that had always been a promise but was never fulfilled, the Reich of synthesis, of uniting contradictions. Whether it would ever become a political reality was by no means certain, for unless approached the right way it would remain a grand illusion; Germany might even perish through the dream of the Third Reich. Moeller agreed with Spengler that not race but the nation and its cultural unity were the key to history and politics. In contrast to Spengler he included Italy among the young nations; the 'socialist foreign policy' he suggested implied an orientation towards Russia and Italy. Moeller's writings, like Spengler's, are full of poetic visions, enormous promises and apocalyptic forebodings. Eloquent in his critique of the existing system, the alternatives he presented made neither rhyme nor reason whatever way one looked at them. It was said about left-wing Weimar intellectuals that their critique of the system was 'purely destructive'; the same applied *a fortiori* to Spengler and Moeller. They were most eloquent in their attacks on liberalism, but they had little to offer of their own. Since Moeller died years before the Nazis came to power he did not directly clash with them as Spengler did. But the praise accorded him after 1933 was lukewarm; it was freely admitted that he had been one of the forerunners of Nazism, but in some ways he did not fit into the Nazi scheme of things and thus came to be more or less ignored in the real Third Reich.

Spengler and Moeller dominated right-wing thought during the early Weimar period. Later on a great many others joined the campaign against the 'ideas of 1918' – liberalism, social democracy and parliamentarism. They were a mixed lot: novelists and metaphysicians, journalists and legal philosophers. With very few exceptions none of them later joined the Nazi Party; one was assassinated in 1934, several were sent to prison or to concentration-camps and most were at one stage or another attacked by the Nazis. Quite a few of them realized soon after the 'national revolution' that they had been grievously mistaken in supporting Nazism. Others reacted like the novelist Hans Grimm, who told Hitler that he would always serve the same cause as the Führer but he would 'never belong to him'. But whether Grimm formally belonged to the party or not is largely immaterial; his *Volk ohne Raum* became one of the basic articles of faith of the extreme right. As a young man Grimm had spent some thirteen years as a merchant in South Africa, and this country, as well as the neighbouring German colony of South-West Africa, provides the historical background to his best-known novel, the *Magic Mountain* of the right (it ran to 1,300 pages and sold 700,000 copies). Of all the right-wing books of the interwar period *Volk ohne Raum* is one of the most readable and most powerful, despite its nationalist perversion, its relentlessly didactic approach, its utter lack of humour. It has a certain elemental force which the slicker products of the modish right lacked.

Most right-wing thinkers preferred, like Hans Grimm, not to be identified with any specific political party, certainly not with National Socialism. Nazism had no elaborate philosophy nor indeed did it need one; individual Nazis such as Alfred Rosenberg (author of *The Myth of the 20th Century*) tried their hand at producing a systematic *Weltanschauung*, but we have it on the authority of Hitler that he never bothered to read the book and there is no reason to believe that other Nazi leaders acted differently. Plodding, earnest, humourless, Rosenberg was a bit of a laughing-stock among the Nazi leaders.

Much of the intellectual spadework for the 'revolution of 1933' was done outside the Nazi movement. 'We are glad about the growth of National Socialism', Edgar Jung, one of the spokesmen of the right-wing intelligentsia, wrote in 1932; 'we have greatly contributed towards it especially among the educated classes. However, when due respect is paid to the popular movement and the militancy of its leaders, it is still true that they have no right to consider themselves the salt of the earth and to belittle or denigrate their intellectual pacemakers.' Jung was killed by the Nazis in 1934, but what matters in this context is neither Nazi ingratitude nor the subsequent fate of other right-wing thinkers, but their historical role as gravediggers of Weimar; in this respect Jung's assessment is not far from the truth.

It was a collective endeavour, carried out by a motley crowd. Some of the fighters on the battlefield against liberalism and democracy were eccentrics or lone wolves, such as Ludwig Klages; others belonged to various circles of likeminded individuals such as the neo-conservative *Herrenclub* in the early years of the Republic or the later *Tat-Kreis*. Some were fairly close to the church, such as Wilhelm Stapel, a Protestant, or Othmar Spann, the semi-official Catholic social philosopher; others preached neo-paganism. Some were romantics, others essentially nihilists, such as Ernst Jünger; some were in the tradition of nineteenth-century reactionary thought, others frightened their conservative colleagues with their sympathies for Bolshevism. To classify them and their changing views would not be a very rewarding task. All that needs to be stressed in the present context is that there was unanimity among them about certain basic beliefs: nationalism, the conviction that parliamentary democracy was wholly unsuitable for Germany, the belief in the need for strong, authoritarian government. It would be comforting if all of them could be written off as backwoodsmen, eccentrics or charlatans. But this was by no means the case; while the right-wing intelligentsia had a greater share of crackpots than the left, it also had in its ranks men of great erudition, fine intellect and an original frame of mind.

However baneful the influence of Carl Schmitt, the legal philosopher, no one in his right mind could dismiss him as an intellectual lightweight. His critique of the Weimar Republic was closely reasoned, based on a wide reading in history and political philosophy. Where Moeller had published impassioned appeals ('Liberalism has undermined cultures, destroyed religions and fatherlands. It is the decomposition, the self-surrender of mankind'), Schmitt conceded that Liberalism (and its political concomitant, parliamentary democracy) had played a positive role during the past century, but asserted that it was quite incapable of solving the problems of modern mass democracy. For this reason the shortcomings of the Weimar Republic were not accidental, they were the logical outcome of an unsuitable political order. If democracy was (or aimed at) the identity between rulers and ruled, it did not follow that liberalism was the only approach to a democratic order: 'Bolshevism and fascism are like all dictatorships anti-liberal, but not necessarily anti-democratic.' In Schmitt's philosophy the state takes the central place. Its main task is not to administer but to serve as a centre of power engaged in a struggle against other centres of power. Thus the state is born out of enmity; if wars ceased, there would be no need for a state; the very idea of the state presupposes the notion of politics, and politics is governed by the conflict between friend and foe. Liberalism, with its belief in harmony in both domestic and foreign policy, had failed to understand what politics was really about. It envisaged the state as a community of interests, at most a social community. But in fact a state was much more than that; it was entitled to expect its citizens to fight and if necessary die for it. The Christian 'Love thy enemies' ethic applied to the private, not the public enemy; serious political conflicts could not be settled by discussion and persuasion, as liberalism assumed, but by struggle and war. For this reason Schmitt had nothing but contempt for Weimar parliamentarism; the parliament was not really democratic because the deputies were puppets manipulated by party organizations, not 'representatives of the whole people subject only to their own conscience', as the Republic's constitution had proclaimed. Really important decisions were taken outside parliament. At the same time Weimar parliamentarism weakened the state: the important thing in politics was taking decisions; those who spent their time in endless parliamentary debates were simply evading taking a decision. Every political order rested not on certain generally valid norms but on a basic decision, something which the bourgeois mentality was incapable of grasping.

Schmitt's critique of liberal democracy and the Weimar state delighted the right and had a profound influence on a young generation of academics. It could not however be accepted by the Nazis without reservations, because by putting such strong emphasis on state power the theory downgraded two other concepts dear to their hearts: race and *Volk*. Furthermore, there was a nihilist element in Schmitt's philosophy. It justified war, but it did not necessarily prove that Germany's cause was just or that war waged by another nation against Germany was evil. What appealed to the Nazis in Schmitt's doctrine was the quasi-scientific justification of dictatorship, for the rejection of the liberal state led logically to an authoritarian order. Schmitt had argued that a minority might well under certain circumstances represent the popular will; other right-wing thinkers went even further, maintaining that it was ludicrous to assume that the popular will was the sum total of votes in an election – as if one vote was equal to another. Such an electoral system would result in the victory of soulless party-machines; it was a mechanical process bound to give power to the irresponsible, inferior elements in the community. Hence the conclusion that political parties were Germany's misfortune; whoever destroyed them by fire and sword would be doing a noble deed.

What would become of individual freedom once there were no longer elections, political parties and a parliament? The right-wing ideologists had a ready answer. Following Spengler, they maintained that the Prussian system provided an 'inner freedom' despite the harsh outward discipline. Together with some Protestant theologians they developed a new argument according to which freedom was by no means identical with the outdated liberal concept of individual liberty: a man could be really free only in a collective, at one with his people. A new and higher political order would give freedom to the oppressed nation and thus provide happiness for the whole.

Such ideas were bound to fall on fertile ground in a country in which parliament and the political parties had never been popular; they were regarded by most educated people as a divisive factor, an attitude which the Germans shared with Rousseau. Since a state could not be strong unless the people were united, and since a powerful state figured much higher in the German scale of priorities than individual freedom, appeals for doing away with the 'parasitic parties' and the parliamentary talking-shop would always earn applause. Strong leadership was natural, whereas parliamentary discussion, give-and-take and compromises, were artificial and undesirable.

Schmitt's doctrine was perfectly rational, once one accepted its premises – a kind of Hobbesian anthropology, involving certain basic assumptions about the low value of individual freedom and the overriding importance of the state. Other leading thinkers of the right saw the salvation of mankind in extreme irrationalism. Among the characters in Musil's *Man without Qualities* figures a philosopher by the name of Meingast who wishes mankind would once more acquire a 'powerful myth' (*ein kräftiger Wahn*). Meingast was a character based on Ludwig Klages, who had been a leading member of the George circle, had settled in Switzerland in later years and is now mainly remembered as a pioneer in the field of graphology. The title of his chief philosophical work, published in three volumes between 1929 and 1932, conveys the message: *The Intellect as Adversary of the Soul*. Taking Nietzsche and vitalism in its extreme form as a starting-point, he maintained that morality was an odious invention of Jews and Christians, contrary to the heart, which was the essence of man. The decline of mankind thus started not with the Enlightenment but at least two thousand years earlier, when the elemental forces were first harnessed and the attempt was made to 'discipline the soul' with Socratic rationalism and the Old Testament creed of free will. Seen in this light all culture is destructive; it makes man a soulless auto-maton, it transforms the earth into a super-Chicago with a few scattered agrarian oases. Technical civilization will bring this orgy of destruction to its logical conclusion by annihilating nature and life altogether. Despite his antisemitism and his fanatical irrationalism, Klages was not an altogether desirable ally from the Nazi point of view. His basic approach was pessi-mistic, for he believed that the process of the destruction of the soul had gone too far and could no longer be arrested; the last opportunity to halt and reverse the process had been missed. Furthermore, Klages's philosophy was essentially individualist and anarchistic. He regarded man as a beast of prey but for that very reason opposed any attempt to tame, discipline and repress him, sometimes in terms reminiscent of latterday neo-Marxist writings on alienation. Such views were bound to be rejected by a mass movement like Nazism, based on strict discipline and blind obedience.

Klages was preoccupied with cosmic problems and hardly ever bothered to comment on current affairs. But his contemporaries, who shared the fashionable belief in the destructive power of the intellect, drew political conclusions. There was a certain logic in it, for the idea of irrational man does not go well with a policy of tolerance and humanism. This is not to say that accepting the limits of reason was necessarily a step towards barbarism; accepting the Id did not make Freud sing its praises. The Expressionists, irrationalist in inspiration, tended politically to the left; Theodor Lessing, once a friend of Klages, who developed a philosophy in some respects quite similar, was considered by the Nazis to be one of their principal enemies and they had him assassinated in his Czechoslovak exile. It was one thing to accept the idea that man was more primitive and less rational than a previous generation had assumed, quite another to relish this discovery.

While many left-wing intellectuals were pronounced Francophiles, hostility to France and everything France stood for was a basic element in the creed of the right. Moeller published long tirades against France ('the profiteer of history'), arguing that the very belief in the possibility of a reconciliation between France and Germany was treasonable. According to Stapel, editor of the *Deutsches Volkstum*, a French-German accord was an 'empty dream'. Ernst Niekisch, spokesman of the 'National Bolshevists', wrote that 'to destroy the republican system in Germany is tantamount to the destruction of the outposts of France within our own nation'.

Thus, with all the internal divisions, there was a consensus on certain basic tenets among the right, whether conservative or radical in inspiration. The attitude to France is one example; the belief in the leader principle another. This refers to the expectation that a *Führer* would arise to lead the people out of its present misery to a better future, the belief in a saviour, more deeply rooted in German history than elsewhere and reinforced by the breakdown of parliamentary democracy. This longing was by no means limited to extreme right-wing groups. The youth movement and the George circle had done their share in preparing the ground, even though the concept of the *Führer* presented in their speeches and writings had little in common with the real Führer who came to power in 1933. Wilhelm Stapel, in a book on *The Christian Statesman*, predicted that the coming leader would not flatter the masses. He would be both paternal and tough. Imbued with soldierly spirit and exerting charismatic power, he would be ruler, warrior and priest all in one. He would be a man fully conscious of his mission and would come to power by popular acclaim. But what if the *Führer* were to fall short of these high standards? This question seems not to have occurred to the ideologues of the right. Since the Weimar Republic had produced few leading personalities, the popularity of the *Führer* myth was not difficult to understand. But precisely because the right-wing thinkers took a dim view of human nature, it is surprising that not one of them seems to have considered the possibility that the long-awaited *Führer* could turn out to be a demagogue, a charlatan, perhaps even a criminal. Once established in power, who would be able to stop him?

Following Spengler, the right-wing thinkers all agreed that the *Führer* would be mainly concerned with foreign policy. Politics is foreign policy, wrote Edgar Jung; this was Germany's fate and its mission in the world. As the central power in Europe it was to see its aim in the restoration of the Reich. Hated and persecuted by the other nations, with artificial frontiers that could not be defended, the *Führer* was to make Germany the dominant force on the continent. This meant that Germany had to expand – a perfectly natural course of action for those who believed in the mission of the master race. The conservative-Christian thinkers, on the other hand, felt that some justification was needed and invoked the idea of a divine Reich, the benefits of which should be shared with other nations under Germany's wise and just rule. They argued that Germany was called upon to unite Europe under its leadership because it constituted the only effective bulwark against the spread of Bolshevism.

Mention has been made of the impact on right-wing doctrine of racialist thought as it had been systematically developed before the First World War. But racialism as a science was propagated only by the Nazis and by some sectarians. Most intellectuals of the right thought that German superiority was rooted in historical-cultural ideas rather than in something biologically definable. This was true of Spengler and Moeller, as well as of Schmitt, Stapel, Hielscher, the brothers Ernst and Friedrich Georg Jünger and other advocates of the new nationalism. Antisemitism was not the cornerstone of their ideology; they did not like the Jews and would refer to them with contempt. But Rosenberg's idea of the Jew as the 'world enemy' found few converts among them. Even Stapel, one of the most antisemitic writers on the right, would engage in public debates with Jews – something which no Nazi would have done.

Economic and social problems were of no great interest to the thinkers of the right, with the exception of the Catholic advocates of the *Ständestaat*, who wanted to reconstruct society largely on a medieval pattern. Carl Schmitt referred on one occasion to Rousseau's dictum that only slaves were concerned with finance. For the true patriot, let alone the true statesman, this was a job best left to specialists. Foreign policy was fate, economic policy a bore. Underlying this assumption there was also the belief that Germany's economic problems could not be solved within the borders fixed in the Versailles treaty and that for this reason, if for no other, it had to expand.

Economics could be ignored while the going was good, but after 1929 this was no longer possible. Thus by the sheer logic of events the *Tat* circle became the most influential group on the intellectual right. The *Tat*, founded before the war, devoted its pages largely to cultural comment and various unpolitical reform movements. It fell on evil days and when Hans Zehrer took it over in 1929 its circulation had fallen to 800 copies. Within three years it became the leading intellectual monthly, with a circulation exceeding that of *Tagebuch* and *Weltbühne* taken together. Zehrer was not yet thirty at the time; his closest collaborators, such as Fried and Wirsing, were in their early twenties. This group of young people infused a new dynamic spirit into right-wing thought, seeing their main task in rigorously working out an economic doctrine which at that time (they ruefully admitted) could be found only on the left. They predicted the coming demise of the capitalist order when the crisis had just begun and they welcomed it: the chaos was a blessing in disguise, because out of it a new order would be born. A revolution was needed in place of the abortive one of 1918.

It had never been fashionable on the right to defend capitalism; Sombart and others had attacked it as plutocratic and feudalist. The right-wing critique of the evils of capitalism had been outspoken and the theories about the rule of finance capital, about late ('senescent', 'moribund') capitalism, were reminiscent of Marxist writings. But once it came to outlining alternatives for the economic order, the right had little to offer but platitudes about an 'organic' German (national) socialism, which would create a harmonious society free of class struggle; spiritual values, not considerations of profit and efficiency, would shape its life. By 1929 such meagre intellectual fare was regarded as inadequate by the more intelligent sectors of the right.

The *Tat* critique of capitalism was far more radical. The journal gave chapter and verse to document the great accumulation of wealth in Germany and the fraudulent manoeuvres of the big concerns: 110 families owned most of Germany's property; 80 per cent of the population owned nothing at all. How in these circumstances could one continue to argue in favour of capitalism? The pauperization of the middle classes and their political radicalization were the outstanding facts of social life. The situation of the white-collar workers was much worse than that of the industrial workers, for the latter had strong organizations of their own; but who was there to take care of salaried employees who found themselves out of work? The spokesmen of the *Tat* left no doubt that the system was not merely unjust but that it was doomed – free trade had come to an end, there was no longer the stimulus of free competition. Since fundamental technical discoveries could no longer be expected, the industrial revolution which had once given the great impetus to the growth of capitalism had played itself out. *The End of Capitalism* was the title of Ferdinand Fried's bestseller, published in 1931.

The editors of the *Tat* propagated a modernized form of mercantilism and a policy of autarky as the panacea for Germany's economic problems. They did not want foreign trade to cease altogether but advocated economic planning and a state foreign trade monopoly. In this way enough would be exported to pay for the import of essential raw materials. They hoped that their programme would gain the support of those sections of society which had been 'pulverized' as the result of the struggle between capital, industry and organized labour: white-collar workers, small entrepeneurs, the intelligentsia, part of the peasantry and, above all, the young generation. A new elite based on this 'third force' would emerge and lead the country towards a better future.

This prospect may have seemed plausible enough in 1929. Three years later it appeared that the extreme forces of the right and left had benefited from the chaos and that there was to be no 'third force'. The *Tat* still argued that a majority of Reichstag deputies had been elected on an anti-capitalist platform; unfortunately they were quite unwilling to reach a compromise on the basis of the *Tat* programme. In these circumstances the idea of a dictatorship from above gained ground: Hindenburg and the Reichswehr were to take power and to pursue a policy such as had been outlined by *Die Tat*. There was no alternative: the parties were corrupt, parliament impotent. Hence the mood of confidence which made Zehrer write in September 1932: 'We are today just about to reach our target. The great turning-point has been reached.' The *Tat* pinned its hopes on Schleicher (the 'social general') who lasted exactly two months as chancellor. Hitler's victory meant that the *Tat* circle ceased to exist; Zehrer disappeared from the political scene altogether; some of his collaborators found a comfortable niche in the Third Reich, but none of them attained a position of power and real influence.

The ideas and activities of the *Tat* reflected fairly accurately the anti-capitalist aspirations and the anti-liberal mentality of the younger generation. They provided an ideology which was far more sophisticated than that embodied in Hitler's vague social and economic programme. What bothered liberal critics was perhaps not so much the anti-capitalist sentiments of the *Tat*, which were fairly widespread in the country, but the contempt with which these young ideologists dismissed the heritage of freedom and liberty, and their naive belief in the omnipotence of the state to 'save the country'. Like other right-wing intellectual groups, the *Tat* suffered from strange delusions as to their own political importance. As one of its leaders said after the war: 'We made a totally mistaken appraisal of Nazism, and did not know about the real power of this movement. We thought that these people were not sufficiently intelligent, and we believed that intelligence was of importance in politics.' Seen in retrospect, the anti-parliamentarism of the *Tat*, its belief in a planned economy and the other ingredients of its programme were not an exclusively German phenomenon. There were interesting parallels elsewhere in Europe, such as the French Ordre Nouveau, or Mosley's New Party in its early stages.

Nor was National Bolshevism something specifically German; similar moods and trends existed in other European countries. In Germany the 'left people of the right' were found mainly among the younger generation. They saw in France, and to a lesser degree in England, the principal enemy; the West was corrupt, the antithesis of Germany and all it stood for. On the other hand Germany had much in common with the Soviet Union, such as, for instance, an interest in keeping Poland down. Germany and Russia were the 'young peoples' about whom Moeller had written, to whom the future belonged. The National Bolsheviks admired Lenin and Stalin, strong, purposeful men who had led their country towards a national renaissance, very much in contrast to the decline of the Western democracies. For some right-wing thinkers the idea of an alliance with Russia was seen as largely tactical, but the National Bolsheviks genuinely wanted a Soviet-German axis based both on an affinity in outlook and on long-term common interests. As one of them wrote: 'If we take our place in the great phalanx of proletarian and oppressed peoples as Lenin – one of the greatest of us – commanded, we do this out of sincere conviction, not for tactical reasons.' They were quite certain that the national elements in Bolshevism would ultimately prevail over its professed internationalism. Subsequent events were to show that this assumption was not altogether fanciful. The West, as the National Bolsheviks saw it, was synonymous with the American way of life, Chicago gangsterism, the Versailles treaty, bourgeois materialist society, Jewish liberalism, decay and decadence. The East, as Goebbels wrote in the 1920s, was 'Germany's natural ally against the diabolical temptations and corruption of the West'. Radical slogans put out by these circles, such as the call for a united anti-capitalist front of workers, peasants and soldiers, caused much discomfort to the traditional right, which stoutly maintained that Bolshevism was a mere disguise for the Jewish drive to world domination and that there could be no collaboration with the Soviet Union. But the National Bolsheviks were not impressed by the strictures of Rosenberg and other professional anti-Bolsheviks; they distrusted and despised the reactionaries almost as much as the representatives of the 'system'.

National Bolshevism was not represented by a political party, a homogeneous bloc, but consisted of dozens of little sects. Its ideological spectrum reached from Ernst Jünger, who played with it for a time, to Ernst Niekisch, who took it far more seriously. For Jünger, Russia was the representative of the will to power; the Soviet Union fascinated him simply because it was less boring than the Western system. At the same time he had little use for Leninist ideology. Niekisch on the other hand tried to provide a synthesis between the extreme nationalism of the right and revolutionary communism. An erstwhile Social Democrat, he had been involved in the Bavarian revolution in 1918–9 but left the SPD because it had not taken a strong stand against the Versailles peace treaty and also because he rejected Marxist internationalism, which was still part of its ideology. Niekisch called upon German youth to spit out all 'Roman' influences; for him Paris was the home of all the enemies of the white race; it would cease to be the *de facto* capital of Germany only when it went up in flames. He rejected the ideas of 1789, published antisemitic propaganda and favoured a totalitarian state; 'even the most barbaric means are justified when they are necessary in the national interest', he once wrote. But at the same time he argued that the spirit of Potsdam, the great ideal of every true German patriot, had found its reincarnation in the Russia of the day. His pro-Soviet sympathies increased over the years; ultimately he came to believe in historical materialism and ridiculed his erstwhile allies for claiming (as he himself had done) that Old Prussia had been a socialist state when in actual fact it had been feudal and patriarchal.

The 'left people of the right' emphatically rejected the idea that 'international Bolshevism' rather than international finance was Germany's main enemy. They were antagonized by the zigzagging tactics of the German Communist Party, but the idea that Germany was a proletarian nation and that it needed a real social revolution strongly appealed to them. These articles of faith at one time had supporters even among the left wing of the Nazi party. If National Bolshevism did not become a political force, this was partly the fault of the German Communists, who were doctrinally far too rigid to make political use of the anti-capitalist ferment on the right. True, they made certain concessions to German patriotism, such as publishing a programme for the 'national liberation of the German people', and they opposed reparations. But in the last resort the Communist Party could not jump over its own shadow; it was not a German national party but the German branch of the Communist International. Its dynamism and its discipline strongly impressed the National Bolsheviks, but its policy was made in Moscow, not in Berlin. With all their sympathies for the Soviet Union, the National Bolsheviks could not accept essential parts of Marxist-Leninist ideology, such as historical and dialectical materialism; they did not deny the existence of the class struggle, but they still regarded national solidarity as the ultimate aim. Such basic differences in ideological outlook could not be overcome.

A review of right-wing thought in the Weimar period shows as much divergence as consensus. Only a few right-wing intellectuals believed that a return to the monarchy was possible or desirable. Their critique of the 'system' was radical but they had only the haziest ideas about the future of their country; their concessions to socialism were largely verbal. They were counter-revolutionary in as much as they rejected the 'Western ideas' of the eighteenth and nineteenth centuries, 'arid intellectualism', liberalism, parliamentary democracy. They virtually monopolized nationalism, and what united them was the belief that the 'system' was so corrupt that any political order that succeeded it would be an improvement on Weimar. They played an important role as pacemakers for the Nazis by spreading ridicule and contempt for democracy among the German middle classes, but they had no direct influence on the course of events.

4
The Rise and Decline of the Avant-Garde I: New Writing and the Stage

On the evening of 9 November 1918, the day the Republic was proclaimed, a hastily convened 'Council of Intellectuals', consisting mainly of avant-garde artists, met in the Reichstag building to assess the situation and to decide on a common course of action. That this was not a representative cross-section of the German intelligentsia hardly mattered; no one was likely to ask for formal legitimation in those turbulent days. The Council demanded the abolition of all academic institutions, the nationalization of all theatres and of the free professions, and the immediate convocation of a world parliament. Art, they said, should be brought to the people and the world should be changed through art. Most of those who had come to this historic meeting were Expressionists; so far as they were concerned the political revolution was merely a postscript to the cultural revolution which had taken place a decade earlier.

The periods of cultural history hardly ever coincide with those of political history. It is as pointless to investigate diplomacy in the period of Impressionism as it is to write on the history of art in the era of Stresemann. Roughly speaking, the great break with cultural tradition occurred, in Germany as elsewhere, between 1905 and 1914; this decade, incidentally, was also a revolutionary period in the social and natural sciences. The new wave of experimentation manifested itself first and most powerfully in painting, but it was to affect literature and music no less radically. In painting, the modern movement had its beginnings with Cézanne and Van Gogh; the dramatic break with tradition came with the exhibitions of the Fauves from 1905 onwards. Then Cubism became the fashion for a while; the term was coined by Matisse in 1908 in a comment on a picture by Braque. (In England the new movement was known as Vorticism.) In Germany the term 'Expressionism' was first used by Wilhelm Worringer in 1911 to define the new fashions in literature.

The transition in music was less abrupt. Debussy's *Pelléas et Mélisande* was performed in 1902, Ravel's String Quartet the year after, and some of Satie's compositions date back to an even earlier period. The real break came after 1908 with the appearance of atonal music, such as Schönberg's *Drei Klavierstücke* and Alban Berg's String Quartet op. 3, and with Stravinsky's *Sacre du Printemps*, which provoked a scandal at its Paris première. In 1909 the first Futurist Manifesto called on its followers and well-wishers to live dangerously, to destroy museums and libraries, to awaken literature from its long sleep and to turn it into a 'mad movement'. The Futurists also praised war, aeroplanes and racing cars ('more beautiful than the *Victory of Samothrace*').

The origins of modernism in literature are the most diverse but also the least tangible. They can be traced to Symbolism, to Rimbaud and even to the eighteenth-century *Sturm und Drang*. In Germany the element of generational revolt was of considerable importance: the modernists were all born between 1875 and 1890; they were a generation with very marked differences from the one which preceded them. The German Expressionist painters and sculptors were strongly influenced by the French, a debt which they freely acknowledged. Foreign models had less impact on music, and scarcely any on literature; writers, unlike composers and painters, are by the very nature of their medium less open to foreign influences.

Péguy's observation not long before the First World War (that the world had changed less since Christ than during the previous thirty years) applies, *mutatis mutandis*, to cultural life in Germany. The gap between the avant-garde and the public grew immeasurably during the decade before 1914. True, every new revolutionary movement in cultural history has been received both by its exponents and its enemies as something quite unprecedented and has initially generated a great deal of opposition. But there was one fundamental difference between this and previous such occasions. The plays of the German Naturalists and their successors, such as those of the young Gerhart Hauptmann, shocked many spectators, who reacted violently ('filth is not art') to the portrayal on the stage of poverty, alcoholism and prostitution. But however outraged they were, they had no particular difficulty in understanding the new trend. On the other hand, Kandinsky's first abstract compositions or the poems of August Stramm (*Du*) were beyond their comprehension; they simply did not make sense and the public suspected that someone was perpetrating a huge joke on them.

The decade before the outbreak of the war was very prolific; most of the important works by Expressionist writers and artists in fact predate 1914. When the war ended, some of the leading practitioners of the new movement were no longer alive. The painters Franz Marc and August Macke had been killed in the war, as had the poets Ernst Stadler, Gustav Sack, Alfred Lichtenstein, Ernst Wilhelm Lotz and Stramm. Georg Heym was drowned in 1912 and Georg Trakl had taken his own life. Die Brücke, founded in Dresden in 1905 by several students of architecture, including Karl Schmidt-Rottluff, Ernst Ludwig Kirchner and Erich Heckel, had been dissolved eight years later following a dispute; and the Munich Blaue Reiter circle ceased to exist during the war when some of its leading exponents, being foreign nationals, had to leave Germany, while others were killed in the fighting. Herwarth Walden's *Der Sturm* and Franz Pfemfert's *Die Aktion*, the most important periodicals devoted to Expressionism, had been founded in 1910 and 1911 respectively. Even earlier, in 1909, Kurt Hiller had founded the Neue Club in Berlin. There was hardly any author of renown in the 1920s who had not been published in one of these periodicals well before 1918. The Expressionists, as a rule, wrote poems and plays. It is almost impossible to point to an Expressionist novel, with the possible exception of one of Döblin's early works, and *Perrudja*, by Hans Henny Jahnn, which was published much later; the medium apparently did not lend itself to the Expressionist style.

All the features which characterized Expressionism had existed well before the war. The chapter-headings in a famous Expressionist anthology, published in 1920, are revealing: 'Fall and Cry', 'The Awakening of the Heart', 'Appeal and Revolt', 'Love Man'. The vocabulary of Expressionism had not changed – it still abounded in words like cry, torment, abyss, darkness, love, brother, soul, mankind and goodness. What was new was the discovery of politics by German Expressionists during the war – hence the meeting in the Reichstag on 9 November. True, even before 1914 the Germans had been more socially conscious than the French modernists, among whom Rouault was a rare exception. But this was a matter of nuances; we have it on the authority of Wieland Herzfelde, one of the pillars of the left-wing modernist movement in the 1920s, that before the war he and his friends never bothered about politics and hardly ever read newspapers. What Hans Richter said about the Dadaists applies by and large to the Expressionists as well: that they reserved their enthusiasm for the SELF, working out its own laws, its own form and its own justification, free from guilt and remorse.

To try to define Expressionism is a thankless task, given the inchoate character of the movement. Furthermore, what characterized Expressionism in literature did not necessarily apply to the Blaue Reiter. Eventually the term became a catch-all for the younger generation of writers, artists and composers, active just before and after the war. When Gottfried Benn, who had been one of the most promising younger members of these circles (a *Medizyniker*, as an early critic called him), wrote that Expressionism had no specific characteristics of its own, he was exaggerating – but not that much. It is certainly far easier to state what Expressionism was not and did not want to be. It totally rejected accepted aesthetic standards: the painters were fascinated by ugliness; the composers threw harmony overboard, gradually moving towards dissonance; the poets and playwrights were preoccupied with the madness of great cities, parenticide and rats emerging from rotting corpses. If there was peace and even a certain joy in Macke's famous picture *Mädchen unter Bäumen*, the poems were far from idyllic. Trains

fall from railway bridges (Jakob van Hoddis), the sun stinks
(J. R. Becher), in San Francisco the moon bursts asunder
(Lichtenstein), we are dirt and we do not want to be anything
else (Benn). Underlying all this was the wish to shock a self-
satisfied, satiated world and the artists' enemies, which included
the state, the middle classes, the philistines and authority in
general. To achieve this aim the Expressionists had to make
themselves heard, and thus both their ecstasies and their
agonies were several decibels louder than those of their pre-
decessors. But it would be unfair to describe them as a group of
pranksters whose main aim was to shock society. They had
sincere, deeply-felt views, even though these were not always
easy to express. They believed that only the substance mattered,
not the outward form. Beauty was a lie, ugliness was true,
because it depicted man in all his weakness and spiritual
poverty. The purpose of art was not to cater to aesthetic taste
but to give expression to the most basic religious, individual and
social experiences. If Rilke had said that beauty was the
beginning of horror, they went one step further: real beauty
was in the horror of tormented individuals, in the loss of equilibrium and symmetry. There was in Expressionism as in other
radical movements a search for roots, a desire to return to
beginnings. Since real primitivism could no longer be found in
their own milieu, they looked for it in Africa and in China, in
the world of the child and in lunatic asylums. Some latterday
critics have detected Gothic and Nordic-Scandinavian influences in Expressionism; others have pointed to the presence of
Mediterranean elements. This applies mainly to the painters;
the Expressionist writers faced problems of a different nature.
Language, they agreed, had to be liberated. But some were less
radical than others in this respect, perhaps because they realized
that with the destruction of syntax and grammar they would
effectively cut themselves off from communicating with anyone
but a few like-minded spirits. They had to choose between the
radical new form and the dream of helping towards the creation
of new man, of 'changing everything'. Expressionism was a
middle-class youth movement, part of a worldwide revolt which
had its roots in boredom and dissatisfaction with the *juste milieu*
– a *Wandervogel* of sorts on a higher level of intellectual sophistication and creativity. Like the *Wandervogel* it contained a great

many incompatible elements. To some it was an end in itself, to others part of a general revolution; the fascination which the great city exerted on some (Marinetti's *passione per la città*) was matched by the abhorrence of those who saw it as an all-devouring Moloch, the symbol of the coming apocalypse (Brecht, Becher, Trakl, Toller). Like the *Wandervogel*, Expressionism was idealistic and regressive at one and the same time. It was a revolt against the falsities of bourgeois existence and against intellectualism; it led anywhere and nowhere. It was a breathless movement, strangely fascinated by fast trains, a theme recurring in the works of many Expressionists, including Benn, Stadler and Wolfenstein.

Underlying it there was a free-floating, aimless militancy. As Georg Heym wrote in his diary in 1911, at the age of twenty-three: 'Most of all I would like to be a lieutenant of the cuirassiers. But the day after I want to be a terrorist.' And on another occasion in the same year: 'I suffocate in the superficial enthusiasm of this banal age. For I need tremendous outside emotions to be happy. In my daydreams I always see myself as a Danton, or a fighter on a barricade; without my Jacobin hat I cannot envisage myself. Now I hope that there will at least be a war. But even that is not to be.' The same young poet also wrote in his diary: 'I would be a great poet but for that swine – my father [*mein schweinerner Vater*].' This recalls Kafka's letter to his father (which was never sent), and the plays on parricide from Hasenclever's *Der Sohn* to Bronnen's *Vatermord*. This theme is central to the whole movement (Sorge's *Der Bettler*, Werfel's '*Not the murderer, the victim is guilty*', Kafka's *The Judgment*): the tyrannical fathers brutally suppressed the individual character of the sons, they were cruel and bloodthirsty; they had sent the sons to the senseless slaughter in 1914. 'What should I do?' asks the son in Hasenclever's play; his friend answers: 'Destroy the tyranny of the family. . . . Remember that the fight against the father is like taking revenge on the princes in a former age.' But most of the plays on parricide had been conceived or written before the outbreak of a war which the sons had welcomed as a liberating act. 'We knew it, this world of peace', wrote Thomas Mann during the war; 'we suffered from this horrible world more acutely than anyone else. It stank of the ferments of decomposition The artist was so sick of this world that he praised God for this purge and this tremendous hope.'

Were German middle-class fathers more evil than fathers in general? Siegfried Jacobsohn, the editor of the *Schaubühne* (predecessor of the *Weltbühne*), noted after watching Hasenclever's play that a father was neither good nor bad, but became so only in the perspective of the son. The young rebels of 1914 were not in fact exposed to greater tyranny at home than previous generations. If the fathers were authoritarian, the sons had the same streak. Heym's father ('the swine') tried his best to help his son who almost ruined his career when, as a young practitioner of law, he destroyed a file which baffled or bored him. Becher senior, also a judge, rescued his son from the clutches of the law, pleading mitigating circumstances after the young poet had killed a prostitute and then tried to commit suicide. There were more such cases and it is a moot point whether fathers or sons were the greater sinners against elementary human decency. It is likely that the rebellion against the fathers gathered momentum because parental authority had weakened, was open to question; revolutions do not occur when the rulers are strong and self-confident. An acute analysis of the new father-son relationship was provided shortly after the war by Heinrich Mann, Thomas's elder brother. The severest critic of Wilhelmian society, who in *Professor Unrat* (filmed as *The Blue Angel*) had described one of the petty tyrants of that age, was in many ways the idol of the younger generation. Yet writing about 'tragic youth' in 1922 he noted that they were not victims of oppression:

They are the opposite of democrats, they want to change everything, even against the wish of the majority. They want the absolute and will follow those leaders who, they think, are the most strong-willed. They are saturated with hatred. But the older generation has a bad conscience, and never punishes them. All protests, all threats and actions of the young are directed against the older generation and its way of life. The old note all this carefully – and give them even more freedom of action. If shots are fired, they frown and wait for the next shooting. They go to the theatre and warmly applaud the plays about the most popular of subjects – parricide.

Heinrich Mann's description of a generation of permissive parents strikes a familiar note. Would Heym really have been a greater poet but for his father? Or was it the conflict with an oppressor, real or imaginary, which made him a writer?

Expressionist literature is no longer read, and it has been argued that this was the fault of Hitler, the resentment of the petty bourgeoisie, and the narrow-mindedness of the so-called educated classes who rejected it because its style did not conform with classical tradition. But Expressionist painting did have a revival, and if the Expressionist plays have been forgotten this is because most of them did not evoke much of a response when they were first performed. Tucholsky noted that the public watching Toller's *Die Wandlung* remained silent and cold, though it had doubtless come to applaud. The Expressionist plays were bad theatre. Once one had seen two or three of them, one had seen them all; the pathos and the monologues of nameless persons were digestible only in small doses. It remains to be said that for many of these writers Expressionism was just a stage in their development; there are Expressionist elements, for instance, in the later Döblin and in the early Brecht, but they no longer predominate.

Writing many years later about the 'greatness and decay of Expressionism', Georg Lukács interpreted Expressionism as a movement hesitating between proletarian revolution and bourgeois reformism, something akin to the position taken by the Independent Social Democrats. But such attempts to classify in political terms a basically non-political movement are quite misleading. The war had made the Expressionists more committed to public concerns than before; they believed that mankind would emerge more humane from the purgatory. But it did not take them long to realize that the power of the *Geist* which they had thought would change the world was very nearly nil, and that the world of brotherly love of which they had dreamt was farther away than ever. Some of their periodicals and yearbooks continued to appear, but by the mid-1920s Expressionism was irrevocably dead.

The place of Expressionism in German cultural history is disputed to this day. It was a movement in the Romantic tradition, perhaps the most extreme form of Romanticism that ever existed. The tendency to put the inner experience above the outer life was typically Romantic, as was the attempt, often unconscious, to recapture the religious (or quasi-religious) ecstasy of the Middle Ages. Expressionism reflected a general fear, a *Lebensangst*; all its practitioners complained about the sickness of the age, about its mendacity and the chaos of human life. (The term 'alienation' was not yet widely used.) 'How sick all living things seem to be', wrote Georg Trakl, one of the most gifted of the school. But the Expressionists were themselves part of the chaos and the disease, and while the rottenness of the age was frequently held responsible for personal difficulties, it was also a convenient alibi; for all one knows, the struggle against the age may have served as an escape-valve for the destructive forces which might otherwise have turned inward. To say this is to defend neither the boredom of the prewar era nor the senseless slaughter of the war. The Expressionists were a sensitive seismograph of their age; at their very best they were almost as moving as some of the seventeenth-century poets, writing after the great holocaust of the Thirty Years War. The main weakness of the movement was that it knew no bounds – a frequent German failing. It lost control over its emotions, became inchoate and incoherent, could no longer speak clearly to the outside world. Had Expressionism been just another avant-garde trend, this would have mattered little. But precisely because Expressionism wanted to change life itself and not just provide a new art-form, it cannot be measured by purely aesthetic standards. Expressionism, as Döblin said years later, was *Gärung ohne Richtung* – ferment without purpose.

The subsequent fate of the Expressionists is of some interest. A few (such as Hanns Johst) later went over to Nazism, others to Stalinism (Becher and Brecht, to name only the most important). By 1930 all these had, of course, outgrown their Expressionist beginnings and did not particularly like to be reminded of what they later regarded as their youthful aberrations. Yet others (such as Benn, Nolde and Barlach), who in later years had a good deal in common ideologically with National Socialism, were rejected by the Nazis and even persecuted because their art was not in accordance with the Nazi aesthetic ideals; it, too, was *entartete Kunst*. Most Expressionists were and remained unpolitical. Not all of them continued to write and to paint. Those who did made their mark, individually or in groups, in the history of Weimar culture will reappear at later stages of our account.

THE DADA INTERLUDE

Towards the end of the war Expressionism was outflanked by a far more radical group, which claimed in its manifesto that Expressionism had not fulfilled the expectations of a new art 'which burns the essence of life into our flesh'. This was Dada, which originated among a small group of refugees from the war in a Zürich cabaret. It promised a new and primitive reaction to the reality of the modern environment. Life appeared to the Dadaists to be a simultaneous 'muddle of noises, colours and spiritual rhythms', in other words the most consistent manifestation of anti-art. *Kunst ist Scheisse*, they said – art is shit. A typical Dada poem read as follows:

Gadji beri bimba
glandridi lauli lonni cadori
gadjama bim beri glassala
glandridi glassala tuffim
(Hugo Ball)

Poems of this kind were not altogether novel. In 1905 Christian Morgenstern had written a phonetic poem which began:

Kroklokwafzi? Sememami!
Seiokrontro – prafiplo:
bifzi, bafzi, hulalemi . . .

But Morgenstern did not set out to be the founder of a new literary school, whereas the Dadaists had more ambitious aims – or at least behaved in such a way as to create that impression. There was method in their behaviour, once they had reached the conclusion that the past was senseless and the present unspeakable, Dada's anti-art did not make sense precisely because it was designed to reflect the general chaos. Like the Futurists, Dadaists stood for the destruction of all previous art, but they did not share the Italians' enthusiasm for the great war. Some had gone to Switzerland, others, such as George Grosz, John Heartfield and Wieland Herzfelde, preferred German lunatic asylums to trench warfare. Their politics, if any, were muddled. They sent fraternal greetings to D'Annunzio, the proto-Fascist, on the occasion of his occupation of Fiume. At the same time they were enthusiastic about the Russian Revolution. Their attitude towards politics is strongly reminiscent of the French Symbolists, who thought that the style and the beautiful gesture was all that mattered, and who for that reason sympathized with the bomb-throwers rather than their victims.

The Dadaists certainly had style. In the first number of their Berlin periodical they proposed the introduction of simultaneous poetry as a new form of state prayer, of progressive unemployment by the immediate mechanization of all physical labour, and the 'immediate regulation of sexual intercourse in the Dadaist spirit through a Central Dada Sex Office'. Dada, they announced, was a club which everyone could join, and in which everyone could be president. *Jedermann sein eigner Fussball* was the name of the first Dada periodical, founded by Herzfelde and Grosz. It is now remembered largely because it was the first to use photomontage systematically, though Raoul Hausmann, another Dadaist, later maintained that he had used it even earlier. The first Dada soirées, or 'happenings' as they would have been called in a later age, took place during the last months of the war. After November 1918 these were open to the general public. In one, a race was held between a sewing-machine, operated by George Grosz, and a typewriter, worked by Walter Mehring. From the ceiling hung the stuffed effigy of a German officer with a pig's head, bearing a placard which read 'Hanged by the revolution'. The Dadaists appeared in grotesque masks, with military uniforms, monocles, riding crops, as well as large wooden iron crosses and papier-mâché death's heads. Baader, the *Oberdada*, had leaflets scattered from the air over Weimar when the Constituent Assembly was in session, announcing that he was to be president of both Germany and the world.

Dada has been explained in retrospect as a naturalistic reaction against Expressionism, yet it is more than doubtful whether Dada ever intended to be taken that seriously: it was hardly more than a satirical interlude. It wanted to shock, to caricature both the old regime and the new rulers; it was a huge joke which went on a little too long. As in Expressionism, the

painters who started their career in Dadaism (Grosz, Schwitters) outlasted the writers. Grosz and his friends, the
brothers Herzfelde and Heartfield soon became politically
committed. Their journal *Pleite* (*Bankruptcy*) was one of the few
in Germany to publish the manifesto of the first congress of the
Communist International. And the Malik publishing house,
originally founded by Herzfelde to put out Expressionist and
Dadaist books, subsequently became the most influential centre
for the dissemination of Soviet and communist literature. In
Germany the spirit of carnival became the godfather of
socialist realism.

THE REPUBLICAN CLASSICS

Expressionism was representative of a mood among certain
sections of the younger generation. Its tone was strident, but its
impact on the intelligentsia was limited and shortlived. It did
not even succeed in becoming a cultural counter-establishment.
The real representatives of the spirit of the new Republic were
two men who had little in common, apart perhaps from the fact
that both had left school at an early age, spent some of their
formative years in Italy and were eventually awarded the
Nobel Prize, Gerhart Hauptmann in 1912 and Thomas Mann
in 1929. At this point, admittedly, all similarity ends. Hauptmann, the author of a stream of novels and some verse, was at
his best as a playwright; whereas Mann was a novelist *par
excellence*. For Mann language was a matter of paramount
importance and he took infinite pains to polish his sentences.
Hauptmann's attitude to language was strictly utilitarian, if not
slapdash. They were totally different in character: Thomas
Mann, the intellectual, meditative and basically pessimistic,
with Nietzsche, Wagner and Schopenhauer as his great heroes;
Hauptmann, a natural talent, optimistic in outlook, a writer
who did not read many books and who was in no need of
philosophical inspiration.

At the time Hauptmann's prestige was far greater, and not
just because he had started his literary career some fifteen years
earlier. He was a man with a sunny disposition, successful in all
his dealings; everything he touched turned to gold – or so it
seemed. He was the 'secret emperor' of Germany, an 'Olym-

pian', a latterday Goethe, the conscience of the nation. His books sold well and several were made into films. The president of the Republic and even General von Seeckt, the chief of staff, went out of their way to honour him. He lived in grand style wherever he happened to be – in Berlin, Italy, Silesia or at a resort on the Baltic coast. Yet he was more of a symbol than an intellectual influence. His important work had been published in the 1890s, starting with *Vor Sonnenaufgang* in 1889, *Die Weber* (1894), and *Die versunkene Glocke* (1896). *Die Weber* was a moving play of social protest, of a realism, freshness and daring such as had not been seen for generations on the German stage. Old Theodor Fontane immediately spotted the rising of a new star; having seen Hauptmann's first play, he wrote that he found in it everything that he had liked in Ibsen – without Ibsen's weaknesses.

Hauptmann was the only German Naturalist writer of originality and real stature, and his works had tremendous appeal from the very beginning. In his later writings he demonstrated an astonishing versatility, showing the capacity to adapt himself to all the prevailing styles of the day, including Neo-Romanticism. He wrote elaborate fairy-tales, comedies and tragedies, psychological novels and a philosophical epic. But he no longer produced anything of even remotely equal importance to his early plays; some of his works were poor by any standard. But the critics, some of whom had been slow to recognize his immense talent, went on making the genuflexions almost mechanically and shouted *O altitudo* whenever another mediocre novel by Gerhart Hauptmann was published. The public's instinct was healthier: it continued to admire the early Hauptmann, but his later output was much less widely read and towards the end of his life his prestige dwindled rapidly. For the right Hauptmann's patriotism was suspect and his work was thought to contain unhealthy, decadent elements; for the left he was an opportunist who did not hesitate to make his peace with Hitler. For the young writers he was an outdated, slightly ridiculous figure; for the conservatives he was far too modernist. Hauptmann himself realized that he was no longer fashionable; 'my period ended with the burning of the Reichstag', he once told a friend. His era as a vital cultural influence had ended before 1914. However during the 1920s Gerhart

Hauptmann was still a name to conjure with, not because of anything very profound or provocative he wrote or said but because of his very presence. Thomas Mann depicted him somewhat maliciously in *The Magic Mountain* as Mijnher Peeperkorn. Settembrini, the fiery intellectual, contemptuously called him 'a stupid old man' who would utter trivial things with an air full of meaning. Yet at the same time he is described as a man of consequence, exuding authority, commanding respect and overawing even the ideologists and the *littérateurs*, who felt that this pompous figure had a trace of something which they lacked – greatness. Gerhart Hauptmann was the most representative figure of Weimar cultural life: he had welcomed the First World War with some patriotic poems which were quickly forgotten; five years later he welcomed the Republic with equal enthusiasm – it was the most important event in a thousand years of German history. Hauptmann's olympian detachment made life in the Third Reich bearable for him.

Thomas Mann was a far more complex personality. He had made his contribution to the war effort with a long political tract, *Betrachtungen eines Unpolitischen*, expressing chauvinistic feelings in a highly civilized way. He later said that it had been a mere rearguard action, but this was certainly not how his contemporaries interpreted it. The right-wingers, who had welcomed it, never forgave him for subsequently betraying the cause of German nationalism and becoming one of the main pillars of the Republic. When the war broke out the author of *Buddenbrooks*, not yet forty years of age, was already one of Germany's most widely-read and respected authors. Unlike Hauptmann, he was never a heartwarming writer; his all-pervasive irony always kept the reader at a distance. Mann's novels were admired, but there was never full identification with the author. *The Magic Mountain* was outstanding among his works after the war. Published in 1924, Mann had worked on it for more than a decade. If *Buddenbrooks* was the great novel of the decline of a family over three generations, *The Magic Mountain* was a panorama of the decay of a whole world: a Marxist could see in the novel a near-perfect mirror of the gradual downfall of the bourgeoisie. But Mann would have angrily rejected any such categorizing; in his political essays he was guardedly optimistic about the future of Germany and the world. There was hope, provided the forces of unreason and darkness could be overcome; the world was simply going through an 'adaptation neurosis'. He was a conservative at heart, a *Bürger*, a member of the class which had created the only cultural values in existence. If there was to be political and social change, as many as possible of the old values had to be incorporated into the new order. What Lisaweta (in *Tonio Kröger*) said to her friend, Tonio, refers also to the author – that he was, in the last resort, only a bourgeois who had strayed among the artists, rather than an artist in bourgeois clothing.

It would be a futile enterprise to look for a clear, consistent pattern in his thought. A conservative socialist in politics, a conservative innovator in literature, a believer in progress who drew his inspiration from Schopenhauer and Richard Wagner – the contradictions in his mental make-up were those of the culture of his time. His works included idylls (like *Königliche Hoheit* or *Herr und Hund*), and books permeated with his fascination for death, like *The Magic Mountain*. All this made Mann Weimar Germany's greatest and certainly its most interesting writer. But he could not be its spokesman and teacher, *magister Germaniae*. For that function someone far less complex and much more single-minded was needed. With all his enormous gifts, he had the German talent of making easy things complicated and obvious matters tortuous and obscure. To sell democracy to his compatriots (in *Von deutscher Republik*) he invoked poor Hölderlin as an early champion. In a famous lecture on Freud, he explained psychoanalysis as an heir to German Romanticism. But to his eternal credit he was one of the very few writers of the Republic who had the courage to stand up and be counted. Many years later he wrote to his children Klaus and Erika that the state of Weimar perished 'not without our own fault'. The cultural elite of the Republic had been deficient in leadership and in a sense of responsibility. Freedom, Mann said, was too often abused, not treated with the necessary care and seriousness.

But had there ever been cultural leadership? After 1918 Thomas Mann realized much more acutely than most that there was a close relationship between culture (*Geist*) and politics, the fateful importance of affairs of state, and he blamed his colleagues (and the German middle classes in general) for staying aloof. He saw in the Weimar Republic a framework which made possible a more or less harmonious coexistence between culture and politics, between art and reality. These were valuable insights, all too rare at the time, but they were not reflected in his novels. The great writer was neither educator nor prophet. He wrote about the innermost self and his assumption that, as he once wrote, this would somehow result in something of great national importance was quite mistaken.

The abundance and variety of German literature in the 1920s was such that any short account is bound to distort the general picture. The first Weimar had consisted of a small group of people, Klopstock and Wieland, Goethe and Schiller and a very few others, who knew each other intimately. The second Weimar had few if any giants who impressed their character on the epoch, but there were a great many interesting writers, poets and playwrights. There was little cohesion among them, the left and right-wing writers were not often on speaking terms, there was a Berlin literature and a regional literature, and each little coterie was deeply absorbed in its own affairs. There was no spiritual or geographical centre. In the Romanische Café in Berlin one would have looked in vain for Gerhart Hauptmann or Hermann Hesse, for Stefan George or Franz Kafka. These four – to choose at random writers who were, broadly speaking, contemporaries – might have known each other by reputation. That they were familiar with each other's works is by no means certain. It would not have occurred to them to go out of their way to look for each other's company, to exchange views and experiences or to discuss their works. The literary periodicals expressed the views of small groups or political parties, or (such as Fischer's *Neue Rundschau*) featured the authors of a certain publishing house. There was no great representative journal in which literary figures would appear irrespective of style and orientation. The most comprehensive periodicals were Efraim Frisch's *Neuer Merkur*, with a circulation never exceeding 1,400 copies, which went out of business in 1925; and Willy Haas's *Literarische Welt*, which appeared during the last years of the Republic.

Germany was very much absorbed in its own affairs, and Vienna and Prague seemed farther away than before 1914. Rilke died in 1926 and Hofmannsthal in 1928; most of their important works had been published before the war, and the same is true of Schnitzler. Their impact on German literature was still great but they were not really part of the Weimar scene in any meaningful way. Karl Kraus continued to publish his *Fackel*, the most idiosyncratic of German periodicals, the most irritating and the wittiest. But he too was mainly preoccupied with Viennese cultural and social life and only infrequently found the time to pursue his running fight with the Berlin critics. Kraus intensely disliked Kerr, and of the younger ones Tucholsky, just as he had hated Harden. There were endless quarrels, and occasionally lawyers were instructed and courts of honour convened; but the literary public no longer followed these exchanges with bated breath.

Kafka, the shyest of men, died in 1924. Hardly any of his writings appeared during his lifetime; even by 1930, after the publication of *The Trial* and *The Castle*, his work was known only to a small circle. Franz Werfel, also a native of Prague, will be remembered for two long novels published in 1929 and 1933 respectively – *Verdi* and *Die vierzig Tage des Musa Dagh*, but he too was an outsider so far as Weimar Germany was concerned. Among the pioneers of the 'new novel' two other Viennese, Robert Musil and Hermann Broch, were the most outstanding; Musil lived in Berlin for many years and the action of Broch's trilogy of disintegration (*Die Schlafwandler*) takes place in Germany. But Broch was published only in the 1930s and Musil was known at the time only to the cognoscenti.

Even if we ignore for our present purpose German-language writers who belonged to other cultural centres, the situation is only slightly less confusing. Stefan George and Hermann Hesse were two of the most important literary figures alive at the time, but they were not really part of the literary *Betrieb*, nor did they have the slightest wish to be. (They probably never met, although they were born within a hundred miles of each other. These facts bear mentioning; it is highly unlikely that leading French or English writers of the nineteenth or twentieth century would never have met.) For Hesse redemption was to be found in escape from time, and for George in the creation of distance between himself and the world; solitude was an essential part of his existence as a writer.

George was the poet and anti-Naturalist *par excellence*; as a young man he had lived in Paris and was strongly influenced by Baudelaire and Verlaine, whose work he translated. He searched for new poetic forms and a new vocabulary, but unlike the French Symbolists he was also strongly attracted by the classical tradition. In 1892 he founded a literary journal (*Blätter für die Kunst*) around which, over the years, a growing circle of friends, admirers and disciples gathered. A writer of great power, George believed in the vision of the poet, in a new aristocracy of the spirit, in great heroes dwelling far from the madding crowd. He advocated a new ritual, a secret priesthood of an elaborate cult with himself as its high priest. Eventually he became the only German writer of his time who established a literary school and deeply influenced literary criticism (Friedrich Gundolf, Ernst Bertram), historians (Kurt Breysig, Ernst Kantorowicz) and even sociologists (Georg Simmel). His works and those of his circle were frequently attacked, but its members were far too disdainful to engage in polemics. Some of these attacks were clearly misguided; since the *Reich* and even a *Führer* figured prominently insome of his poems, George was believed to be a sympathizer of National Socialism. But his *Reich* was not of this world, and when the Nazis came to power he went to Switzerland, where he died. More justified were the critics who pointed to the precious, stilted and even insincere elements in his and his disciples' writings. The circle lived in an ivory tower transplanted into a lunar castle, mistaking the world it had created for the real world; and it was of course deeply shocked when under the impact of cruel realities the tower collapsed.

When Hermann Hesse celebrated his fiftieth birthday in July 1927, a critic wrote that his time was already past, whereas George's great age of fame and influence was yet to come. Yet four decades later Hesse is more widely read than ever, both in Germany and abroad, whereas the study of George is more or less confined to professional students of German literature. Born in Württemberg, Hesse had settled in Switzerland before the war. His early novels dealt with subjects not unlike those pre-occupying the young Thomas Mann – the conflict between the world of the artist (who in Hesse's novels also happened to be often a vagrant) and the bourgeois. But Hesse's interest in the outside world (unlike Mann's) gradually diminished and his novels became 'biographies of the soul'. His work likewise reflects the disintegration of the old world of European certainties. He too refuses in the end to give in to bleak despair, though he moves perilously near it: the life of the Steppenwolf is that of a self-confessed candidate for suicide. To a larger degree than Mann's, Hesse's novels are an account of his inner life and its many crises. The influence of Jungian analysis is marked – in Goldmund searching for the eternal mother, a theme that had already appeared in *Klingsors letzter Sommer*; in *Siddhartha*, which introduces Indian and Far Eastern religious themes; and in Harry Haller, the Steppenwolf, who comes to symbolize the neurosis of a whole civilization. At the time, young Germans were influenced not so much by Hesse's philosophical novels but by *Demian* and *Zarathustras Wiederkehr*. *Demian* is a novel of adolescence, describing how young people grow up and achieve through suffering and disappointment an inner freedom which makes it possible for them to face realities. *Demian* was published under a pseudonym and it was generally believed that its author was a very young man telling the story of his own life. In fact it had been written by a man well into his forties who had remained young at heart and who believed in the mission of the young generation. Thomas Mann wrote many years later that *Demian* had an electrifying effect because Hesse touched a certain nerve with uncanny accuracy; the book was 'a message from very deep down'. Hesse himself later said that he had hoped to help his compatriots to understand how they too had been guilty, and that it was wrong on their part to go on cursing the wicked war, evil enemies and the horrible revolution. He was, needless to say, quite unsuccessful as a political educator and he soon gave up his mission. It was more than a little ironical that this least political of writers, who more than anyone else tried to distance himself from time and space and listen to the voice of his innermost self, should show more wisdom and humanity than most of his contemporaries at the two great moments of truth in Germany history. In 1914, after the outbreak of war, he published an article in Switzerland invoking Schiller's Ode to Joy ('Freunde, oh nicht diese Töne') against the prevailing hate-mongering, the chauvinism displayed by writers and academics in his native country, which of course made him a traitor in the eyes of the super-patriots. In 1931 Hesse resigned from the Prussian Academy of Literature because the Republic, as he wrote at the time, was not republican enough and did not combat the new aggressive spirit in the universities. Hesse's posthumous popularity in America, Japan and elsewhere is based partly on a misunderstanding. But the fact that in the 1960s a great many young people in faraway countries believed they had discovered a message in his novels was not entirely fortuitous. He had pre-empted certain themes which appealed to a later age, such as the early hippie in *Knulp*, the message of salvation from the East in *Siddhartha*. He had expressed the mood and the spiritual pilgrimage of another period also deeply afflicted with neurosis; he was the writer of adolescence *par excellence*, of idealistic pathos and of black despair, of the collision between youthful dreams and repulsive realities. Such a writer was bound to be rediscovered sooner or later and to find new disciples.

George and Hesse were remote from the literary storms that from time to time shook the German literary scene. If there was a *Zeitgeist* (a proposition which cannot be accepted without major reservations), its more typical representatives were writers such as Heinrich Mann, Jakob Wassermann, Alfred Döblin, Arnold Zweig and to a certain extent Leonhard Frank and Lion Feuchtwanger, to choose just six out of a much greater number camping on the slopes of the Weimar Parnassus. They were by no means generally accepted by the German reading public; on the contrary, their very names were anathema to wide sections of the educated middle classes. True, Anatole France and Romain Rolland were never popular among followers of Action Française, but the French man of letters was not to such an extent ignored by a public hostile to his political views. Germany was less tolerant; these writers were rejected by the right partly because they were Jews, partly because they were in basic sympathy with the new era which had been ushered in by the country's defeat. They had been opponents before, now they belonged to the republican cultural establishment.

With all the differences in approach and style there were

certain features in common to these writers apart from their political orientation: they mainly wrote novels, hardly ever poetry, and if they dabbled in drama they did so without conspicuous success. Most of them were left-wing liberals (four of the six were of Jewish origin), who under the impact of the political and economic crisis moved further to the left though none of them actually joined the Communist Party. (Döblin, who had been a socialist of sorts in his early days, was converted to Catholicism late in life.) All of them emigrated when Hitler came to power. Today they are no longer widely read, and some are virtually forgotten. They were uneven writers: the distance between the best and the worst in Heinrich Mann and Arnold Zweig is astounding. But each of them wrote at least one or two very fine novels which are bound to last irrespective of changing public moods and fashions.

For Heinrich Mann, Thomas's elder brother, the Weimar period was the least productive in his long literary career. He had made his name as a pitiless critic of Wilhelmian Germany, of moral decay and cultural aridity; again in his old age, during the years of emigration, he was to produce another work of real literary distinction – the historical novels on the good King Henri Quatre and his time. In the years between he wrote some indifferent novels and a good many praiseworthy essays in defence of the Republic, and served as president of the literary section of the Prussian Academy. He was at once more bourgeois and more bohemian than his younger brother, more deeply rooted in the nineteenth than the twentieth century. Heinrich Mann was one of the few representative figures of the left, conciliatory by nature despite an often aggressive language; as we have seen, at a time of crisis some misguided colleagues even suggested that he should be president of the Republic. As a writer he was always overshadowed by his brother, unjustly so because he was an author of deep wisdom and humanism and, at his best, a master of the novel who owed little even to the French teachers whom he had studied so closely. Rilke, so different from him in every respect, greatly admired him and asked: 'When did this great artist ever serve his apprenticeship? – referring to the fact that even his early novels reveal an astonishing maturity.

Heinrich Mann was born into a Lübeck patrician family,

every inch the *grand seigneur*, even when blatantly defying bourgeois conventions in his private life. Arnold Zweig's father was a Jewish saddler in a little town in Upper Silesia; the son, who made his literary debut just before the war, was strongly critical of bourgeois society yet at the same time deeply rooted in it and never managed the transition to 'socialist realism' which, in theory at least, he advocated in later life. Zweig's pacifist novel on *Der Streit um den Sergeanten Grischa*, published in 1927, is one of the great German war books, the story of a recaptured Russian prisoner of war who is executed after a long bureaucratic wrangle among the German military command in the east. Everyone is aware that the execution is contrary to international law, but Grischa has to die in order to counteract defeatist tendencies among the German troops on the eastern front. The book's success induced Zweig to make it the starting-point for a whole cycle of novels against the background of the war. The earlier ones (such as *Junge Frau von 1914*) have something of the power and freshness of *Grischa*; the later books are embarrassingly bad and make painful reading. Zweig, even more than Heinrich Mann, did not fare well in later years at the hands of the critics, who were at the most willing to concede that at his best he was an accomplished storyteller. It is an unfair judgment, for with all his misguided intellectual pretensions, his moments of vanity and insincerity, his place in German literature should be assured; one can think of few panoramic works of similar quality in which a whole period of Germany history was mirrored.

Zweig and Feuchtwanger were fascinated and horrified by antisemitism and their own personal dilemma as Jews in German society; in Feuchtwanger's case this is reflected in his famous historical novel *Jud Süss*, the seventeenth-century court Jew (1925), and in his books on the struggle of the Jews against the Romans – the Josephus trilogy (1932–6). Like Zweig, Feuchtwanger warmly supported Soviet policy in later years; his apologia for the Moscow trials and his glorification of Stalin (*Moskau 1937*) are among the worst that have been written on the subject. But on the whole neither man's writing was shaped by ideological considerations, and with due genuflexions to dialectical materialism (and in Zweig's case to psychoanalysis) it remained essentially traditional and even old-fashioned.

Feuchtwanger's most interesting novel of the Weimar era is *Erfolg* (1930), describing the rise of the Nazi Party in his native Bavaria during the early postwar years. In East Germany Feuchtwanger is now held in great esteem and some of his novels have attained the status of modern classics. In a large West German history of modern literature his name is mentioned just once – as a *littérateur* who for a certain time was on friendly terms with Brecht. Yet he was neither a giant nor a marginal figure but a master of the historical novel who succeeded in recapturing the colour, spirit and moods of periods long past.

Jakob Wassermann has fared worse in the eyes of posterity. At the time his eagerly-awaited psychological novels were huge successes with both the critics and the public; Thomas Mann wrote that Wassermann could tell a story better than himself and Hesse thought him one of the greatest living writers. Reread now, the weaknesses of these novels are, with a very few exceptions, glaring. There was in them, to quote Thomas Mann again, not only profound moral seriousness and deep vision but also a great deal of empty pomp and solemn idle talk. They attracted the contemporary reading public, but the pathos of the 1920s has not stood the test of time well. Wassermann was a modest and sensitive man, deeply unhappy despite his immense success, a good friend, helpful to younger writers – not a frequent occurrence in German literary life then or indeed at any time. Compared with the writers after 1945, he was a giant.

Like Thomas Mann and Hesse, Leonhard Frank, one of the very few German writers of working-class origin, always wrote essentially about himself; unfortunately there was not a great deal to write about. He had been a mechanic, a chauffeur and a painter before he wrote his first and best novel, published just before the outbreak of war. *Die Räuberbande* is the story of a gang of youngsters in his native Franconia who act out their Wild West fantasies in terms familiarized by Karl May, whose exotic novels inspired several generations of German schoolboys and adolescents. It is a sad and moving tale of youthful hopes, illusions and disappointments, of growing up and of the clash with reality: the young rebels all rejoin society; the most gifted of them, an artist, commits suicide. During the war Frank lived in Switzerland; his collection of short stories *Der Mensch ist gut*

(1920), a fiery attack on the senseless slaughter of 1914–8, is again devoted to the ideals of the young generation. In the new world envisaged by Frank there will be universal love and all men will be brothers. Tall, elegant, slightly sinister-looking, Frank became a central figure in Berlin literary society in the 1920s; he wrote about the working class and the unemployed (*Von drei Millionen Drei*), and one novel which was made into a memorable play (*Karl und Anna*). But fame had come too early, and he was somewhat embittered that his reputation did not continue to grow. He remained a radical at heart, a writer with considerable native talent who hardly developed after having made an astonishing debut on the literary scene.

Of those mentioned so far Alfred Döblin, a practising physician, is the most difficult, complex and indeed contradictory figure; no two of his works are in any way similar. He began as an Expressionist (or late Impressionist), but both his approach and his subjects underwent constant change. He tried his hand at a new-style historical novel (*Wallenstein*), was attracted by religious and exotic themes, ancient worlds and fantasy landscapes. He wrote allegorical novels and parables as well as a naturalistic account of the failure of the revolution of 1918. His most widely-read book, both in Germany and abroad, was *Berlin Alexanderplatz*, unrivalled in world literature as a symphony of big city life; a funny and tragic book, with the loneliness of the individual as its leitmotif. Döblin, the epic writer, did not believe in individual heroes: 'I am an enemy of the personal factor', he wrote on one occasion; 'it is all swindle and lyricism.' Yet unlike Dos Passos's trilogy, written during the same period, there is a central story and even a hero; poor Franz Biberkopf, just released from prison, desperately trying to make his way in the big city jungle. It is a deeply moral tale set against an underworld background, describing a life without aim or purpose, with all tremendous rhythms and dissonances of the metropolis. It was the only time that the big city had come alive in German literature; perhaps the first time since Balzac in world literature.

These then were some of the leading writers of the Republic. Some themes recur in their work and their moral preoccupations are similar; their novels and plays deal with the innocent victims of a hostile or simply indifferent society (Heinrich

Mann's *Madame Legros*, Wassermann's *Der Fall Maurizius*, Zweig's *Grischa*). Yet the conclusions drawn are not necessarily similar: Madame Legros, the Paris draper, saves a prisoner of aristocratic origin because she is a decent and courageous human being; she refuses to take part in the storming of the Bastille. Nor does injustice make a revolutionary of Etzel Andergast (in Wassermann's novel). Young Bertin, on the other hand, who has witnessed the Grischa travesty of justice from close quarters, gradually turns into an active critic of the whole system. But in general the writers of the Republic were not preoccupied with the world around them; paraphrasing George Lukács's thesis about the German novel, it could be said that its main weakness was its inability to give literary expression to the problems of contemporary Germany. That there was no Balzac or Dickens among them, drawing their inspiration from the current scene, rich, full of passion and conflict, is not surprising: the giants of literature are sparsely sown. But the Weimar writers did not know their own country well, and their world was a very small one, poles apart from the rest of the people. The idea that the life of a politician or a businessman, for instance, could be a fit subject for a work of literature would have been rejected out of hand; they did not know that world nor were they eager to become acquainted with it. If they had a message to convey they chose past ages for their background; they preferred either cosmic-abstract topics or the problems of the individual. The realistic novel of which Fontane had been the last great exponent seemed to have come to an end; there was no German *Les Thibault*, nor even a Duhamel, a Romains or a Galsworthy. One can think of a number of reasons for the lack of interest in contemporary subjects: there was the need to recover from the war, physically and spiritually; there were objective difficulties involved in approaching the new reality, which was far more complex than the old one. After the publication of *Berlin Alexanderplatz* a critic wrote that the old novel had been an epic-dramatic mixture in which it was, in all probability, impossible to convey any longer what was most significant. Perhaps it was a correct observation, perhaps a mere alibi; the *Human Comedy* of the Weimar Republic at any rate was never written, nor even a cycle on its *Hommes de la bonne volonté*.

The writers of the younger generation were less afflicted by doubts about the future of the novel and their métier. They believed they had something of importance to say because their experience differed in essential respects from that of the old-established writers. More or less simultaneously with the appearance of Neue Sachlichkeit in painting and architecture, a new realism and sobriety was introduced into German literature, very much in contrast to the ecstatic style of the immediate postwar years. The war novels which now began to appear heralded the end of the postwar period – the war experiences had been digested and now found literary expression. Some of these writings condemned the war, directly or by implication; others glorified it; and lastly there were those, perhaps the majority, which with all their criticism were basically unpolitical and, preoccupied with the fate of individuals, left open the question whether it had all been in vain. To the anti-war literature belongs the most successful book of all, Remarque's *All Quiet on the Western Front*, in the words of the author 'neither accusation nor confession' but the story of a generation 'destroyed by war, even though it may have escaped its shells'. Despite a certain sentimentality and immaturity it was a powerful indictment of the senseless slaughter and it offended nationalistic circles. 'This is what war was really like', hundreds of thousands of Germans said after Remarque's novel, which was the great bestseller of the 1920s. The author had some difficulty in finding a publisher, for who would want to read about the war ten years after? *All Quiet on the Western Front* became the forerunner of the second and main wave of war books. There was Ludwig Renn's *Krieg*, all the more effective because it described events with an almost total lack of passion. Other noteworthy books were Plievier's novel about conditions in the navy in 1918 and Edlef Köppen's *Heeresbericht*, describing the glaring discrepancies between the official communiqués and the reality of the front line. Ernst Glaeser's *Jahrgang 1902* was the story of a boy who grew up against the background of disintegration and total disillusion.

The literary merit of these books varies; as human documents all of them were of considerable interest. They told the story of the generation which had gone out to fight, having been taught that a hero's death was both beautiful and proper (*dulce et decorum est*). But the vision of a quick victory and a fine death soon gave way to the bitter experience of a world which seemed to bear Dante's inscription over the entrance to Hell: *Lasciate ogni speranza* (to quote from the *War letters of Fallen German Students*, a widely-read book, first published in 1928). It is possible to understand the spirit of the twenties without George, Hesse and *The Magic Mountain*; it cannot be understood without reference to the mood of the survivors of Langemark, Verdun and the Somme. There was in some quarters a reluctance to believe that the years of suffering and sacrifice had been in vain. The heroes of the national war novel (Zöberlein, Schauwecker, Beumelburg) saw the war as a time of supreme trial; the home-land had to be defended against a world of enemies. They had fought for a greater and better Germany; if they had failed it was through no fault of their own. They may have had their doubts about the conduct of the war and they did not belittle its horrors. But above all they recalled that the war had brought out idealism and solidarity, had shown in innumerable acts of courage the heights to which the soul of man could rise – to quote E. E. Dwinger, a young chronicler of the war in the east. Above all there had been the true comradeship of the trenches, a sense of community such as had never been experienced before or since. It had been a people's war; men from all classes and backgrounds had come to live and act together in face of a common danger. Out of the experience of the war, the *Fronterlebnis*, the dream of a new, more complete community had been born. For this generation the end of the war had therefore come as a twofold shock: both because it ended in defeat and because the sense of community quickly melted away. They were shaken not so much because the old world had gone up in flames but because the great ideas of 1914 had evaporated into thin air.

As the years passed, the horrors of war receded and a second wave of war books poured forth. Ernst Jünger's *In Stahlgewittern* stands out among them for its detachment and literary merits. The author, unlike so many others, was not a mere civilian in uniform but a young man who had discovered in war his true vocation – to be a soldier. Jünger developed his own philo-sophy: war as such was neither good nor bad, but a natural phenomenon which had to be accepted like a thunderstorm. It was a test in the history of nations in which the fate of the individual (and of hundreds of thousands of individuals) counted for little. It was the hour of truth, not as the official propagandists and hurrah patriots interpreted it but a new Saint Crispin's day to be remembered by that band of brothers to the ending of the world. Jünger's book closes with the words: 'Germany lives and Germany shall not perish.' But it is not certain whether a patriotic slogan provides the key to an understanding of the author's motives. For deep down Jünger remains an individualist who does not care greatly for collective experiences. He simply enjoyed the war, regarding it as a dangerous and therefore all the more attractive sport; he did not hate the enemy, he loved the excitement and the adventure. In other words his approach was basically nihilistic, that of a modern *Landsknecht*. And so, despite his exceptional courage and literary success, Jünger remained a somewhat uncomfortable ally both for the right wing in the Republic and later on for the Nazis; the individualist could not really identify with them. Somewhat akin to Jünger but not quite of the same stature was Ernst von Salomon, an even younger soldier and right-wing bohemian who had missed the *Fronterlebnis* but found his fulfilment in the exploits of the Free Corps after the war had ended.

There is no consensus among students of German literature about the exact date of the demise of Expressionism: was it already dead by the early 1920s or did it continue to exert some influence for a few more years? But they all agree that the agitation which had been so widespread in the immediate postwar period died down as normality returned. The repercussions were felt in literature: language became unecstatic, the treatment of subjects more or less realistic, novels were concerned more with the problems of the day, less with the faraway past and the distant future; there was no longer an overwhelming desire to break away from old forms. The staging of *Zeitstücke* in the theatre was part of this trend, as were writings about young people and their problems. School, the youth movement and the university were among the favourite subjects in the first novels of young writers; on the left a new literature about the proletarian condition came into being (Friedrich Wolf, Anna Seghers, Bruno Nelissen-Haken and others).

The most popular of the writers who made their debut

towards the end of the 1920s were Erich Kästner, best-known at the time for his poems, and the novelist Hans Fallada. Kästner, one of the few genuinely funny German writers, bitterly attacked militarism and brutality (such as he had witnessed during the war), the stupidity of the bureaucrats, the indifference and conventional hypocrisy of the middle classes. He lacked the venom of a George Grosz or a Tucholsky, and is now mainly remembered for his stories for children, of which *Emil and the Detectives* is the best known. The novel *Fabian* describes life in Berlin at the height of the economic crisis; the hero dies trying to save a drowning child; the underlying tone of the novel is one of *Galgenhumor* – there is not much hope for the future but we have to go through the motions anyway. A cheerful pessimist, Kästner was a soloist on a truncated keyboard on which he played with great virtuosity, to the delight of many faithful readers.

Fallada's heroes are the people hit by the depression: the peasants of North Germany, the minor functionaries who have lost their jobs, the ex-convicts. Unstable in his private life and lacking firm convictions, there is nevertheless at times an uncanny accuracy in his portrayal of mood and milieu. His novels are not great literature but give a faithful reflection of the *Zeitgeist. Kleiner Mann was nun?* was the question a great many Germans were asking at the time. Neither Kästner nor Fallada emigrated when Hitler came to power. The latter made a half-hearted attempt to collaborate with the Nazis, and subsequently with the East German authorities. He died of drink and drugs not long after the end of the Second World War.

These then were some of the better-known writers of the liberal and left-of-centre cultural establishment. But the political and cultural orientation of the German *Bildungsbürgertum* was overwhelmingly towards the right, among whom Wassermann, Werfel and Arnold Zweig were ignored, while Thomas Mann and Gerhart Hauptmann had relatively few readers. The literature admired in these circles was not known outside Germany; traditionalist in both style and content, the left dismissed it as outdated and uninteresting. This has also been, by and large, the verdict of history. Since the German middle classes failed, their literature too was found wanting in later years. But this approach does less than justice to a sizable group of writers of some literary distinction who neither defended the Republic nor acted as precursors of Nazism. The books most widely read at the time were not written by the authors mentioned so far; they were Ina Seidel's *Wunschkind* (1930), Hermann Stehr's *Heiligenhof* (1918), Emil Strauss's *Der Schleier* (1920) and the novels of Rudolf G. Binding. These books sold many hundreds of thousands of copies, which none of the works of the republican authors did with the exception of *Buddenbrooks* and *All Quiet on the Western Front*. Carossa should be added to this list, and Wiechert; both had their devoted readerships. They were not at the centre of the republican literary scene physically or spiritually; Ina Seidel was the only one of them who lived in the capital for any length of time. Stehr and Strauss lived in virtual seclusion far from Berlin, did not appear at cocktail parties and literary receptions and remained unmoved by the literary fashions of the day. There was nothing about the sexual problems of the younger generation in their books, or about the deficiencies of the legal system; no socialism and no psychoanalysis. The heroes of their novels were inward-looking, mystics, men in search of god, obstinate fellows – modern Parsifals in quest of some unknown Holy Grail. They were preoccupied with moral conflicts and troubled consciences, they were inchoate and verbose at the same time, very German in their abstraction, their rootedness and sometimes in their dullness. Yet emotionally this literature struck incomparably deeper chords among the German reading public than the Berlin liberal writers. It was the literature of the silent majority (*die Stillen im Lande*), overrated at the time, underrated or forgotten now.

These books owed little to foreign influences, and they were written for a public whose interests in writers other than German was strictly limited. It was not their ambition to be up-to-date, and for that reason they made little impact outside the public for which they were written. But this public was substantial, and so far as it was concerned this was the real German literature.

There were partisan writers of the extreme left and the far right, regional writers (*Heimatdichter*) and, following a religious revival after the First World War, there was also a Catholic literature of some importance. And, of course, there were some

writers who did not fit into any category, and who have therefore been a puzzle to literary critics and historians. All this
reinforces the point already made concerning the abundance of
German literature: collectively this was perhaps its richest
period. It is not easy to think of many novels or poems written
during the 1860s, the 1890s or the 1960s which are worth re-
reading; it is not at all difficult to prepare such a list of works
published during the 1920s. The period was also rich in another
sense: it produced works so different in inspiration, style and
content that it defies generalization. It was not the greatest age
of German literature but certainly the most lively and
interesting.

REVOLUTION ON THE STAGE

Of all the muses Thalia was closest to the heart of Weimar; the
theatre expressed most faithfully the *Zeitgeist*, the stage became
almost a national institution. New plays were hotly debated, as
if they were events of the greatest political or social importance.
A first performance was discussed much more widely than a
first novel, however important, and the reviews were read with
rapt attention. The quarrels between Kerr and Ihering, between Kerr and Kraus, the rivalry between Reinhardt and
Jessner, were events of almost cosmic importance. This excitement, slightly comical as it may appear in retrospect, was not
altogether unjustified, for the German theatre at the time had
the greatest producers and the most gifted actors, and it staged
the most interesting plays. Berlin was the theatre capital of the
world. Furthermore the theatre, unlike the literature, was overwhelmingly republican in sentiment; to a considerable extent
it was socialist and revolutionary. There was a right-wing
literature, but there were no right-wing Reinhardts or Jessners,
no nationalist playwright comparable to those who had their
great successes during that period.

The beginnings of the golden age of German drama go back
to the 1890s, when in Berlin Brahm and Schlenther staged Ibsen
and Gerhart Hauptmann, and the avant-garde theatre of the
day found its most prominent and gifted exponents. After ten
years of apprenticeship in Berlin, Max Reinhardt, a young
Austrian, became chief producer at the Deutsche Theater in

1905–6, staging conventional plays such as Schiller's *Kabale und Liebe*, *The Merchant of Venice* and *A Midsummer Night's Dream* in a very unconventional way. He staged mass scenes such as had never been seen before: twelve hundred lamps burned brightly in the Schauspielhaus, there was colour, air, plants, even real trees. The mass spectacle was born with the *Jedermann* mystery plays and Vollmoeller's *Das Mirakel*, which played in London in 1911 to ten thousand spectators. But it was not just that Reinhardt broke with the tradition of the old intimate court theatre and brought more of everything on to the stage. He was a producer of genius, a modernizer for whom the highest virtue was not to stick too closely to traditional practices – not even to the original intentions of the playwright, especially if he happened to be a classic. Producing plays had been a trade; now it became an art. It was at this time, too, that the separation between stage and auditorium gradually disappeared; for ages it had been as sacrosanct as the frontiers between nation-states. From this it was only one more step to the active participation of the audience in the political theatre of the 1920s.

The history of the theatre of the Republic in the narrower sense begins in 1918 with Hasenclever's *Der Sohn*, Goering's *Seeschlacht* and Unruh's *Ein Geschlecht*. (Military censorship was surprisingly liberal: a sailor in Goering's play says on the evening of the battle of Jutland: 'Oh dear fatherland, we are the swine and we are waiting for the butcher. . . .') The era of the republican theatre ends with the first performance of Gerhart Hauptmann's aptly entitled *Vor Sonnenuntergang* (*Before Sundown*). In between an enormous number of plays was performed – Georg Kaiser alone (admittedly one of the most prolific playwrights) wrote forty between 1905 and 1928. Only about a dozen of these are still staged, and perhaps a dozen more should still be with us but are undeservedly forgotten. But great producers and outstanding actors gave the public memorable performances even of plays not always of the first rank.

The producers of the day were men of great versatility and adaptability: Reinhardt made his mark as a virtuoso of the Impressionist, Neo-Romantic theatre, but he was equally at home in later years in staging Rolland's *Danton* and Shaw's plays. When Reinhardt left Berlin a whole galaxy of younger producers such as Karl Heinz Martin, Heinz Hilpert, Erich Engel, Berthold Viertel, Jürgen Fehling got their chance. Leopold Jessner was the complete antithesis of Reinhardt; his conception of the theatre was different in as much as the emphasis in his Staatstheater was not so much on acting, nor even on the action of the play, but on the basic motive and impulse underlying it, on speed, on certain frequently recurring symbols such as the famous Jessner staircase (when Caesar is killed he is pushed from the top of a big staircase). His stage, unlike Reinhardt's, was not enormous, nor did he use so much machinery. He concentrated on what seemed to him essential, using colour, light, a great deal of movement and the music of the word. Jessner was at his best in staging classical plays such as *Richard III*, *Macbeth*, Schiller's *Don Carlos* and Wedekind, the father of the modern movement in the German theatre.

Beyond these two giants of the Berlin stage there were the youngsters of the revolutionary theatre – Seeler's Junge Bühne gave Brecht and Bronnen their first chances, Piscator's Political Theatre received much support from critics and a public which by no means shared his political convictions. Experimentation was not restricted to Berlin. As we have already seen, many of the most important plays were first performed on provincial stages, which were anything but provincial in their approach and standards. The 1920s were above all an age of abundant acting talent: Werner Krauss and Fritz Kortner, Heinrich George and Eugen Klöpfer, Ernst Deutsch and Gustav Gründgens, Elizabeth Bergner and Kaethe Dorsch, Lucie Höflich, Lucie Mannheim and Agnes Straub – these were just some of the actors and actresses who made their name during this period. Their range was as wide as that of the producers: Werner Krauss was unforgettable as Agamemnon, as Hilse (the old man in Hauptmann's *Die Weber*), and he surpassed himself as the Captain of Köpenick; Kortner's Macbeth fascinated the public and he was equally convincing as Hans Albers's sparring partner in the boxing scene in *Journey's End*.

There were the inevitable rivalries: Reinhardt, some critics said, was simply a decorator of genius catering for bourgeois gourmets ('culinary theatre' Brecht called it). Brecht himself was put in his place for his repeated plagiarism and Kerr admonished him for his lack of originality. *Nur wer die Gähnsucht* *kennt, weiss was ich leide,* he wrote after watching Brecht's *Eduard II* (freely adapted from Marlowe).* Piscator was written off in 1929 as a bore who, having dismantled the traditional theatre, provided the ritual declamation of political slogans as an alternative. The two playwrights who dominated the theatre during the early years of the Republic were Georg Kaiser and Carl Sternheim; the two are frequently mentioned together though they did not really have much in common apart from their age. Kaiser's recurrent theme is the bourgeois who breaks out of the fetters of the bourgeois world and invariably comes to grief. This is the story of the cashier who embezzles money in *Von Morgens bis Mitternachts,* Kaiser's best-known play; the flight ending in ecstatic confession, love interludes and mad dialogues. To escape arrest the hero shoots himself and, falling, comes to rest on a wooden cross. Electrical current in the theatre is cut off, the lamps go out. This, apart from the absence of parricide, was a typical Expressionist play. The chaos, the escape, the confessions and the shock effect – but a play which dispensed with real human beings; concentration on abstractions and on intellectual constructions could not hold the attention of the public, however well-disposed, for very long. Only rarely, as in *Die Bürger von Calais,* did Kaiser overcome this innate coldness and remoteness, which contrasted so strongly with the inner warmth preached by Expressionism.

Sternheim's desire was to be the Molière of his time, but his humour was too corrosive; he had a genuine gift for satire, which found a convenient target in philistine small-town society (*Bürger Schippel, Die Hose*), or (as in *Tabula Rasa*) in the socialist militant betraying his erstwhile ideals. While fairly successful at the time, attempts to revive Kaiser and Sternheim even a few years later were unsuccessful; the mood had changed. Some of Ernst Toller's best-known plays were written in prison where he was confined for his part in the Munich uprising in 1919. He was widely liked and admired; a fighter for justice, a believer in humanity, his works were permeated with youthful idealism but his fame as a writer was shortlived; his first important play, *Die Wandlung,* became a success owing to a producer and an

---

*'Only he who knows yawning as I do, knows what I suffer' – a play on words, referring to Goethe's *Wilhelm Meister*: *Nur wer die Sehnsucht kennt, weiss, was ich leide!*

actor of genius (Martin and Kortner). His later plays on the Luddites (*Die Maschinenstürmer*) and about an impotent war invalid (*Hinkemann*) showed that Toller had been prematurely proclaimed the greatest dramatic genius of the 1920s. 'Provincial pathos', the critics said; 'journalistic cliché', 'penny-dreadful Naturalism', drawing unfavourable comparison with the young Gerhart Hauptmann. Toller had a powerful ally in Alfred Kerr, the leading dramatic critic, who put his work well above Brecht's. But so far as the public was concerned Toller was regarded as a failure well before the Nazi rise to power compelled him to leave his native land.

Mention has been made of the brief glory and the equally quick eclipse of Expressionist drama. This was the play of the father-son conflict, the desperate onslaught against the old world and its political, social and artistic conventions. These plays swamped the stages and the curious public came to see them, wondering whether they would indeed show – as they promised – a road out of the chaos towards a better world. But at best they succeeded only in reproducing the chaos on the stage; the language was incoherent, there was no action and the audience was quickly bored. By 1923 Expressionism in the theatre was finished and the public was eagerly awaiting new plays dealing with real human beings and not with mankind in general. Two new stars began to shine brightly in the post-Expressionist era, Piscator and Brecht, and it is to them that we ought to turn next. Piscator, coming from a well-known family of Protestant churchmen and professors, had been a soldier and was not yet thirty when he arrived in Berlin to revolutionize the German theatre. 'My own life began on 4 August 1914.' With these words he opens his book *Das politische Theater*. The war had been his great teacher.

The first proletarian theatre company opened in Berlin in the spring of 1919. It played in meeting-halls without benefit of professional actors and was a resounding failure. Even the *Rote Fahne*, organ of the German Communist Party which had every sympathy for the new venture, wrote that what Piscator produced was neither art nor effective propaganda. In 1923–4 Piscator was the chief producer of a 'bourgeois' Berlin theatre staging Tolstoy, Gorky and Romain Rolland. A wider public first heard of him when in 1926 Jessner invited him to produce

Schiller's *Die Räuber*, which he did – with Spiegelberg in Trotsky's mask (complete with dinner-jacket, brown homburg, gold-
framed glasses, blond pointed beard, yellow cane). Piscator
made his third and most successful attempt to run a proletarian
theatre in 1927–9. Some of the plays he staged, *Storm over
Gottland* and *The Good Soldier Schweik*, attracted great interest;
the extreme right was enraged and there were debates in parliament. He had not only the support of the Communist Party, but
received financial backing from a rich fellow-traveller as well,
Felix Weil, who also financed the Frankfurt Institut für Sozialforschung. The Berlin critics were all in favour of giving
Piscator a chance, acknowledging his great talents as an innovator. Yet what he wanted to achieve he did not accomplish;
the 'political theatre' was acclaimed almost exclusively by a
bourgeois public; workers seldom if ever found their way into
his theatre, and if they did they hardly ever enjoyed it. It was
Piscator's aim to sharpen the class-consciousness of the proletar-
ians, to make them more militant fighters for the cause of world
revolution. But if the working class went to the theatre at all, it
wanted to see plays of a different kind; all Piscator achieved, in
the last resort, was to induce some guilt-feelings among the
liberals. But since those who came to applaud him were already
psychologically conditioned, this was not too difficult a task.

The political theatre, in brief, had little political effect. Its
main impact was on a small circle of enthusiastic young professionals. Friedrich Wolf, Brecht and Toller wrote for Piscator,
George Grosz and John Heartfield designed the scenery, and
some of Berlin's most promising young actors performed.
Piscator never found the play which would have given him the
opportunity to apply his revolutionary new ideas. He was at his
best staging novels, such as *Schweik* and Plievier's *Des Kaisers
Kulis*, rather than plays. This, of course, was no accident, for
Piscator was more interested in dramatizing the general social
and political context than in the fate of individual heroes, and
he gradually found himself out of step with the party line as the
Soviet stage moved from its early experimental period towards
neo-classicism and his Communist friends withdrew their
support.

Piscator's many interesting innovations included the use of
films projected on to the side of the stage, pictures and subtitles,

even statistics and newspaper headlines. These were shown both during intervals and simultaneously with the performance. He used a revolving stage in the shape of a segmented sphere, platforms which could be raised and lowered, stages with several levels. Like Brecht he regarded the theatre not as a mirror of the times, nor a place for 'creating illusions', but as a means of changing society. The two parted ways later as Brecht chose a more indirect approach (*Verfremdungseffekt*), for instance by transferring the action to faraway countries, while Piscator remained a believer in head-on confrontation with reality. Brecht's method was the more complicated and left him greater freedom as a dramatist. He could be poetic and romantic, could allude to certain events and developments, whereas in Piscator's theatre there was no room for subtlety. Despite the assistance of greater actors and first-rate composers such as Hanns Eisler and Edmund Meisel (not to mention a host of economists and agitprop experts), Piscator's stage, with all its technical innovations, remained one-dimensional. The theatre programmes contained excerpts from the Communist Manifesto and slogans from *Die Rote Fahne*; the prologue (or epilogue) of the play consisted of a speech which made the meaning clear even for those few spectators who may not have got the message. Thus, in Peter Lampel's play on school revolt, an actor appearing on the stage announced that what was wrong with the school could not be remedied by reform but only by world revolution. This proclamation was followed by the singing of the 'International'. Piscator's three business failures could be explained by reference to the hostility of the critics and the growing indifference of the public. In fact he was admired by his peers as a craftsman with many new ideas, but he was too primitive for an educated public and not entertaining enough for the rest. His stage was a mixture of Naturalism and Expressionism, speeches declaimed fortissimo and in easily understandable language: for half-tones, for psychology, there was no room. It was attacked not only from the right; Karl Kraus wrote that Piscator was ruining the theatre; others that Piscator's main achievement was to have shown that the stage could be an effective means for social reportage, thus narrowly confining its function and scope; and there were those who poked fun at the subtitles projected on the screen during the performance – what if similar titles were provided for the classics ('old man starving in prison', 'Luise's lemonade is insipid')? Something was obviously very wrong with a producer who needed crutches of this kind.

It was to Piscator's credit that he proved to his contemporaries that the classics could be seen in a new light, and that contemporary problems could be acted out on the stage. There were no 'beautiful phrases' in his theatre, no pretence of objectivity. But his techniques also meant considerable impoverishment of the theatre. What he wanted to accomplish could be achieved with much less difficulty in the cinema or alternatively in stage-managed political meetings. He saw the possibilities of the cinema but only as a means to enhance the effect of the theatre. But the cinema was a medium in its own right, with potentially a much greater impact on the masses. Had Piscator realized this and had he been given the opportunity, he might have revolutionized the silent film. His attempts to change the theatre were bound to remain no more than an interesting episode in the history of this medium.

Great as the influence of Piscator's theatre was on the professionals, in Germany and abroad, the impact of Brecht's work was even more far-reaching, though his fame as a theoretician of the stage began to spread only towards the end of the Weimar age. Feuchtwanger in his *roman à clef*, *Erfolg*, described him as a young man, unshaven, unkempt, smelling like a soldier straight out of the trenches. He was an actor of genius in his private life as well; when he sang his crude ballads in his shrill voice women literally swooned. Later on he designed for himself a kind of uniform which became something of a Brechtian trademark: cheap steel-rimmed glasses, leather coat and leather cap. He chainsmoked cigars and was known to be very rude to people. Brecht's first performed play was *Drums in the Night* (1922); he was twenty-four years of age at the time and received the Kleist Prize, one of Germany's major literary distinctions, the same year. The critics were not quite certain at the time what to make of him: an Expressionist who was also a Naturalist presenting a revolutionary play without political tendency. The young man obviously had great talent, if only in a mastery of dialogue such as had not been heard for a long time on the German stage. *Drums in the Night* is the story of a soldier returning from the war who finds his bride engaged to another man; he becomes a revolutionary leader but abandons his political career as he regains the young lady's affection. *Baal*, a play written even earlier, was performed in 1923. It describes a rather asocial young poet, who matures from seducing women indiscriminately to killing his best friend, of whom he has become jealous. All this is presented in disjointed pictures – the work of a chaotic talent, a nihilist exuding a feeling of nausea. A rightwing critic called *Baal* a 'mud bath'; but the Communists did not like the play either, and the nihilist streak in Brecht's mental make-up continued to disturb them for a long time. After the performance of the cantata *Mahagonny* (1929), they attacked Brecht as the 'spokesman of a resigned, sceptical bourgeoisie, which is trying to cross the void of its own confusion by performing nihilistic balancing-acts'. In later years Brecht admitted, 'We all suffered [during that period] from a lack of political conviction, and I particularly from a lack of capacity for enthusiasm.'

The turning-point was 1926: 'I am eight feet deep in *Das Kapital*', he wrote a friend. His Marxist studies taught him several important lessons: money rules the world, laws exist only for the exploitation of the toiling masses, big business means robbery, fraud, vulgarity. The Great Depression seemed exactly to bear out the Marxist analysis. Earlier on Brecht had been fascinated by America, the country of the future: 'What men they were – their boxers the strongest, their inventors the most adept, their trains the fastest, and it all had looked like lasting for a hundred years. And now the sudden crash – what a bankruptcy, how great a glory that has vanished!' America – this was the golddiggers' town of Mahagonny, rotten to the core and criminal. But it was not only Mahagonny that went up in flames; the whole capitalist system was doomed. Hence yet another conclusion: mankind was not just moving towards hell, it was in hell already. (This conformed with the political analysis of the German Communists at the time, according to which fascism was already in power.) If so, mankind had to be saved; but since man by himself was both too weak and too shortsighted, he needed leadership and purification through mass action, revolution. This involved violence, even injustice; and it was precisely this aspect which fascinated Brecht the dramatist. In *Die Massnahme* a young Communist acting in conditions

Friedrich Ebert, Reichspräsident until his death in 1925.

3 Karl Liebknecht and Rosa Luxemburg, killed by right-wing terrorists in January 1919.

4 Berlin, March 1919. Government troops on top of the Brandenburg Gates waiting for the Spartacists to attack.

5 Walter Rathenau, the foreign minister for the Republic, was murdered in June 1922.

ALFRED DÖBLIN

BERLIN ALEXANDERPLATZ

DIE GESCHICHTE VOM FRANZ BIBERKOPF

IM

WESTEN NICHTS NEUES

VON

ERICH MARIA REMARQUE

✫

701.—725. TAUSEND

1 9 2 9

IM PROPYLÄEN-VERLAG / BERLIN

Die Weltbühne

Der Schaubühne XXI. Jahr

Wochenschrift für Politik·Kunst·Wirtschaft

Herausgeber·Siegfried Jacobsohn·

Erscheint jeden Dienstag

XXI. Jahrgang   3. März 1925   Nummer 9
Versandort: Potsdam

Verlag der Weltbühne
Charlottenburg·Königsweg 33

27 To the anti-war literature belongs the most successful book of all – Remarque's *All Quiet on the Western Front*,which reflected the new realism of the younger writers.

28 The voice of the intellectual left – *Die Weltbühne*.

29 *Die Linkskurve* was the leading Communist literary journal.

№ 53.

Bayerisches Polizeiblatt.

Herausgegeben von der Polizeidirektion München.

040

10000 Mark Belohnung.

Wegen Hochverrats

nach § 81 Ziff. 2 des RStGB. ist Haftbefehl erlassen gegen den hier abgebildeten Studenten der Rechte und der Philosophie

Ernst Toller.

Er ist geboren am 1. Dezember 1893 in Samotschin in Posen, Reg.-Bez. Bromberg, Kreis Kolmar, Amtsger. Margonin, als Sohn der Kaufmannseheleute Max u. Ida Toller, geb. Kohn.

Toller ist von schmächtiger Statur und lungenkrank; er ist etwa 1,65 — 1,68 m groß, hat mageres, blasses Gesicht, trägt keinen Bart, hat große braune Augen, scharfen Blick, schließt beim Nachdenken die Augen, hat dunkle, nahe schwarze wellige Haare, spricht schriftdeutsch.

Für seine Ergreifung und für Mitteilungen, die zu seiner Ergreifung führen, eine Belohnung von

zehntausend Mark

ausgesetzt.

Solche Mitteilungen können an die Staatsanwaltschaft, die Polizeidirektion München oder an die Stadtkommandantur München — Fahndungsabteilung gerichtet werden.

Um eifrigste Fahndung, Drahtnachricht bei Festnahme und weitmöglichste Verbreitung dieses Ausschreibens wird ersucht.

Bei Aufgreifung im Auslande wird Auslieferungsantrag gestellt.

München, den 13. Mai 1919.

Der Staatsanwalt bei dem standrechtlichen Gerichte für München.

31 Bertolt Brecht, who with Toller wrote for the political theatre of Piscator.

10 After the collapse of the Bavarian Soviet in 1919, Ernst Toller, poet and playright, was accused of high treason for his part in the uprising.

32 A scene from Brecht's highly successful *Threepenny Opera*.

Die neue sozialistische Partei

(Olaf Gulbransson)

BEBELS STIMME AUS DEM JENSEITS:
„ICH KENNE KEINE SOZIALISTEN MEHR. ICH KENNE NUR NOCH SPALT-PARTEIEN!"

56 A cartoon from *Simplicissimus*, 26 October 1931. August Bebel, a former leader of the Social Democrats, looks down to see socialism dismembering itself. 'There are no socialists any more. There are only divided factions.' By 1932 the split between the Communists and the Social Democrats had effectively destroyed the German left.

57 Hitler's election speech at the Lustgarten, Berlin in April 1932. Dr Goebbels stands to the left.

Deutsche Studenten marschieren wider den undeutschen Geist

58 Collecting books of an 'un-German spirit' for public burning in May 1933.

of illegality endangers his comrades by his incautious zeal to help the workers. He has to be executed to ensure the survival of the others. An injustice is committed in the name of a higher justice; Brecht thus anticipated the explanations current among foreign intellectuals in later years to justify the Moscow purges and trials. Yet again, the Communists were not entirely happy about this short play; after all it was not 'typical', merely an extreme situation. Other critics said that it had been inspired not so much by socialism, let alone humanism, but by the conviction that man was born evil, that only by following instructions from above would heavenly mercy be bestowed on him and would he attain a higher, purer ego – the socialist mass-ego. Extreme situations always fascinated Brecht; they offered dramatic possibilities which a 'normal' situation could not provide.

This point is central for the understanding of Brecht. A great many books have been devoted to interpretations of the dramatist, to the connexion between his politics and his artistic work; and a great deal of meaning has been read into sayings which in all probability were just thrown off. Thus, in an interview with a French critic, Brecht said about *Die Massnahme* that it did not mean anything in particular; it was just a limbering-up exercise. Brecht, like the majority of Weimar intellectuals, was basically not a political animal. If the feeling of impending crisis drove many of them into political commitment, this did not endow them with political experience and instinct. The essential element in Brecht was always the anti-bourgeois, anti-establishment, anti-respectability attitude. He was interested not in politics *per se*, but in the endless, intriguing dramatic possibilities contained in politics. Communism attracted him above all because it was, at that time, anti-bourgeois. Fascism also had dramatic possibilities, and it is not unthinkable that Brecht would have become a fellow-traveller like his friend Bronnen whose plays – up to the late 1920s – attracted as much attention as his. The element of violence which fascinated him was certainly even more pronounced in fascism than in communism. But fascism was not sufficiently anti-bourgeois and it was also intellectually too primitive.

The Threepenny Opera, first performed in August 1928, has remained Brecht's greatest success among the wider public; it was a new-style opera with a highly amusing story, dramatic scenes and many hit songs. To make it even clearer that this was a satire on bourgeois society, Macheath, in the *Threepenny Novel* published six years later, is no longer a gangster but director of a bank, the typical, normal bourgeois. But the bourgeois public liked the play tremendously, refusing to take Brecht's politics quite seriously. Basically it was, of course, an anarchistic play glorifying the outcasts of society rather than the proletariat. Brecht felt genuine sympathy for his gangsters, in whom he saw kindred spirits, although deep down in their heart they also yearned for bourgeois respectability. Several years later Brecht returned to the gangster's world in *Arturo Ui*; but this time without much sympathy. The play tries to explain the rise of fascism with reference to the collaboration between the gangsters who dominate the Chicago vegetable market. The predictable result was a failure, both politically and artistically.

Of his poems (*Die Hauspostille*) quite a few deal with the world of the outcasts – prostitutes, criminals and other misfits. It is a revealing fact that Brecht's 'positive' revolutionary heroes such as Pelageya Vlasova in *The Mother* or Frau Carrar (in the play about the Spanish Civil War) never carry quite the same conviction as the gangsters. He was a satirist at heart, who felt a little self-conscious when he had to switch to revolutionary pathos. This was realized by the Communists too, and it helps explain why, up to the end of his life, they did not feel quite at ease about him even though Brecht served the party to the best of his ability. It did not prevent him, however, from emigrating at a time of crisis (like Piscator, Feuchtwanger, Anna Seghers and other German Communists) to decadent America rather than to the country where a new society and a new type of man were said to be in process of creation.

Already during the 1920s Brecht was hailed as a playwright of genius. But not all felt sure about his place in the history of the theatre. Tucholsky, who liked his plays (and his poems), wrote at the time: 'Today he is overrated, one day he will be underrated.' He could not have been more mistaken; Brecht's real rise to fame began only after 1933, but not because of any outstanding successes in his late, 'mature' years: with the exception of *Mother Courage*, none of his later plays was a success with the public. It was Brecht the theoretician of the drama, the

Brecht of the non-Aristotelian 'epic theatre' and the *Verfremd-ungseffekt* who became known, and was imitated, all over the world.

The epic theatre was meant to show man not just in his individuality but in his dependence on society. The 'epic' approach was used also in staging the works of other authors, including some of the classics. Brecht like Piscator wanted to achieve theatrical effect through new means. He also used projections and newspaper headlines but, unlike Piscator, instead of relying mainly on these mechanisms he used traditional dramatic means: chorus, narrator, songs, turning familiar situations upside down, acting through contrasts. Brecht is more objective than Piscator; his actors do not totally identify with the role they are supposed to play but remain narrators, telling their 'story' with a certain detachment. Instead of crossing all his t's and dotting all his i's, like Piscator, Brecht leaves it to the imagination of the spectator to draw the (admittedly obvious) conclusions. Brecht's theatre, in other words, though reducing the element of 'artistic illusion', does not entirely expel it from the stage.

In the last analysis his tremendous impact remains something of a riddle; he did not initiate a school, his innovations were not lasting, the 'epic theatre', broadly speaking, died with him. He was a playwright of great talent; unlike the Expressionists he was able to create living human beings rather than figures who spoke and behaved like automata. A satirist of genius, he staged biting parodies of society; but his plays are uneven in quality. He is admired as an entertainer not a teacher, and performed far more often in the capitalist West than in the communist East. His plays did not reach the working class, and the one which will no doubt live longest is *The Threepenny Opera*. Perhaps the key to his success is in the fact that albeit a communist of sorts, he somehow managed in retaining his individuality not to lose his sense of humour. To the last he remained something of a mystery man, a mixture of great shrewdness and incredible naiveté. One could never be quite certain whether he was serious and whether his plays had a hidden meaning. He deliberately cultivated this impression of the enigmatic genius.

Brecht's fame spread after 1945; during the Weimar era he had been just one of several leading playwrights, and by no means the most successful. Most critics had reached the conclusion by 1930 that the end of the theatre was at hand. Then, in 1931, a play was performed which compelled the Cassandras to eat their words, at least temporarily. Carl Zuckmayer, author of *The Captain of Köpenick*, had made his debut ten years earlier with some indifferent Expressionist plays. To the wider public he became known as the author of *Der fröhliche Weinberg*, which was a tremendous popular success despite right-wing attempts to interfere with the first performance; he also wrote the scenario of *The Blue Angel*, the movie which made Marlene Dietrich famous. Some critics, of course, were not satisfied; his success contradicted all their theories. Zuckmayer, they said, had written a comedy that was at best middlebrow. *Der fröhliche Weinberg* was excellent entertainment; the play ran for almost three years in Berlin and was staged many hundreds of times elsewhere. But it was not a modern play; the author was out to please, not to change the world. It was less easy to dismiss *The Captain of Köpenick*. This is the story of Vogt, the cobbler just released from prison where he has spent, on and off, thirty years of his life, mostly for petty thieving. He cannot settle down because the authorities refuse to give him the documents essential for getting employment and a residence permit in Wilhelmian Germany. One day in October 1906, having bought an old officer's uniform, he takes command of a unit of soldiers marching by in a Berlin street. He leads them to the Köpenick town hall, has the mayor arrested, issues papers to himself, seizes the cashbox and leaves the place in a hansom cab.

This was a play with many facets: slapstick comedy and stark tragedy; there was no element of surprise for everyone knew the story, which was based on a real event. But it gripped the audience like no other play at the time; its construction was perfect, so was the dialogue. It was a phenomenal success and Zuckmayer in his later plays never again rose to similar heights. He had succeeded in showing, without Piscator's machinery or Brecht's theories, that the theatre still had enormous possibilities. The German theatre had been notoriously weak in comedy; now, overnight, it was enriched by one that was bound to last. Again, some of the critics were not content; the play was too perfect, the author was obviously too much in love with his hero. His ideological views were not easily discernible; he had

written a popular play, a *Volksstück*, transcending the traditional divisions of high, middle, and lowbrow culture. Everyone
was made to laugh, and occasionally to weep. It confounded all
the recent theories on the theatre, it was not complicated and
modern enough, it did not represent the *Zeitgeist*. And yet it was
and has remained an outstanding success, even though many
intellectuals refused to accept that a man who was ideologically
uncommitted, who had developed no new theory of the drama,
had managed to write a perfect play. Outside Germany Zuckmayer's fame did not spread; the dialogue in the *Captain of
Köpenick* is largely in dialect, which makes translation exceedingly difficult.

The late 1920s were the age of the *Zeitstück*; former Expressionists and newcomers alike competed in plays on political and
social topics. For a while the sailors' revolt of 1918 became a
popular subject; Toller, Plievier and Friedrich Wolf wrote
plays about it. Others devoted their attention to the problems
of the younger generation (Lampel, Bruckner), the reactionary
abortion laws and the misdeeds of conservative judges. One of
the most prolific practitioners of this genre was Friedrich Wolf,
like Benn and Döblin a physician by profession and a member
of the Communist Party. Some of these plays had a powerful
impact at the time, but their success was short lived.

German theatres were at first reluctant to stage war plays by
German authors; it is revealing that only after the success of
R. C. Sheriff's *Journey's End* was Graff and Hintze's *Die endlose
Strasse* performed by a provincial theatre, and this, too, only
after it had been first staged and widely acclaimed in England.
This is the story of a single army company and reminds one of
All Quiet on the Western Front; it was a realist play of suffering,
pacifist by implication but devoid of a revolutionary message,
a play of resignation. It certainly did not fit in with the concepts of the extreme right but it was not as provocative as
Remarque's novel; first performed in 1930, the play was banned
only three years after Hitler had come to power. During its
short life-span it was performed more than five thousand times.

By and large the critics were not far wrong: the great period
of the German theatre was over by 1930. The reasons for the
decline were manifold: there was, after several years of unprecedented creativity, a feeling of exhaustion. At the beginning

of the decade there had been a whole galaxy of talented young writers (such as Bronnen and Toller) of whom great things had been expected but who had not been able to live up to these expectations. Producers were running out of ideas and most of them also of money; Reinhardt left Berlin, not for the first time; Jessner moved to a less important theatre and Piscator again went bankrupt. There were several younger gifted producers and, of course, many talented actors. In normal conditions, given a short breathing-space, there would have been a theatrical revival. But conditions were not normal, the effects of the depression were much more strongly felt in the theatre than the impact of the inflation ten years earlier. A new novel did not involve a large investment, whereas the production of a new play was expensive. Some of the leading Berlin theatres had passed into the hands of entrepreneurs (such as the brothers Rotter) who were not in the business to lose money. This meant staging safe plays and operas; Reinhardt produced *The Tales of Hoffman* and *La belle Hélène* in 1931, as well as a few musicals. In the end this too was of no avail; the public stayed away and the Rotter concern, together with other theatres, went bankrupt.

Following the Nazi electoral victories producers and actors began to fear for their positions. The theatre of the Republic had been left-wing in inspiration, yet the *Zeitgeist* was veering more and more to the right. Many leading producers and actors were of Jewish origin and thus obvious targets for Nazi attacks. The plays of the 1920s were no longer suitable and the directors were reluctant to produce any new play that was likely to be 'controversial'. The classics again came to the rescue: 1932 was the Goethe centenary, *Faust* I and II were performed all over Germany. A very gifted new Mephisto named Gustav Gründgens came to the fore; he was to outlast the Republic as well as Hitler and to become the idol of the public in postwar Germany. The sound of the death-knell could be heard on the German stage well before 30 January 1933. There was no sudden end, only a gradual decline. The period which had opened so full of promise, and which had at its height realized some of this promise, ended with the proverbial whimper.

5
The Rise and Decline of the Avant-Garde II: Modernism and the Arts

MUSIC IN THE REPUBLIC

In his memoirs Bruno Walter mentions the unprecedented artistic sensitivity, the passionate concentration which was so typical of musical life in the Weimar era. Germany was the country of the leading conductors, the finest orchestras and soloists; its schools provided the most progressive musical education, and the general level of musical appreciation was of the very highest. Visitors to Germany with an interest in music faced an *embarras de richesses*. In 1929, to give but one example, a music festival, the *Festwochen*, was held in Berlin. Special events included performances of *Meistersinger* in the State Opera House (Kleiber), *Rheingold* and *Walküre* (Leo Blech), *Salome* and *Rosenkavalier* directed by the composer; *Don Pasquale* (Kleiber), *Das Lied von der Erde* (Bruno Walter), *The Marriage of Figaro* (Furtwängler), *André Chénier* (George Szell), *The Flying Dutchman* and Hindemith's *Neues vom Tage* (Klemperer), *Rigoletto, Lucia di Lammermoor, Manon Lescaut* and *Aida* (Toscanini). Symphony concerts offered on the same occasion were directed by Stravinsky and Toscanini; Bach's Mass in B minor was performed under the direction of Georg Schumann. Benjamino Gigli sang one evening, Casals played trios with Cortot and Thibaud.

Performing talent in Germany at the time was by no means limited to Berlin; thus Strauss's *Arabella* and *Die ägyptische*

Helena were first performed in Dresden. There was a readiness to give the new music a chance, even on the part of conductors who were by no means in the forefront of modernism. In the Kroll Opera House Furtwängler and Klemperer conducted Hindemith as well as Stravinsky's *Oedipus Rex*, Milhaud and Schönberg, even though the public preferred *Tosca* and *Madame Butterfly*. Bruno Walter, not a revolutionary innovator, conducted Shostakovich's First Symphony at its premiere. Kleiber, another non-modernist, devoted much energy to the first performance of Alban Berg's *Wozzeck*, and Furtwängler did his best to do justice to Schönberg's Variations op. 31, even though the work had already caused a scandal during rehearsals. The international character of Berlin as a musical centre is borne out by the invitation sent in 1926 to the Austrian Schoenberg to succeed the Italian Busoni as head of the composition master-class at the Berlin Conservatory.

In the struggle between the old and the new music Germany was not the main battleground. In music, as in the other arts, the decisive break with tradition had taken place well before the First World War, not in Berlin but in Vienna and Paris. The country of Bach, Beethoven, Brahms and Wagner was showing signs of exhaustion before the turn of the century, a phenomenon not uncommon in the history of even the richest musical cultures. If there was to be another revolution in music, Germany, for once, was not to be in the forefront; at the time it could not boast of more than one or two composers of international stature. Richard Strauss, the son of the greatest French horn-player of his time, was sometimes compared to Goethe, though the parallels with Gerhart Hauptmann, his contemporary, are more striking. Like Hauptmann, he had begun as a revolutionary innovator. The harsh dissonances of his early orchestral works and the deliberate ugliness, the shrillness and difficulty of operas such as *Salome* (1905) and *Elektra* (1909), were considered shocking by many contemporaries. But by 1918 the erstwhile revolutionary had become a classic, and the younger generation of composers found him of little if any interest. So far as the general public was concerned, Strauss's position had become unassailable; the premieres of each of his later operas, such as *Die Frau ohne Schatten* (1919), *Intermezzo* (1924), *Die ägyptische Helena* (1928) and *Arabella* (1933), were major events, though none of them had an effect remotely similar to his earlier works. Strauss's development as an operatic composer from *Rosenkavalier* onwards illustrates the retreat from Wagner to Mozart. This was quite typical of a whole generation of composers (including Busoni) who had grown up under the spell of Bayreuth. Like Gerhart Hauptmann, Richard Strauss was a natural talent; he had no ambition to elaborate new theories of harmony; about art he reflected but seldom, and about public affairs even less frequently. Of the efforts of the younger composers he did not think highly; after listening to young Hindemith's Second Quartet in 1921, he asked the composer, 'Why do you write this atonal stuff? You have talent!'; whereupon Hindemith replied, 'Herr Professor, you make your music and I'll make mine.' Three decades later Hindemith found himself in a similar position, for meanwhile a new generation had grown up which thought his work antiquated. Richard Strauss was at the very centre of the musical establishment of the Republic, even though he lived for years outside the country. From 1919 to 1924 he served as director of the Vienna Opera; after that he travelled frequently abroad.

Strauss enjoyed success and his role as an 'Olympian'; much in contrast to his Munich neighbour Hans Pfitzner, he was a contented and happy man. Pfitzner, also the son of a musician, was always complaining that, like the hero in his best-known opera (*Palestrina*), he was a genius whose true value the world had never recognized. He devoted a great deal of time and energy to fighting the 'modernist danger', and always stressed the specifically German character of his music. With his hypersensitivity, his grumbling and fault-finding, he sorely tried the patience even of devoted friends such as Thomas Mann. Unlike Strauss his fame was restricted to Germany, and within Germany to a fairly small group of faithful admirers, especially among right-wing circles, espousing the cause of a great patriotic composer whose true importance was belittled by the *Kulturbolschewisten*. In fact Pfitzner's lamentations were exaggerated, for leading conductors of the day such as Furtwängler supported him, and it was not their fault if, with the exception of *Palestrina*, none of his works established itself in the repertoire.

By the time the war ended, Max Reger was no longer alive and Busoni, an important influence in the modern movement, had only a few more years to live. Strauss and Pfitzner were past the peak of their careers, whereas Paul Hindemith, by far the most important among the younger composers, was just about to begin his. But Hindemith, too, was not a world figure; before his emigration to the United States his influence was largely restricted to his native Germany. Hindemith's string quartets (especially No. 2 in C major, 1922) established his fame but he also wrote *Lieder*, jazz music, operas such as *Sancta Susanna*, with libretto by the Expressionist poet August Stramm. Hindemith was a composer of many parts who tried his hand in various musical genres and whose work betrays frequent changes in style – perhaps because he considered style less important than technique. He wrote ragtime music, songs for the Berlin cabaret (*Neues vom Tage*), but also set to music the tragic song-cycles of Rilke and Trakl. His work during the 1920s showed affinities with Stravinsky and Schönberg, yet in later years he attacked them in his theoretical writings on the essence of harmony. His two great operas, *Cardillac* (1926) and *Mathis der Maler* (1934), are quite dissimilar in character, and the fact that by the early 1930s it had become more risky in Germany to use the modern style was not the whole explanation. As theoretician and teacher – Hindemith was head of the Berlin Hochschule composition class after 1927 – he had only limited influence, whereas his impact as a composer of modern music was great and in some respects lasting. Of all the Central European modernists he was the one whose work was most accessible – with the exception of Alban Berg's *Wozzeck*.

If the contribution of German composers to the development of modern music was modest, the quarrels about the issues involved raged in Germany as bitterly as elsewhere. Arnold Schönberg was at the very centre of the storm, though by predisposition he was anything but a revolutionary. If Debussy had written that *le siècle des aeroplanes a droit à sa musique*, Schönberg had no intention of entering the history of music as the composer of the aircraft age: 'I hate to be called a revolutionary . . . from the very beginning I had a strongly developed feeling for form and a strong aversion to exaggeration.' He would have agreed with one of his pupils who called him 'the last of the Romantics'. He wrote a large book presenting a new theory of harmony, claiming at the same time that he had done no reading in the history of music. His retreat from tonality came gradually and can be compared with Kandinsky's retreat from figurative art. ('I moved from Expressionism to abstract painting slowly, through endless trial, despair, hope and discovery.')

Schönberg, himself also a painter, and Kandinsky were friends, and in the first *Blaue Reiter Almanac* an essay by the composer on the new music was published. There were close links between the avant-garde in music, in literature and in the visual arts; those involved were all more or less clearly aware that they were part of one general movement. After listening to a Schönberg work in 1911, Franz Marc wrote to his friend Macke that the new music reminded him of Kandinsky. There were no longer consonances and dissonances: a dissonance was simply a consonance more widely spaced. Schönberg would have readily agreed. He introduced the term 'atonality' (which he later came to dislike) in his *Harmonielehre*. Students of the history of music pointed out that dissonances and chromatism could be found in Wagner (whom Schönberg greatly admired) and even in earlier composers; but these had been more or less isolated incidents: the emancipation of music, its progress beyond the confines of tonality, was the work of Schönberg. In the 1920s he went one major step further with the adoption of the twelve-tone technique, or as he called it, 'the method of composing with twelve tones which are related only with one another'. He had no illusions about the radical character of the break this represented; it was the end of harmony, of traditional music as it had been practised and enjoyed for centuries. To his friend, the music critic and historian Paul Bekker, he wrote in a famous letter in 1924: 'I cannot be understood and I content myself with respect.' Yet at the same time he had no doubt that his approach would come to be accepted by all. So far as the avant-garde was concerned this prediction certainly came true, but there was also tremendous resistance and the general public would have agreed with only the first part of Schönberg's statement.

He was attacked both as a charlatan and as the gravedigger of music; the right-wingers attacked his compositions as yet another baneful manifestation of the Jewish spirit in music, although Schönberg's two star pupils and friends, Berg and Webern, who took his techniques even more seriously than he did and thus shocked the public even more, were of impeccable Aryan origin. But just as Schönberg was not a man of the left, his critics were not necessarily fascists and reactionaries. While he and his friends argued that everything new in music had at first encountered violent opposition, the critics maintained that there was a radical difference. Beethoven's last quartets and Wagner's *Tristan* had indeed been at first rejected by an indignant public; but the attitude towards them changed within a few years. Listening to these works a few times made it easier to understand them. No amount of exposure over half a century to Schönberg's music and that of his pupils has brought about a similar change; if the general public had insufficient musical erudition to appreciate Schönberg and his followers, what of the great musicians, from Furtwängler to Bruno Walter and Casals, who also dissociated themselves from atonality?

The arguments of the advocates of modern music were remarkably similar to those put forward by the protagonists of modern painting. Historical norms are no longer valid, modes of expression change rapidly, art need not be generally understood to be great, it need not illustrate an idea nor does it have to display fidelity to nature. It does not have to be beautiful, but it ought to be profound. If the nineteenth century was 'overly harmonious, it is not surprising that in the twentieth century the pendulum has swung the opposite way' (Franz Roh). These observations on twentieth-century German painting fully apply to modern music.

During the 1920s the fate of modern music was still very much in the balance. Schönberg was sensitive to antisemitic attacks, as his letters to Kandinsky show, but the charge that his music was un-German he did not take seriously; in conversation with one of his pupils he said in 1921: 'I have discovered something that will ensure supremacy for German music for the next hundred years.' However there were attacks from all sides, and also desertions from his own camp. Hanns Eisler, an erstwhile pupil, became a Communist and collaborator with Brecht, and as a result had to forswear his past because 'dodecaphony' was a mortal sin in the eyes of his new comrades. Eisler, in turn, influenced the American composer Marc Blitzstein and Alan Bush, the English left-wing composer, both of whom were studying in Berlin at the time.

Among the most effective protagonists of the new music were the conductor Hermann Scherchen and Paul Bekker, author of a famous Beethoven biography and music critic of the influential *Frankfurter Zeitung*. A great deal of passion, indeed fanaticism, was injected into these disputes; there was slanging and vituperation of every sort. Thomas Mann, in his story of Adrian Leverkühn, has provided a memorial to that age of bitter strife from a vantage-point that was not too friendly. Essentially, the debate continues to this day. Some critics see in Schönberg's work the last link in a chain that began with Wagner's *Tristan*, the dissolution of tonal harmony, the road to chaos. Others regard him as one of the greatest pioneers in the history of music. Schönberg's music has remained difficult to understand; only a few of his works, such as *Gurrelieder*, *Verklärte Nacht* and *Pierrot Lunaire*, have become part of the concert repertoire.

Other minor and less radical modernists fared no better. Kurt Weill's *Royal Palace* (1927) and *Mahagonny* (1930) were rejected by the public; Ernst Krenek's jazz opera *Jonny spielt auf* (1927) encountered both enthusiastic acceptance and violent rejection. The jazz invasion of the early 1920s will be described in a different context; if it did not succeed in the opera houses, jazz triumphed in the dance halls and even National Socialism had to make some concessions in later years to the new style in popular music.

To a certain, albeit limited extent, atonal music can be interpreted as the impact of Expressionism on music. The works of Schönberg, Webern and Berg convey apocalyptic visions, the intimation of catastrophe; they resemble similar presentiments in the works of contemporary poets and writers. Schönberg, Webern and Hindemith chose texts from Georg Trakl for their songs – though it is only fair to add that they were equally fascinated by the poems of Rilke and George.

The musical crisis was part of a larger cultural upheaval, but the problems of music were specific, rooted in the very nature of the medium. Attempts to explain it in political or psychoanalytical terms were not very illuminating. Typical of this kind of comment was young Wiesengrund-Adorno writing on the 'social situation of music' in 1932; he claimed that Stravinsky reflected upper-middle-class ideology much more accurately than Richard Strauss, that the petty-bourgeois elements among the public rejected the esoteric Schoenberg and the melodious Hindemith alike, that the absurd hit songs of the time contained sadistic elements and manifested anal regression. If there was a connexion between music, psychoanalysis, politics and economics (which is not certain), the composers and conductors were among the last to perceive it. What Bruno Walter wrote years later applied to most of his colleagues as well: that he was always totally immersed in his art and that there was no corresponding awareness of his duties as a citizen. Conscious republicans and democrats like Fritz Busch were a rare exception. Busch writes in his autobiography of a festival at Leipzig in 1923 in honour of the Republic which stuck in his mind because the speaker called the Chancellor of the day a living corpse:

> While I stood petrified at my desk, my indignation at the disgraceful situation began to grow. Quite incapable of pulling myself together, I began the Fifth Symphony. After the first movement I threw the stick away and went out. How could I conduct music ... when thousands of so-called educated men allowed abuse of a government we had assembled to celebrate to pass without contradiction? The audience dispersed when I did not come back. I expected my dismissal next day, or at least disciplinary action. But once again nothing happened.

Incidents like these occurred with increasing frequency as the decade drew to its close.

MODERNISM IN ART AND ARCHITECTURE

Germany had produced Bach and Beethoven, Goethe and Schiller, Kant and Hegel, but there were no German Leonardos or Rembrandts. Suddenly, during the first decade of the twentieth century, Germany moved to the forefront of modern art. Nor was interest in the new departures in the visual arts limited to a handful of avant-garde artists and critics, as in other European countries. The first German autumn salon in 1913 provided a panorama of modern art such as had never been shown anywhere else before.

Thus 1918 was no more a watershed in the visual arts than in literature. It is difficult, in fact, to think of a single major artist of the 1920s whose pictures had not been exhibited before the war, and some of the pioneers of the modern movement were no longer alive when peace came. Nevertheless, the 1920s were not a mere epilogue to the revolution which had taken place before the war. It was a decade of change and new departures. If by 1930 the work of Brecht, Döblin or Werfel no longer betrayed substantial traces of their Expressionist beginnings, the same applies, *a fortiori*, to Klee and Kandinsky (who had belonged to the Blaue Reiter in Munich), or to Nolde (who had for a while been a member of the Brücke). Beckmann had been a leading Expressionist; subsequently he became one of the most representative figures of Neue Sachlichkeit, which was the very antithesis of Expressionism. There was continuity, but only within strict limits. What has been said about Expressionism in literature applies by and large to its impact on the visual arts. The modern movement transcended the traditional borderlines between the plastic arts, literature and the theatre. Kokoschka, Kubin and Meidner provided illustrations to the books of their friends, the poets and novelists. Writers and artists belonged to the same circles in Munich and Berlin, they contributed to Herwarth Walden's *Sturm* and Pfemfert's *Aktion*. They signed the same manifestoes and collaborated in staging plays. Even if Kokoschka had not painted a single picture, or Barlach worked on a single sculpture, their names would still figure in the annals of contemporary German literature. In later years the Bauhaus spent a great deal of time and effort on dramatic experiments. Moholy-Nagy, to give but one example, was stage designer for the Berlin State Opera and for Piscator's theatre. Klee was a gifted musician, so was Herwarth Walden. On the other hand, most important composers were at one time or another guests of the Bauhaus. If modern German painting was more international in outlook than German literature, this has to do with the very character of the medium; for obvious reasons there was no 'international style' in literature as there was in architecture. Even the most German painters were open to foreign influences: the Far Eastern themes in Nolde's work are unmistakable, as is the inspiration Barlach drew from Russia. Both had spent part of their apprenticeship in Paris. Kirchner, perhaps the most gifted of the members of the Brücke, spent the last twenty years of his life in Switzerland and painted some of his finest pictures in France. But he always considered himself a German painter, and despite all foreign influence there was indeed something specifically German in his work and that of his friends. The German artists felt they had a message of their own and their own ways of expressing it.

When the war ended, the three leading figures of the older generation of painters were still alive and active. Liebermann, Slevogt and Corinth had helped to pave the way in the transition from academic to modern art; they had been the rebels, the secessionists of the 1890s; the impact on them of French Impressionism is unmistakable. Liebermann painted some of his finest portraits in the 1920s and Slevogt continued to work as an illustrator up to his death in 1932. But of these three only Corinth was regarded by the younger generation as a truly modern painter; the other two were, after all, rooted in the nineteenth century. Kirchner said about Corinth that he had been 'just average' and became truly great only in later life with his hymns to nature, when his colours became richer and less conventional and his portraits 'projections of the inner man'. Yet Corinth by no means regarded himself as an Expressionist; he called the painters of Die Brücke 'men of Hottentot naiveté', who had been unduly influenced by French fashions. Liebermann, hard as he tried to be fair to the young modernists, followed their efforts without great sympathy. *Kunst* after all comes from *können*, he wrote to a friend after 1918: 'If it were derived from *wollen*, we would call it *Wulst*.' In his eyes, and those of other men of his generation, it simply was not enough to be inspired and to aim high. So far as sheer ability was concerned, they did not think highly of the younger generation.

If 1918 was not the decisive turning-point in the history of modern German painting, it was still a date of importance. There was the impact of the war and, above all, the general climate had changed; after 1918 there was far wider recognition of modern art. Wilhelm II had proclaimed that any art which ventured 'beyond the laws and limits imposed by Myself' was no longer art. The artists ignored him and went on to draw, paint or sculpt as they saw fit; but the directors of museums, with a few exceptions, belonged to the old school, and even if they were not unsympathetic to the modern trends they could not always show it. Among the public, interest was aroused only slowly; the painters of Die Brücke did not sell a single picture before they moved on to Berlin in 1910. Painters such as Kirchner, Schmidt-Rotluff and Heckel were autodidacts, and this too was held against them. After 1918, on the other hand, museums started buying modern art, exhibitions were arranged. Yesterday's outsiders became the new insiders. Modernists became members of the Prussian Academy; Dix and Hofer were made professors in Berlin, Klee in Düsseldorf, Beckmann and Baumeister in Frankfurt, Schlemmer and Mueller in Breslau, Kokoschka in Dresden. By and large the avant-garde had become respectable. Recognition outside Germany took much longer; the German painters and sculptors – in contrast to the architects – were not thought to be of merit and interest. It was not until well after the Second World War that they were discovered abroad.

Before 1914 the two most significant groups of artists were those around Die Brücke and the Blaue Reiter. For many years the former remained less well known, and it is easy to see why. For there is a line leading from the Blaue Reiter to Surrealism and abstract art, styles much more familiar to the international public than the approach of Die Brücke, rooted in the tradition of the late Middle Ages (Dürer, Cranach, Grünewald). Quite independently of Paris, the artists of Die Brücke discovered African and Oceanic primitive art and Etruscan sculpture. They tried their hand at woodcuts as well as lithography. Each summer they went to a lake not far from Dresden or to the North Sea, which had a peculiar attraction for them. After their move to Berlin, city scenes became a favourite subject for some of them; Kirchner's *Street Scene Berlin 1913* is a typical attempt to depict not only individuals but the relations between them. Their work, like that of the Expressionist poets, reflects the general feeling of malaise, the nervousness and the inner unrest; and there were apocalyptic undertones. They were at the same time both fascinated and horrified by the big city. During the early years the styles of the members of Die Brücke were remarkably similar; there were certain differences, but the common elements were much more marked. After their split in 1913 they drifted apart. Max Pechstein was an adventurous painter, a *fauve*, consciously drawing upon primitive art in his younger years, yet at the same time a little more conventional than the others and thus more accessible to the public. Following in Gauguin's footsteps, he went to a South Sea island just before the outbreak of war. At the time he was considered to be the most Expressionist painter of them all; towards the end of his career he became the most academic. Kirchner fell seriously ill during the war, moved to Davos in 1917, and spent the following twenty years up to his suicide in 1938 in and out of Swiss nursing-homes. He was the richest in ideas of the group and developed his own highly individual form of Cubism; his Swiss landscapes and his illustrations to Georg Heym's *Umbra Vitae* are among the finest creative achievements of German painting in the 1920s.

Heckel was in his early years the most romantic and pessimistic of the group but also the one most interested in politics. Like Beckmann, he was fascinated by the world of the circus and the variety theatre – clowns and white circus horses appear frequently in his pictures. During the 1920s the Expressionist element gradually disappeared; his German landscapes became more Fauvist and his graphic art more decorative. Typical of his early pictures was *Zwei Männer am Tisch* (1912), which might well illustrate a scene from Dostoevsky; the landscapes painted in his later years reveal a more realistic style, less isolation and even a certain lyricism.

Schmidt-Rotluff, equally important as a painter and a graphic artist, showed in his early pictures Cubist influences, whereas in his religious canvases (*Christus*, 1918) produced after the end of the war the monumental element predominates. He was opposed to programmatic painting; to a query from a journal in 1913 he replied: 'Of myself I know that I have no programme, only the inexplicable nostalgia to grasp what I feel and to find for it the purest expression.' It is interesting to compare his credo with that of Otto Mueller six years later: 'My main aim is to express with the greatest possible simplicity the impression of a landscape and human beings; my ideal was and is the art of old Egypt, even from a purely technical aspect.' His postwar pictures are softer and more joyous than those produced earlier (*Frauen am Meer*, 1919; *Abend am Meer*, 1919); the Italian landscape had an exhilarating effect on his work. In these later pictures there is little of the erstwhile Expressionist spirit of the 'salvation-through-suffering' mood, so typical of the years just before and after the war.

Emil Nolde was somewhat older than the other members of Die Brücke and he joined them only for a short while. He was one of the most individualistic of German painters, even though his beginnings were similar to those of most of his contemporaries: realist painting, a stay in Paris, the impact of Post-Impressionism. Around 1905 he developed a highly individual style in his religious and grotesque works (the most famous of which was his *Last Supper*). These pictures, often primitive, with glaring colours, express inner feeling with demonic strength. Christ and the apostles are shown with such ugliness and distortion that the church authorities found it necessary to intervene; his *Life of Christ* had to be withdrawn from an exhibition of religious art in Brussels in 1912. Although he was of peasant origin, the most 'Nordic' of all German painters and, apparently, an early member of the Hitler movement, his work was not only banned by the Nazis but he was forbidden to paint altogether. He lived to the ripe old age of eighty-eight and continued to paint almost to the end of his life, very much in the style he had developed fifty years earlier.

If Nolde's contact with Die Brücke was tenuous, Kokoschka, Beckmann and Hofer were not connected with any group. Oskar Kokoschka made his name in Vienna in 1908 as an Expressionist playwright, and at about the same time, 'like a maniac, jumped into art' (Paul Westheim). His early work as a painter is a little uncertain, expressing a desire to shock the philistine through various eccentricities. During the 1920s there was distinct progress towards objectivity, especially in his landscapes and city pictures, but also in his portraits. Of all the artists hitherto mentioned, Kokoschka was the one with the greatest psychological curiosity and also one of the most politically aware. His sitters (as in the famous picture of Auguste Forel) come out like X-ray portraits, psychological horoscopes. One critic commented that Kokoschka gave even to his landscapes a portrait-like quality, trying to discover and express the *genius loci*.

Carl Hofer was a man of paradoxes: 'He seeks beauty and meets caricatures. He is fundamentally a conservative and experiments even in his seventieth year' (Will Grohmann). Born in southern Germany, he spent five years in Italy as a young man and then five years in Paris. Yet apart from a certain influence which Cézanne exerted on his work, it is impossible to classify him: he did not belong to any specific school and had a style which was entirely his own. 'One ought to have the courage not to be modern', he once said. He was a restrained, sober painter and his main interest was the human element; the *Couple at the Window* (1925) and *Carnival* (1928) are good examples of his style. In 1952 he wrote that Naturalism had always been alien to him, and that Impressionism did not touch him: 'The ecstasies of Expressionism were not to my taste.' He was, as he said on one occasion about himself, a romantic in search of the classic.

Max Beckmann, six years younger than Hofer, is the painter of clowns, actors, dancers, of masked balls and carnivals. It is interesting to compare his *Paris Carnival* (1930) and his *Ladies at the Window* (1928) with Hofer's paintings. His early pictures were in the Impressionist tradition, but there was a radical change during the war. His name is usually mentioned together with those of Otto Dix and George Grosz as one of the representative painters of Neue Sachlichkeit. Yet in essential respects he differed from them, above all in the grotesque allegorical figures which inhabited his dream world, as well as in the Gothic, vertical structure so typical of his pictures. Perhaps his finest work was produced in the 1930s; the philosophical and historical triptychs, with their masterful use of colour. Some critics detected in them a return, albeit on a limited scale, to his Expressionist beginnings.

The Blaue Reiter, based in Munich, consisted of a group of friends very different in approach and temperament but united in their opposition to 'official art'. They were influenced by French painting to a larger degree than the Brücke, but they did not just copy the Fauves. Kandinsky was the oldest of the group and its outstanding theorist; the name 'Blaue Reiter' was derived from one of his pictures. Yet when he developed his revolutionary new techniques, and painted his first abstract compositions of crossing lines and vivid colours to which he gave musical names or numbers, the others by no means slavishly followed him. Marc painted a few abstract pictures,

Macke experimented with the style but returned to representational art, and for Klee, Kandinsky was a friend but not a model or a master.

The Blaue Reiter was short-lived but is of interest in view of the subsequent work of some of its members. Kandinsky inaugurated the abstract revolution with his book: *On the Spiritual in Art*, in which he developed his basic views – that the essential element in art was not form but the artistic content. Explaining his gradual retreat from objective painting (which lasted about four years, from 1910 to 1914), he wrote that the observer has to learn to look at the picture as the graphic delineation of a mood, not as the depiction of objects. The real work of art comes into being in a mysterious way, 'out of the artist'. He is not just entitled but obliged to deal with form (and with colour) as is necessary for his purpose. The aim is not the imitation of nature but the presentation of the 'inner world'. Hence the affinity of abstract painting with modern music, which can express the new rhythms much more easily. Kandinsky's theories attracted great interest and his book was translated into many languages. His drawings were at first much less in demand. Years later, writing about his first exhibition, he noted that the public had been rather well educated: the pictures had to be wiped dry every evening because so many people spat at them; at least nobody had tried to cut them to ribbons. Kandinsky went to Russia during the war but returned to Germany in 1921 and became a teacher at the Bauhaus. His work in the 1920s shows a preoccupation with geometric forms, probing deeper and deeper into a secret world.

The war and the revolution of 1918 produced new preoccupations but not a new style: 'We carried out our revolution a long time ago', wrote Alfred Kubin at the time. Political organizations mushroomed and various manifestoes were issued. Like the Expressionist poets and dramatists, the painters were now more than ever before in search of the new man. But with all the appeals for socialism, world revolution and 'political art', the underlying inspiration was mystical, even religious, rather than political in character. 'Suns and moons are our pictures', proclaimed the manifesto of 'Absolute Expressionism' published in *Der Sturm*: 'There is no longer I and thou, only eternity and our road to the stars.' Lunacharsky, the Soviet cultural commissar, was not far wrong when he saw in the tendency towards mysticism, whether Christian or Far Eastern in origin, a typical reflection of the postwar German situation, the depression and the mood of despair. But one should not press the analogy too far, because left-wing mysticism and eschatology had their origins in the prewar period; this, after all, was what Expressionism had been about. The main importance of the activities of the 'revolutionaries of the spirit' united in the Novembergruppe and the Arbeitsrat für Kunst was the endeavour, successful on the whole, to popularize modern art and to reform the cultural policy of the state. As a pressure-group they made their mark; the director of the Berlin National Gallery, who had faithfully obeyed the Emperor's wishes, now opened a special gallery to show the works of the younger painters. Evening classes were organized for the public and many exhibitions arranged.

The underlying assumption was that art, which had served a small section of society, should be restored to the people: 'Art and people should become one.' Ludwig Meidner said that there was a sacred solidarity between poets, painters and the poor. The bourgeoisie lacked sincere respect for art, it knew no love, only exploitation. The worker on the other hand was said to respect the *Geist* – that magic word which dominated all contemporary discussions. Pechstein denounced the glorification of the art of antiquity and expected from the Republic not just a healthier attitude towards art but also the beginning of a 'new unified' epoch in the history of art. Fashionable acceptance of socialist tenets and its mingling with religious themes is reflected in the first publication of the Arbeitsrat für Kunst, with its cover picture by Feininger: 'The Cathedral of Socialism', showing three shining stars over a medieval church with three towers. These were the aspirations of the moderates; the radicals argued with George Grosz that art was unnatural, the artist a maniac, a sick man ('art is now an altogether secondary affair'); mankind could well do without it. Grosz berated his colleagues who had not left their ivory towers: 'Your brushes and pens should be weapons but they are empty blades of straw.' Makart, the nineteenth-century painter whom they despised, had after all been sincere in his way, expressing the nostalgia as well as the reality of middle-class life. The Expressionist anarchists on the other hand, with their snobbish and peculiar ideas, expressed nothing but their own irrelevant selves and it was time to put a stop to this. Some leading artists, such as Kubin, remained aloof from these debates, deeply suspicious about the intrusion of politics into art. Klee too expressed opposition in principle to all majority judgments on art.

As modernism advanced, the hostility towards it grew, mainly but not exclusively among right-wing circles. The critics condemned the new fashions as gangsterism, un-German, a ferment of decomposition, Bolshevist. They attacked the government with increasing vehemence for promoting the work of evil bunglers and foreign swindlers (such as 'Idiotinsky'). As they saw it, modern art had sunk to the level of primitive African and Oceanic tribes; worse still, it bore a distinct resemblance to the paintings of the inmates of lunatic asylums. Others, less extreme, were willing to give modern art a chance but warned against replacing the dictatorship of the official art of yesterday by the tyranny of a new school; they feared that the public, afraid of being out of step with new fashions, would swallow the new creed hook, line and sinker. In fact, much as the revolutionaries disliked the patronage of the bourgeois public, there was no noticeable enthusiasm for Kandinsky and Klee among the working class. It was the same story as in the theatre all over again. The leading Communists had no great interest in art and took their cue from the Soviet Union. While experimentation was in fashion in Moscow they were fairly tolerant; later they became arch-conservatives, bitterly opposed to modern art. Thus the artistic avant-garde learnt by bitter experience that a revolutionary in politics could well be a conservative in his cultural tastes. The leading Social Democrats, in so far as they had cultural interests, were not enamoured of modernist trends either; but despite this lack of enthusiasm they were helpful on many occasions and appointed a *Reichskunstwart* who was sympathetic to the avant-garde. So far as appointments to the Academy of Arts were concerned, the policy was conciliatory: modernists were appointed but also an equal number of traditionalists.

The revolutionary groups which came into being in 1918–19 were short-lived; they disbanded after a year or two and the artists ceased to publish their manifestoes. But one of the new ventures was to last for more than a decade; the Bauhaus, which will be discussed below, became a focus of modern architecture, attracting much attention in Germany and abroad. The idea of the Bauhaus had been defined in Gropius's appeal of 1919 that architects, sculptors and painters ought to return to craftsmanship, that there was no essential difference between artists and craftsmen. The artist was simply a craftsman on a higher level. This approach was based on ideas put into practice in the two previous decades by Van de Velde in Brussels and Weimar. But only the Republic made it possible to carry out these experiments on a broader basis and to pursue them much further than envisaged by the precursors. The political constellation was auspicious but this was merely a precondition for success. The Bauhaus would not have achieved what it did but for the fact that there were many gifted artists willing to collaborate in the new project.

The impact of modernism did not bypass art history; the theorists and historians, without necessarily identifying themselves with any specific group or style, had done much of the spadework for the recognition of modern art. Among the pioneers was Julius Meier-Graefe, with his work on the Post-Impressionists (Cézanne, Van Gogh). The French painters were at the time acclaimed by a wider public in Germany than in their native country. As a result many of their works found their way into German museums and private collections; the trend was reversed only when the Nazis began to purge the museums. Germany produced some of the world's leading art journals, such as Westheim's *Kunstblatt*, Flechtheim and Wedderkopp's *Querschnitt*, and the more conservative *Kunstwart*. Worringer's influential work *Abstraktion und Einfühlung*, first published in 1907, demonstrated that abstraction had been used freely in ancient and medieval art; Carl Einstein's *Art of the 20th Century* (1926) and Max Dvořák's *Kunstgeschichte als Geistesgeschichte* (1921), with its emphasis on El Greco and Breughel as precursors of modern art, were other milestones in making modernism respectable.

After Expressionism had been proclaimed dead the only bone of contention among the theorists was whether it was merely a movement that had expired or art in general. While this debate was still continuing the new realism (Neue Sachlichkeit) appeared on the scene. There was near-unanimity about the causes of this new phenomenon. Kandinsky referred to the political situation, to *Angst* and insecurity. Franz Roh, who published a book in 1925 called *Nach-Expressionismus, Magischer Realismus*, described the new trend as the result of widespread disappointment, social and artistic. Hartlaub, another art-historian and head of the Mannheim museum, who had coined the term 'Neue Sachlichkeit' in 1923, referred to the resignation which had spread as the grandiose utopias of 1918 had not yielded the expected changes. It is relatively easy to point to manifestations of Neue Sachlichkeit in architecture, whereas the impact of the movement on painting and sculpture was on the whole limited and brief. The name mentioned most frequently in this connexion is that of Otto Dix, and the portrait of his parents is probably the best-known example of the new style. His early work reflects the horrors of the war; there are strong elements of social criticism, for instance in scenes from a a bordello (*Zuhälter und Nutten*, 1922). These pictures are suffused with a spirit of brutality, yet when criticized Dix said with disarming naiveté that he had not been aware of this and had only wanted to paint *Stilleben*. Schrimpf and Alexander Kranoldt were other representatives of Neue Sachlichkeit, and to a certain extent also Oskar Schlemmer, one of the pillars of the Bauhaus. They are sometimes lumped together as the 'monumentalist branch' of Neue Sachlichkeit, but apart from the fact that all three were purged by the Nazis they did not have much in common. There are strong plastic elements in their work and there is a connexion between Schrimpf, Kranoldt and contemporary Italian schools. But their pictures, and particularly Schlemmer's frescoes, also contain strong symbolical and mystical elements which are not at all in the realist tradition.

Neue Sachlichkeit, in brief, was a short interlude. To some it recalled the lost illusions of a generation, for others it was the return to a greater measure of realism, if not of academic painting, and to still others (such as Dix) a transitional stage towards a latterday, modified and restrained form of Expressionism. Its impact, at any rate, was not as acutely felt as, and much less lasting than that of Surrealism, which appeared in France at about the same time.

Beyond these groups and schools there were individual painters defying classification; partly because they went their own way, partly because they continued to change and develop throughout their working lives. Paul Klee is the most obvious example; born in Switzerland, he exhibited some of his early pictures with his friends of the Blaue Reiter and in 1921 he joined the Bauhaus. He was the most erudite of German artists of the period, anti-monumentalist *par excellence* and opposed to the idea of functionalism in art. Yet at the Bauhaus he taught not only abstract painting, but also headed the weaving class. Gropius called him the 'highest moral court of appeal'. There are certain similarities with Kandinsky, on whose later work he had a certain influence. Like Marc and Kandinsky, he was influenced by Delaunay, the great innovator of colour, and his linear method also has a certain affinity with the abstract artists. Yet his sense of humour and above all his wealth of ideas and ways of expressing them were unique among his contemporaries. He was the first and for many years the only painter who studied the drawings of children and of psychotics and who tried to find connexions between painting and the world of science. In his theoretical work there are frequent references to biology, mathematics and physics; he was deeply interested in the structure of the atom and the theory of relativity. At the same time he always stressed the close relationship between painting and music. He was one of the most difficult of modern painters, as well as one of the most influential. On Klee's tombstone in Basle there is an inscription from his diary: 'In this world I am altogether incomprehensible. For I live equally with the dead and those as yet unborn.' Klee wrote that art transcends the object, both the real and the imaginary. More than other modernist writers, he suspected that the symbols and the messages of art would not find a public to which it would convey a meaning. Thus, in a lecture given in 1924 but only posthumously published ('On Modern Art'), there are the deeply pessimistic words: *Uns trägt kein Volk* (We are not rooted in the people and not supported by it). His oeuvre, more than that of any other painter, reflects the basic dilemma of modern art.

The authors of the manifestoes of 1918 were clearly over-optimistic with regard to the coming 'unity of art and people'.

Strange as it may appear in retrospect, they were genuinely unaware of the fact that the distance between the avant-garde and popular taste had grown immeasurably and that the doctrines preached by the right were much more in line with popular taste. The pseudo-realistic and monumental style developed in the Third Reich did not encounter widespread derision, as modern art so often did. The dilemma of modernism was not, of course, an exclusively German phenomenon, but it emerged nowhere more sharply than in republican Germany.

The violent reaction to modern art affected even the new style in architecture. It was easy to poke fun at the paintings of Kandinsky or Klee and the collages of Schwitters: there was, after all, a world of difference between a Kandinsky composition and the picture of a traditional painter. On the other hand the difference between a Gropius building and that of a less innovative architect was, in comparison, much less striking. Both, by necessity, had doors and windows, walls and a roof. At worst, the anti-modernist could argue that a sloping roof was better suited to the German climate than a flat roof because it provided better drainage for rain and snow. And yet the attacks on modern architecture were as acrimonious as the criticism of serial music or abstract painting. This is all the more surprising since the architectural style had not remained static, and few buildings designed in 1930 resembled those of 1905; moreover even some of the most bitter enemies of the new architecture had been innovators in their younger years. The attacks were directed above all against the Bauhaus, though at no time did it monopolize German building; it consisted of a small group of people more interested in experimentation than in obtaining commissions, but its indirect impact in Germany and later abroad was substantial and lasting.

The beginning of the new style can be traced back to well before the First World War. The prevailing fashion in German architecture during the last decades of the nineteenth century was, as elsewhere, ornate, over-decorated, with many turrets and gables. But around 1900 a gradual break in tradition set in, partly under the influence of Jugendstil, partly in order to make building simpler and less expensive. Examples of the new approach were Messel's Wertheim department store (1904), Bonatz's Stuttgart railway station (begun in 1913), and some of the buildings of Hans Poelzig and Peter Behrens. At an exhibition in Cologne in 1914 of the Deutsche Werkbund, a group of architects and craftsmen who wanted to improve industrial design, the new style was already very much in evidence. One of the centres of the new movement was Weimar, where Henri van de Velde ran the local arts and crafts school. Van de Velde believed in much closer cooperation between the various arts, and when with the outbreak of war he had to leave Germany, he suggested Walter Gropius, then aged thirty-one, as his successor. Gropius had been an assistant in the office of Peter Behrens, a Berlin architect, together with Mies van der Rohe and Le Corbusier; he had already made his mark with the design of the Fagus factory buildings just before 1914 and also with some interesting constructions at the Werkbund exhibition in 1914. These designs revealed concern with social and hygienic considerations, a tendency towards simplicity, and a stress on the use of 'new materials' (steel, glass, concrete); all these features foreshadowed the main characteristics of the architecture of the 1920s. Gropius served in the war and thus could assume the directorship of the Weimar school only in 1918. Within a few years he made it the most prestigious – or as others would say, controversial – institution of its kind in Europe.

Gropius believed in what he called the 'total work of art', the *Gesamtkunstwerk*. The term was not entirely new; Wagner had used it, though in an entirely different context. Gropius was referring to the building of cathedrals in the Middle Ages, when artists and craftsmen of various specializations had closely collaborated under the direction of the architects. He was convinced that a similar concept could be made to work in the twentieth century and that by a collective creative effort of architects, sculptors and painters a return to the crafts – and to craftsmanship – could be effected and the isolation of the various visual arts overcome. Vaguely similar ideas had been voiced by William Morris, but unlike him, Gropius was not a romantic; he accepted that the Bauhaus would have to come to terms with the machine age. This implied not only the use of new materials and methods of construction but also mass production. One of the central ideas of the Bauhaus was 'community building'; as Gropius saw it, this was not just a technical problem but above all a political, social and economic challenge. Hence a new concept of town planning – very large blocks and terraces oriented to the sun: 'Just as the Gothic cathedral was the expression of its age, so must the modern factory or dwelling be the expression of our time: Precise, practical-functional, free of superfluous ornament, effective only through the cubic composition.' In accordance with the *Zeitgeist*, the educational work of the Bauhaus called in rather sweeping terms for a 'complete spiritual revolution' in the individual, a new style of life to help overcome the fragmentation of human existence.

Considering that the Bauhaus was not a giant institution, such a programme seemed over-ambitious. Over the years it had on its staff altogether some five hundred graduates; but if they were few in numbers they had tremendous enthusiasm. Lothar Schreyer, one of the masters, later wrote about the 'fire of devotion to an idea' inspiring all of them: 'We felt that we were literally building a new world.' There was an abundance of talent: the famous introductory course was given by Johannes Itten and later by Josef Albers (who specialized in glass, furniture, and wallpaper design), and by Moholy-Nagy (the head of the metal workshop who also did important original research on photography and was a stage designer). In addition to Klee, Kandinsky and Oskar Schlemmer, there were Lyonel Feininger (master of graphic painting), Marcel Breuer (master of interiors), who designed the first tubular steel chair, Gerhard Marcks (head of the ceramic workshops), and Gropius's two successors, Hannes Meyer and Mies van der Rohe, both leading architects. Visiting lecturers included Theo van Doesburg, Stravinsky, Hindemith, Bartók and many others.

The question whether the Bauhaus teachers should be called masters, professors or have any rank at all was a matter of dispute during the early days. Opinions were divided, Marcks admitted that he had once used the professorial title in order to get a maid for his wife, but apparently without much success; and, anyway, 'I feel just as stupid as a professor as I do as a master.' Kandinsky dismissed the matter as irrelevant.

Among so many geniuses there was bound to be trouble. The first major controversy arose between Gropius and Itten, who believed in spontaneity (to the extent that he did not correct the apprentices' mistakes). A theosophist, he started his classes with

Mazdaznan and breathing exercises. It should be mentioned in passing that theosophy and Far Eastern religions, fashionable at the time in Western Europe, had a considerable impact on artists, including Kandinsky, Brancusi, Malevich, to name but a few. Gropius maintained that art and technology constituted a new unity, whereas Feininger stressed that they remained essentially different in their function. He wrote in a letter in 1923 that Gropius more than the other masters had an eye for realities; his main concern was to get outside commissions to secure the survival of the Bauhaus. But Feininger was not entirely happy about this state of affairs. In his view – and Kandinsky and Schlemmer took a similar position – the policy of the Bauhaus should not be directed by such immediate practical ·considerations. Such criticism did not in any way diminish his personal admiration for Gropius. 'He never complains', Feininger wrote his wife in 1923, 'never seems exhausted or embittered. He works until three in the morning, hardly sleeps at all, and when he looks at you his eyes shine more than anyone else's.'

When Gropius left in 1928, and with him Breuer and Moholy-Nagy, personal differences with some other masters were involved, but they were apparently not the decisive factor.

Gropius named Hannes Meyer as his successor, a suggestion he was soon to regret. Swiss-born, Meyer was a Constructivist, a friend of El Lissitzky, and he wanted to apply Marxist-Leninist principles to architecture. He advocated 'scientific building', and he was far more interested in technology than in art. 'Building is only organization', he wrote in 1928; and 'paint for us is just a means to protect materials.' If Gropius had found it difficult to keep so many geniuses happy, Meyer could not possibly succeed; he was replaced in 1930 by Mies van der Rohe, the 'classicist among the modernists' or, as others called him, the 'anatomic architect'. Mies had matured more slowly than Gropius but was eventually recognized as a master of equal stature. He built the German pavilion at the Barcelona world exhibition in 1929 which in its design and its original use of materials (steel, walls of yellow onyx) became a landmark in the history of architecture. He was perhaps best known at the time as a furniture designer (the 'Bauhaus chair'). After having left Germany, not without some hesitation, in the late 1930s, he became even better known for his architectural work in Chicago, New York (the Seagram Building) and Mexico City.

The activities of the Bauhaus provoked bitter attacks from many quarters. The original impulse for the establishment of the institution had come from the government of Thuringia, but so far as the conservative city fathers of Weimar were concerned the Bauhaus was not really wanted. Local artisans were afraid of competition, while the extreme right claimed that most of the pillars of the Bauhaus were Jews and foreigners (which was quite untrue). According to these critics, the cubic forms of the housing models advocated by the Bauhaus were a regression towards the primitivism of inferior races. It was attacked as a hotbed of communism, even though, with the exception of Hannes Meyer who came into prominence only after the Bauhaus had left Weimar, none of its leaders was a Communist. As a result of the constant attacks, the Bauhaus moved to Dessau in 1925–6 where Gropius had built for it a glass-and-steel complex which was one of the architectural wonders of the 1920s. Its new, official, name was Hochschule für Gestaltung. The attacks on the Bauhaus had helped to spread its fame all over Germany; Einstein, Gerhart Hauptmann and others signed appeals on its behalf. But its days in Dessau, too, were numbered as Nazism gained strength and Hitler's local representatives bitterly fought this loathsome manifestation of *Kulturbolschewismus*. In 1932 the Bauhaus was transferred to Berlin and soon after it was dissolved.

Thus the opponents of modern architecture had at last succeeded in their struggle. Schultze Naumburg, the most vocal enemy of modern architecture in Germany, had called it 'a battle of life and death' against the evil dream of government buildings which looked like factories and churches which could easily be mistaken for movie-houses. The Bauhaus, that 'cathedral of socialism', resembled a synagogue in his eyes. But Gropius and Mies, Feininger, Hannes Meyer and Itten, were of impeccable Aryan origin, and even the *Völkische Beobachter*, the chief Nazi mouthpiece, had in the early days some good words for the Bauhaus. It referred to its staff as people who had turned their backs on the false individualism of the prewar period and created highly functional and relatively cheap housing. The subsequent attacks on the Bauhaus and all it stood for were at least partly motivated by professional envy on the part of those who spearheaded the campaign and who, incidentally, failed to become, as they had hoped, the leaders of German architecture in the Third Reich.

Important as the Bauhaus was, the history of modern German architecture cannot solely be written in terms of Weimar and Dessau. Some of the leading architects of the period such as Bruno and Max Taut, Erich Mendelsohn and Ernst May, Hans Scharoun and Martin Wagner, while in broad sympathy with its aims, never belonged to it. They had ideas of their own about the metaphysics of architecture, about geometry and 'organism'. Bruno Taut was the most extreme theorist among them, the creator of a utopian ('alpine') architecture, replete with references to light and crystal. He was dreaming of a world without private property and without marriage, a world no longer dominated by big cities. In his *Stadtkrone* he proposed the erection of community buildings in the heart of the new cities with houses of crystal at their very centre. (He had built such a glasshouse for the famous 1914 Werkbund exhibition.) Such outlandish fantasies would have been easily dismissed but for the fact that Taut was also an excellent and eminently practical architect and designer, the builder of some of the biggest housing projects in Berlin, such as the *Hufeisen* in Britz. Taut, May and a few other leading architects went to the Soviet Union as consultants but did not stay for long.

Most members of the Bauhaus eventually found their way to the United States. Mies continued to build in Germany but in 1938 he too left his native country. In America their talent found real scope, both as teachers and as practising architects. While Breuer and Mies had been influential theorists before 1933, their practical experience had been very limited. The former had built altogether three houses in ten years, the latter seventeen, but half of them for display at exhibitions. If the attempts to revive the Bauhaus in America were unsuccessful, the impact of the former members of this circle on the development of modern architecture was considerable: they were the pioneers of a new idea. As Mies said in a speech on the occasion of Gropius's seventieth birthday: 'You cannot exert such influence with organization, you cannot do it with propaganda. Only an idea spreads so far.'

Seen in retrospect the architecture of the 1920s exerted a more lasting influence internationally than any other aspect of Weimar culture. The impact of German literature, however interesting, was for obvious reasons limited; rooted in a specific situation, it was not for export. The German stage, from Reinhardt to Brecht, radiated a greater influence but the theatre, too, could not always transcend the obstacles of language, national character and tradition. German musical life excelled more on the level of performance than in creative innovations. Only in architecture did something akin to an international style come into being at the time, and the Germans made a decisive contribution towards it.

Measured by the unrealistic expectations of the manifestoes of 1919, German architecture was not a success. It did not radically change the world; it only designed ways and means of improving it. The general mood of the builders of the city of the future was antibourgeois, yet it was precisely among the bourgeois that they found their supporters and clients; in this respect, too, they did not fare differently from the revolutionary writers and painters. It will bear repeating that political radicalism and artistic avantgardism do not by any means go hand in hand. The artists who were most revolutionary in their outlook and approach, such as Klee and Kandinsky, were the ones least interested in the political future of mankind; their main concern was with the problems of the individual.

*   *   *

From what has been said so far a more or less clear pattern emerges: Republican Germany was the main battleground between the modern movement and the forces of tradition in literature, the theatre, the visual arts and to a certain extent also in music. What predestined Germany for this role? The constraints of Wilhelmian Germany disappeared after 1918, but these constraints had never been really stifling; what the Kaiser said was largely ignored by writers, artists and composers. Modern art, after all, was born in the decade before, not after the war. Certain sections of the German intelligentsia were more uprooted than their contemporaries in France, Britain or the United States and thus more open to new influences. Their break with traditional values was more radical, their desire to experiment more ardent. The fact that Germany had lost the war was of considerable relevance. There was the strong Jewish element, as so often in the forefront of avantgardism. But the role of the Jews in the visual arts was minute; Karl Hofer noted in a letter to a Nazi official in 1933: 'Next to the army no field was as *judenrein* as the visual arts.' Only a relatively small part of the German intelligentsia was in sympathy with the revolutionary artistic ideas, and some erstwhile revolutionaries later deserted the avant-garde.

The break in historical continuity was more palpably felt in Germany after 1918 than in other Western countries. But such breaks had occurred in various countries on previous occasions in history, without necessarily resulting in a cultural revolution. It was in all likelihood just a favourable constellation which made Weimar culture possible: an abundance of talent as well as of sources of conflict, combined with the political freedom which made experimentation possible. With all its defects the Weimar Republic was more sympathetic, or at least less antagonistic, to modernism than any other political system of the day. The preconditions for a cultural revolution existed in Germany at the time, which is not to say that it was bound to happen there and then.

6
Universities in Opposition

Weimar culture was conceived outside the schools and universities and it never penetrated the academic establishment to any depth. The prevailing mood in the universities was anti-republican almost from the very beginning; if academics supported Weimar it was usually in a half-hearted way. The Weimar age is of enduring interest because, with all its fads and absurdities, it witnessed the emergence of the first truly modern culture; German universities on the other hand were never hotbeds of revolutionary new ideas. True, the scientists were changing the world without realizing it, but there was nothing specifically German about their discoveries. Dialectical theology preoccupied some minds, *Wissenssoziologie* was debated by others, and existentialism intoxicated and confused some young philosophers in Freiburg, Heidelberg and Berlin. But at the time these were little more than storms in academic teacups; they proceeded, as the German saying goes, almost 'behind closed doors'; non-theologians, non-sociologists and non-philosophers became aware of these developments only years later.

The opposition of so many academics to the Weimar Republic and all it stood for does not imply that the great majority of professors were Nazis or Nazi sympathizers. On the contrary; among the historians and the philosophers, among the economists and sociologists, there were at most two or three party members, and these were marginal figures in their respective fields. (There was one prominent Nazi physicist and one mathematician.) Right-wing apologists have not failed to stress this fact, but the paradox is more apparent than real. While many professors did not fully identify with Nazism, in which they discovered various flaws, and which was anyway too radical and vulgar for them, their attitude to parliamentary democracy was one of disgust and open hostility; they ignored Hitler but attacked the Republic. If there was not a single Nazi among the history professors before 1933, there was not a single socialist either, and only a handful willing to defend the Republic against its detractors. The majority was reactionary *tout court*, the minority was *vernunftsrepublikanisch*, pro-republican because they accepted it as a political necessity, rather than out of instinct or deep moral conviction.

This split in the academic community dates back to the First World War, and in a deeper sense it has to be traced to an even earlier period. The German academics had by no means always been blind servants of autocracy, preachers of militarism and chauvinism. In the 1830s and 1840s they had been in the forefront of the struggle for freedom and democracy; by and large, it was only after 1871 that they made their peace with the establishment. In 1863 Du Bois Reymond, the famous physiologist, deplored the inferior quality of German revolvers when an attempt to assassinate Bismarck failed. A decade later he referred to German university professors as the intellectual bodyguard of the Hohenzollern. In their great majority the academics were *kaisertreu*, believed only in power politics and in Germany's civilizatory mission; their speeches on the Kaiser's birthday excelled in a jingoism which differed from that of the philistine only because they were replete with references to past history, philosophical allusions and a surfeit of Greek and Latin quotations. They were not necessarily members of the Conservative Party, but in their radical nationalism they sometimes went well beyond it. There were some left-of-centre critics but their impact was insignificant.

The outbreak of the First World War produced an orgy of chauvinism, and in July 1915, in the so-called Seeberg memorandum, 352 professors submitted an annexationist peace programme going far beyond the proposals of the government of the day. Belgium, it was argued, had no right to exist, large parts of France and Russia were to be incorporated, and unrestricted submarine warfare was to be declared forthwith, well before the military leadership decided on this dangerous course of action. Chauvinism also prevailed in the academic community in Britain and France, even in Russia and the United States, but the German intellectual war effort had an intensity unrivalled elsewhere. Later on, after the first flush of patriotic enthusiasm had disappeared, there was a parting of the ways. The moderates rallied and by 1917 their numbers were about equal to those of the extreme annexationists. Among them were many of the most respected intellectual figures of the day: Delbrück and Lujo Brentano, Max Weber and Troeltsch, Meinecke and Oncken. But the moderation of the moderates was relative; few of them believed in peace without any annexations, and even fewer supported a radical democratization of German domestic politics.

The military defeat and the revolution of 1918 were regarded by the overwhelming majority of German professors as an unprecedented disaster and they differed only as regards the explanations provided. Some argued that Germany's idealism and will to power had been wanting; the theologians, not surprisingly, argued that the German people had been punished for not taking its religion sufficiently seriously. Only a minority of moderates, such as Troeltsch, were willing to put much (or most) of the blame on the country's leaders, their policy of aggrandizement in foreign affairs and their unwillingness to carry out overdue reforms at home. Troeltsch believed that it was pointless to oppose 'world democracy' because it was the wave of the future; Meinecke maintained that any attempt to restore the old regime would divide the nation irrevocably. The Republic, according to this line of reasoning, was for Germany the least divisive political order; but it had not carried the day in the view of Meinecke and likeminded spirits because it was an irresistible force, it had prevailed simply because the old powers had collapsed. Meinecke was a *Vernunftsrepublikaner*; in a dialogue published not long after the end of the war he admitted that there was no warmth in his advocacy of democracy, only rational, utilitarian considerations. 'You have married the Republic without loving it', the other participant in the dialogue says accusingly of his friend.

Delbrück, another great historian and the editor of the

Preussische Jahrbücher, was similarly ambivalent in his attitude towards democracy and the Republic. During the war he had courageously attacked the Pan-Germans, but this did not make him an admirer of the Weimar constitution, nor, in particular, of the new parliamentarianism which he said was a breeding-ground for corruption. He sharply criticized the anti-patriotic character of the new regime as manifested, *inter alia*, in the abolition of the black-white-red banner. Max Scheler, a convert to Catholicism, had welcomed the war as a 'metaphysical awakening' and had been an ardent annexationist while the going was good. He accepted the Republic later on, but with even more reservations than Max Weber, who suggested a plebiscitarian *Führer* democracy which he thought would not have as many ill effects as parliamentarianism. Hans Nawiasky was a liberal Munich law professor who in later years became one of the chief targets of Nazi propaganda at his University. Yet comparing the constitution of 1871 with that of 1919, Nawiasky noted that while the former symbolized the achievement of the highest national aspirations, the Weimar constitution was a child born of sorrow in which no one rejoiced.

If those who accepted democracy were half-hearted in its defence, the former annexationists were beset by no scruples in ther unbridled campaign of vilification. Von Below, Dietrich Schäfer, Johannes Haller and others devoted much of their energy during the 1920s to the attempt to show that Germany, undefeated on the field of battle, had been stabbed in the back by defeatists and traitors. They attacked 'black' and 'red' internationalism and of course the Jews – everyone who had been an obstacle to victory. For without victory there was no power, and without power no culture, no prosperity, no national existence.

This then in briefest outline was the attitude of the right-wing nationalists in the academic community throughout the Weimar period. The Republic, democracy, liberalism were both the cause of Germany's downfall and the main obstacle to its revival as a major power. Many of these inveterate and un-compromising enemies of the new order hailed from families which under the monarchy had provided the manpower for the middle and higher ranks of officialdom; they belonged, in the words of one observer, to a caste which had become redundant and was doing its best to poison the political climate. The situation was anomalous in as much as the anti-republican professors were employees of the Republic. Yet, while insisting on every occasion on their rights and privileges, they were unwilling to concede to their employers even a minimum of loyalty.

The departments of history, law and German language and literature were among the staunchest bulwarks of the old order, with the Protestant theologians not far behind; the Catholics were on the whole less radical, many of them belonging to the Centre Party which was part of successive government coalitions. Philosophers and sociologists, with a few exceptions, kept out of the political battles. But even among the natural scientists, among geographers and professors of medicine, there were not a few who used every opportunity to attack the 'system' and to talk with nostalgia of the good old days. 18 January, the day the Second Reich was founded in 1871, was still celebrated in the universities, as was the anniversary of the battle of Sedan. With tears in their eyes and in trembling voices the patriotic professors mourned the horrible tragedy that had befallen the *Vaterland*; with sacred fervour they denounced the criminals responsible for the disaster and who now, to Germany's everlasting shame, constituted the government. True, the speeches usually ended on a note of confidence and reassurance: a great country like Germany could not be kept down for ever by the forces of evil at home and abroad; one day it would rise again. In 1925, when Reinhold Seeberg, the author of the annexationist memorandum of 1915, became rector of Berlin University, he composed the inscription for the memorial to the students killed in the war: *Invictis victi victuri* – to the undefeated, those who have been defeated but will be victorious again.

This, then, was the spirit prevailing in wide sections of the academic community, and it need hardly be stressed that a political orientation of this kind was invariably coupled with the strongest aversion to 'Weimar culture'. The very same professors who used the university as a forum to attack the new democratic order at the same time complained bitterly about what they called the progressive politicization of the university. Their own views on the state of the nation in general and the state of the universities in particular were, as they saw it, unpolitical because they were so completely self-evident; in a similar spirit, Thomas Mann had called his famous wartime tract *Betrachtungen eines Unpolitischen*. But the demands of democratic ministers of culture who wanted to appoint a few socialist professors, to establish several chairs of sociology, to democratize the rigidly hierarchical structure of the university, who suggested making higher education accessible to wider sections of the population – these were dangerous partisan views which threatened academic freedom. And so the tocsin was sounded: the government wanted to impose its views on the academic establishment. In fact the only censorship inside the universities was the one exerted by the professors themselves, and this was applied only vis-à-vis the left. In 1921, when the Freiburg legal philosopher Herman Kantorowicz criticized Bismarck and particularly the annexation of Alsace-Lorraine, he was immediately asked by the Freiburg senate to desist from 'any further political activity'. No right-winger, however extreme, was ever subjected to such sanctions.

The attitude of the mandarins towards the Republic's first minister of culture, Adolf Hoffmann, was one of open contempt, because he had been a mere manual worker (albeit a printer) and because his spelling was erratic. The second, Konrad Haenisch, a right-wing Social Democrat and a mere journalist, was not held in high esteem either, though he went out of his way to appease the conservatives. The third, C. H. Becker, could not easily be dismissed as an illiterate meddler for he was a colleague, an orientalist of world renown. For this reason he was hated all the more as a renegade who wanted to destroy the hallowed traditional structure of the university. Becker moreover had dared suggest that standards at the universities had fallen and that arid specialization had taken over. It was an obvious case of fouling one's own nest.

The professors were opposed to university reform for various reasons: it would have affected the traditional monopoly of the *Bildungsbürgertum*; inside the universities it would have broken the stranglehold of the full professors, relatively few in number, who were running the universities and on whose goodwill everyone else was dependent. These *Ordinarien* were the main advocates of self-rule. Their attitude was once compared by the philosopher Jaspers to the (territorial) behaviour of the monkeys on the palm trees in the sacred forest at Benares. Each monkey had his own palm tree and to the outside observer the whole scene seemed very peaceful indeed. But the moment one tried to climb up another's tree, all hell would break loose, coconuts would fly through the air and there would be general mayhem. A professor would not as a rule intervene in the affairs of a colleague, on the tacit assumption that this would guarantee the fullest freedom of action for himself. It will be easily understood that Becker's plan met with stubborn opposition. If the minister argued that state and society had changed and that the university could not forever remain out of step, the professors countered that the old university was German in spirit and furthermore had functioned well. Why should it try to adapt itself to the new system, which was neither German nor workable?

The extreme enemies of democracy in the university were a minority, but their shrill denunciations seemed to dominate the scene. The majority was unpolitical, which usually implied an instinctive anti-republican bias. In their rare public appearances the defenders of the new state lacked conviction and fighting spirit; they were always willing to compromise.

Thus when a pro-republican association of university teachers was founded in 1926, Friedrich Meinecke made a plea for co-operation 'in national harmony with our reactionary colleagues'. This desire for tolerance and collaboration was not however shared by the other camp, and the association was short-lived. There were a few men of staunch democratic convictions such as Gustav Radbruch, a law professor who later became minister of justice, the political scientist Hermann Heller, as well as some sociologists and economists; most of them were Jews and were thus doubly exposed to the attacks of right-wing professors and students. Through their writings and lectures the reactionary professors exerted considerable influence on several generations of students. Men in their fifties and sixties, they were products of the Wilhelmian period, unable and unwilling to adjust to a new era. The students had grown up in very different times, and if Weimar literature were a good barometer they should have revolted against authority. But it was only on the stage, not in the real world of the Weimar Republic, that the sons were killing the fathers. In so far as the students were not apathetic, interested mainly in finishing their studies as quickly as possible, their ideological orientation resembled that of their teachers. Only towards the end of the Republic, under the impact of the economic and political crisis, did more radical views prevail, and then reactionary gurus were overtaken on the right by the more aggressive Nazis.

The following table shows that there were substantial fluctuations in university enrolment:

1907:	63,000
1913:	78,000
1919:	111,000
1923:	125,000
1925:	89,000
1928:	112,000
1931:	138,000

There was, naturally, a sharp decline in the number of students during the war, and an equally natural steep rise immediately after, but it is surprising that the number should have fallen during the years of economic stabilization. The number of women students grew slowly, reaching 15 per cent of the total by the early 1930s. Before the war a substantial part of the students had come from rich families, whereas after 1918 the overwhelming majority came from middle-class homes. Since the middle classes were profoundly affected by the postwar economic upheavals, the life of the average student in the early 1920s was very different from the carefree existence led by previous generations. Suffice it to say that the average income of a German student in 1921 was 4,000 marks, whereas the minimum needed at the time to make ends meet was, according to official statistics, 8,200 marks. A survey disclosed that three thousand cases of tuberculosis had been detected among students. For a great many of them the main concern during the immediate postwar period was to find a room and to get at least one hot meal a day. Paraphrasing Brecht, they could have said: *Erst kommt das Fressen, dann die Politik.*

Before the war a working student had been a rare exception. In the early 1920s on the other hand, and again during the depression, the *Werkstudent*, washing dishes, working on building sites or as a mechanic, became a frequent sight. In the summer vacation more than half of the students went out to work not because they were attracted by manual labour but simply because they needed the money.

Given the change in the social composition of the student population, and the widespread poverty, it may seem puzzling that every other student should still have belonged to a 'corporation'. The corporations were divided into those which engaged in duels and those which did not; in a bygone age they had been the symbol of 'feudal' student life, of beer-drinking, various curious customs, and substantial monthly remittances from home. After the war the character of the corporations underwent change and their importance in student life decreased appreciably. There were few working-class students; Haenisch's statement soon after the war that he was aware of only three such students in all of Germany was an exaggeration; there were in fact a few thousand. But it is true that students from low-income groups (workers, peasants, poorly-paid state employees) did not constitute more than 5 per cent.

The first reaction of most students to military defeat and revolution was one of utter bewilderment. Initially, even the conservatives among them seemed willing to give the Republic a try and favoured the convocation of the (Weimar) Constituent Assembly. But debate over the terms of the Versailles treaty brought many of them into sharp conflict with the new regime. Moreover the Burschenschaft, the main student organization, disapproved of the new black-red-gold banner of the Republic, which was more than a little paradoxical because these had been for a century the Burschenschaft's own colours, the symbol of the struggle for German unity.

In 1919–20 the students were called upon to join the border defence units in eastern Germany to prevent the seizure of German territory by the Poles. Noske, who signed the appeal on behalf of the government, stressed that the German people was fighting for its national existence; unfortunately it would be impossible to establish special student units, for the workers deeply distrusted the students, who were thought to be anti-working-class in their outlook. Noske argued that these prejudices were unjustified but subsequent events spoke against him, for most students volunteered for the Free Corps and other right-wing law-and-order groups. The swing back to the right was unmistakable. At the second national students' convention in Göttingen (July 1920), the *völkische* students were already the strongest group; the same year the Burschenschaft, once a liberal, even revolutionary force, adopted the Aryan paragraph, excluding Jews from its ranks. Subsequently the Gymnasts' and the choral societies followed suit. If none the less the more extreme demands of the right were not accepted by the rest, it was mainly due to the war veterans, who were on the whole a restraining influence in student politics – very much in contrast to the younger students, who had just missed the war and wanted to compensate for this by a display of super-patriotism. By 1923 most of the ex-soldiers had graduated and it was left to the small and not very active republican student associations and the larger Catholic student groups to oppose the activities of the anti-republican camp.

Since the views of the anti-democratic elements in the universities did not differ in essentials from those of the right wing in general, a detailed description does not seem to be called for. Typical for the philosophy of these circles was their extreme irrationalism, the belief that 'scientific objectivity' in politics was as reprehensible as socialism or pacifism, the assumption that the country needed fanatical conviction rather than objective analysis. It was only logical that many students should decide not to participate in the annual celebration (on 11 August) of the Weimar constitution, for 'we combat the constitution, we do not celebrate it'. Not only the 'stab in the back' myth, but the call for a *Führer* and a *Reich* was sounded among the students earlier and with greater shrillness than in the country at large.

Attacks on Jewish students occurred at various German universities after 1919; they were neither widespread nor large-scale in comparison with the academic pogroms which took place in Austria and some East European countries. But Germany after all was not Rumania; nothing like this had happened before the war; some explained it with reference to the general deterioration in standards of civilized behaviour, others pointed to the growing number of Jewish students (including some from Eastern Europe) and to the fear on the part of non-Jewish students of stiff competition in their subsequent careers. The real reasons were probably more complex for, paradoxically, the pro-Nazi vote was strongest in universities in which there were few if any Jews (such as Greifswald, Rostock or Erlangen). Again, within the universities the Nazis scored highest in the very faculties in which there were hardly any 'non-Aryans' (forestry, veterinary medicine, etc.). But whatever the reason, antisemitism was deeply rooted. Even the Catholic student organizations decided to adopt the Aryan paragraph, and it was only as the result of considerable pressure on the part of the clergy that it was partly revoked. A curious compromise was reached: Catholics were not permitted to attack other Catholics because they were of Jewish origin, but neither were they under any obligation to accept them as members of their association.

The radicalization of the student body manifested itself in many ways. When Walther Rathenau, the foreign minister of the Republic, was killed in 1922, many students and their organizations expressed sympathy with the assassins. Demonstrations were directed against Jewish and left-wing professors because they had spoken without due respect of those who had fallen in the war (Gumbel at Heidelberg), had attacked Hindenburg, who was not even president at the time (Lessing at Braunschweig), or had advocated pacifism (Dehn at Halle). The victims of these attacks could not count on the support of the academic authorities or of their colleagues, for (it was argued) it had been their own fault for provoking the students by expressing views bound to offend every German patriot.

By 1927 the patience of the government had run out and it decided to withdraw recognition from the Deutsche Studentenschaft, the largest of the student associations, not because it openly defied the republican institutions but because of the violent character of its demonstrations against its opponents. The Nazis were not even the dominant group at the time, but just one of several right-wing extremist factions. Hitler's followers emerged as the strongest political force among the students only after 1929. In the 1929 elections to the student bodies the Nazis first gained the majority in Erlangen and in eight other German universities, not counting Vienna. At ten more universities they attracted more votes than any other list. Their success was all the more remarkable because their student association had no more than three thousand members at the time. The 'silent majority' did not bother to take part in the elections; in most universities not more than 30–35 per cent of all students voted, and in some the percentage was even lower. However, militants usually prosper at a time of crisis; the right-wing radicals came to dominate the scene in the German universities to the extent that the others were unorganized and so, in the final analysis, did not count.

Having said all this, it remains to be noted that for every lecture that was disrupted, a thousand took place without any disturbance. It was perfectly possible to study at a German university during the 1920s without ever coming across manifestations of chauvinism and racialism. Professors prepared their lectures and busied themselves with their research, students did their homework, or refrained from doing it because they were engaged in more rewarding activities. Even though the university establishment was on the whole reactionary in character, the universities were not political organizations and most of their time and energy was devoted to non-political activity. It was only on certain occasions that the deep-seated hostility to the system appeared in the open. Towards the end of the first postwar decade, under the impact of the political and economic crisis, the universities became the scene of violent demonstrations. There was no battle; the contest had been won by the Nazis hands down.

*   *   *

No account of cultural life in Germany in the 1920s can afford to ignore the work done in the institutions of higher learning. But a detailed and systematic survey of this kind would be largely irrelevant in the context of the present study, which deals with the specific character of German culture at the time rather than the research done, *grosso modo*, all over the world in academies, universities, laboratories and libraries, from Harvard to Tokyo. German astronomers did important work during the 1920s: Baade discovered Hidalgo, the planetoid farthest from the Sun, and the Zeiss planetarium was built in Jena. O. H. Warburg did pioneering work on the physiology of tumours and Domagk was the first to develop the sulfonamides in 1932. There was a great tradition in these fields, and if the war had interrupted research and resources had been diverted, there was every reason to assume that work would be continued with undiminished vigour after 1918. Advances were made in astronomy, medicine and other fields, but they are outside the compass of our study. But even if the historian restricts his field of vision to those breakthroughs which were of more than specialized interest, he faces certain difficulties which are well-nigh impossible to overcome. Even if he could analyse the ideas of Husserl and Heidegger, of Planck, Einstein and Heisenberg and a great many others in a few pages, he cannot even with a minimum degree of assurance indicate where some of these ideas fitted into the general picture, which for want of a better term is usually called the *Zeitgeist*. For unfortunately it cannot be taken for granted that Weimar culture was a giant jigsaw-puzzle in which all pieces, ordered with patience and ingenuity, will eventually fall into place. There were common patterns and links, but there was also disorder and asymmetry; and if some of the pieces cannot in the end be made to fit a general pattern, it may not be the fault of the historian. Perhaps there was not one *Zeitgeist* but several?

German historiography may be a good starting-point for our *tour d'horizon*, not because of outstanding individual achievements or because the profession as a whole initiated revolutionary new departures. The state of historiography is of interest because it shows most clearly the way its practitioners had been affected by the outcome of the war and reflected so accurately the malaise of the unloved Republic. Not that the German historians were engaged in writing the history of their own time; with one exception – the ideological struggle against the Versailles treaty – it is difficult to think of major contributions to contemporary history. German historiography in the 1920s was still distinguished by a preoccupation with the past of its own country; moreover, few historians were interested in anything but political and cultural history. There was no opposition in principle to economic and social history; it simply did not interest most of the leading historians. By and large, the study of social factors was thought to be the domain of sociology, which, some historians conceded, would perhaps one day be able to develop certain general concepts concerning society and social history and thus act as a corrective to a historiography traditionally preoccupied with the unique and the specific.

The defeat of 1918 was a great blow even to those historians to whom it had not come as a surprise. The idea that all may not have been well in Wilhelmian Germany, that the defeat may not have been an accident and that the recent course of German history had to be reconsidered in a new light, was faced by many of them only with great reluctance. Leading historians such as Erich Marcks, Georg von Below, Dietrich Schäfer and their pupils continued to maintain that Bismarck had been absolutely right, that his prescriptions and method for the unification of Germany had been the best if not the only possible ones, that Germany's great misfortune had been its internal division into dozens of small principalities and its resulting weakness. They found that no major mistakes had been committed in the conduct of German foreign policy; the outbreak of the war was mainly, if not wholly the fault of Germany's enemies, who had followed with suspicion and envy the emergence of a major power in the heart of Europe. These historians glorified the state, *raison d'état*, power (which meant, above all, military power); they believed with Ranke in the primacy of foreign policy, regarding war and conquest as inevitable and not undesirable concomitants in the development of a nation. Their attitude to democracy and the Republic was wholly negative. If they drew a conclusion from the war and its outcome, it was simply that Germany had not been relentless enough in waging war, and that as a result of disunity and treasonable activities the home front had not been sufficiently strong.

Another group of historians, which included Meinecke, Hermann Oncken and Otto Hintze, did not share their colleagues' blind admiration of Bismarck, nor did they idealize the Wilhelmian state. When Meinecke wrote his great book on *Staatsräson* he did not play down the excesses of Prussian militarism. Some of his colleagues also recognized the fact that the Germans with all their virtues had shown a regrettable lack of civic courage: the willingness and ability to stand up, when necessary, against officialdom, the establishment, popular opinion, however unpopular such a stand might be and whatever its consequences. These historians freely admitted that the old elite, with all their sterling qualities, their sense of duty and their incorruptibility, had all too often shown a deplorable lack of initiative, imagination, independent thought, and were on the whole men with rather limited mental horizons. However, the self-criticism of these historians did not necessarily make them any more well-disposed towards France, Britain and Germany's other adversaries. They too mourned Germany's abject fall; they still believed in the continuity of German history and thought that the catastrophe had been caused by a concatenation of tragic circumstances. The basic difference between them and the revanchist historians was that they accepted the Weimar Republic, whereas their colleagues opposed it as an artificial, 'unhistorical', anti-German creation.

It is difficult to think of any major left-wing contribution to the historical debates of the period. History did not figure high on the scale of priorities of intellectuals tending to the left, and in any case the historical establishment would have resented (or ignored) any intervention from these quarters. Towards the end of the decade a few younger historians made their heretical views known, but they had not the slightest impact on the historical profession. In so far as there was a revisionist approach, a tendency to debunk the heroes of yesteryear, it manifested itself in popular biographies, which had an astonishing success during the 1920s. This literature, needless to say, was rejected out of hand by conservatives and historical materialists alike. Thus the conservative historians pursued their traditional preoccupations in relative quiet, with hardly any outside interference and with a minimum of controversy inside the profession.

If German historiography during the 1920s was, on the whole, inward-looking, and thus of only limited interest to foreign historians unless Germany happened to be their special field of study, art history was cosmopolitan in outlook. This discipline, heir to a rich tradition from Winckelmann onward, continued to flourish during the period. True, there was nothing specifically 'Weimarian' about it; the leading teachers in the 1920s such as Wölfflin or Goldschmidt were sexagenerians, and the Warburg Institute in Hamburg, which became one of the main centres of study in the field, had been founded by the heir to a banking fortune well before the First World War. The history of art is a fairly specialized subject, and in the hands of some of its practitioners it became esoteric as well. Even in this field the political storms of the age were felt from time to time. Racial doctrines made certain inroads, giving rise to such questions as: was it the 'Dinaric blood' in Albrecht Dürer which attracted him to Italian art? The Wölfflin school was mainly interested in accounting for stylistic change, whereas the circle around the Warburg Institute concentrated their work on the survival of antique elements in medieval art (Warburg, Saxl, Panofsky), which led them to another interesting area, namely the connexions between 'Northern' and 'Southern' art, more specifically the presence of non-Italian elements in the Italian Renaissance. These studies, interesting as they were, were ultimately less significant than their general endeavour to extend the frontiers of art history, investigating topics which had been ignored hitherto in professional circles: mythology, astrology, magic and the occult sciences in general. This novel approach attracted philosophers and psychologists; Cassirer's studies on mythical thought and symbolic forms were largely written at the Warburg Institute. When the Nazis came to power their purge of German museums was directed above all against the 'decadents'. But the history of art was also affected, and there was a mass exodus of art historians, Jewish and non-Jewish. Britain and the United States benefited from the migration and the golden age of German art history came to a sudden end.

*   *   *

The more adventurous spirits in the universities preferred sociology to history, for this, to use a later idiom, was where the action was, or at least the great debates. Germany had been one of the cradles of modern sociology and the years just before and after the First World War were the most productive in the history of the discipline. The first convention of German sociologists took place in Frankfurt in 1910 with Simmel, Sombart, Tönnies, Max Weber and Troeltsch among the principal speakers. The work of these leading sociologists largely belongs to the prewar era: Simmel died in 1918, Max Weber in 1920, Troeltsch in 1923, Max Scheler in 1926; Tönnies's and Sombart's more important works had also been published before 1914. But Weber's great work, *Wirtschaft und Gesellschaft*, was published only posthumously (in 1922); and in general, the seminal works of the first generation of German sociologists reached a wider public only after the war. The debates sparked off by their writings did not come to an end during the Weimar period, but, as in the case of Max Weber, continue to the present day. Most striking about the founding-fathers of German sociology was their breadth of interest compared with the specialization which prevailed subsequently. Max Weber was equally at home in history, law, economics, philosophy and theology; he wanted to understand how modern society had come into being and how it functioned, and narrow specialization was obviously not the right approach to that end. None of the founding-fathers had been trained as sociologists; like Freud, they were the creators of a new field of study and research. In some cases their pioneering work was done outside the academies: Max Weber, Scheler and Vierkandt did much of their important work in the seclusion of their studies because each, for different reasons, was for long periods prevented from teaching at a university. Scheler and Troeltsch were philosophers with a special interest in theology; Simmel was also a philosopher, but inclined towards literature; Sombart's and Brinckmann's main interest was economic history; Vierkandt had started his career as a geographer and ethnographer, Franz Oppenheimer as a physician. This may explain the great sweep of their works but also a certain amateurish naiveté, the belief that they had discovered the key to an understanding of society – or even to remodelling it: Tönnies with his *Gemeinschaft* and *Gesellschaft*, Oppenheimer with his constant emphasis on ground rents, Vierkandt with the 'group'. Seen in historical perspective, their discoveries were of limited value only, which does not mean that they should be belittled. For these were early days in the annals of sociology, when all kinds of approaches and avenues had to be explored, and when no one could be certain whether any one of them would lead into a blind alley or herald a major advance.

Sociology in Germany, more than in any other country, was in its early phase preoccupied with (or, as others thought, plagued by) philosophical problems. The very substance and function of sociology was in dispute. Was it to be *ancilla historiae*, the servant of history? Was it to be an independent scholarly discipline or a branch of the philosophy of culture? Was it to move in the direction of pure theory or towards empirical research without any specific theoretical basis? Sociology was under attack not only by the historians but also by philosophers such as Dilthey, who called it a 'gigantic chimera' (*Traumidee*). Since the German sociologists took this critique more seriously than their French and British counterparts, they became entangled in unending and often inconclusive debates about subject-matter and methodology, and about the essential nature of knowledge in general.

Being the heirs to a great philosophical tradition, the Germans refused to find out by trial and error whether a particular method worked; this would have been vulgar, philistine positivism. They had to know *a priori* whether it could work and this was the origin of the famous *Methodenstreit*, the dispute on method that was to last for decades and which, in the words of Schumpeter, was so much wasted energy. Schumpeter may have exaggerated the harmful effects of these philosophical disputations. They would have been of value if they had established no more than the fact that there are various sociologies, just as there is more than one way to philosophize.

Of the great German sociologists of the first third of the century Max Weber was by far the most important. His work on the spirit of capitalism, on the struggle for power in the modern state, on political leadership (charisma) and types of authority was highly original and stimulated further research: the use of 'ideal types' has become part and parcel of modern sociology. But above all he was at the centre of the dispute about 'value-free social science'. Weber's demand that the social sciences should maintain absolute objectivity struck many of his contemporaries as a contradiction in terms, for was it not beyond dispute that the social sciences differed in their basic character from the natural sciences? They pointed out that Weber himself did not renounce political activity (he accepted, not without a struggle, the Weimar Republic), even though he could not prove scientifically that his position was the right one. Could it really be argued that politics, science and morals were totally unrelated things? And how could the social responsibility of sociology be asserted if it was to be value-free? Weber's dilemma has remained that of successive generations of sociologists who agreed with him that sociology should not be a speculative philosophy of history, and that it could not be a science without applying scientific standards. But on the other hand experience, common-sense and the exigencies of life had shown that a 'polytheism of values' would lead to dangerous relativism and ultimately to anarchy.

Ten years after Weber's death Karl Mannheim, in his *Ideology and Utopia*, tried to resolve the dilemma. If, according to Marx and Freud, to Bergson, Pareto and other leading students of man and society of the past century, all knowledge was tied to one's class situation (or alternatively to one's sub-conscious), there was no objective truth and there was little purpose in pursuing rational study except perhaps in the natural sciences. Mannheim's ambition was the wholly laudable one of trying to transcend relativism by incorporating the irrational factors into a new framework. Basing himself on Marx and Weber, and developing certain ideas first advanced by Max Scheler, he conceded that thought was existentially connected with social position. Everyone sees only that part of the societal entity towards which he is orientated anyway; ideologies are superstructures, in the Marxian sense. If intellectual activity is simply a response to a political situation, then one *Weltanschauung* is as good as another and it is simply a matter of taste which one is preferred, just as children (or adults, for that matter) may prefer one kind of ice-cream to another without being able to account objectively for their preference.

Mannheim thought he had found an ingenious way out of the dilemma, for there was one stratum in society which had no clear, distinctive class interests but was free-floating – the intelligentsia. The intelligentsia alone could study reality objectively; it alone could see the truth, the total social reality. This concept of the sociology of knowledge was attacked from both ends of the political spectrum – from the right because it led to moral relativism and because it was just a rehash of historical materialism; from the left because it had the additional drawback that it undercut Marx's position, turning Marxism into an ideology rather than a science – unless one was willing to interpret Marxism as a movement of the intelligentsia rather than the working class.

Different schools coexisted in German sociology during the Weimar period. Almost every university practised a different approach or, at any rate, put the emphasis on a different aspect. Leopold von Wiese's school in Cologne was concerned with the analysis of interpersonal relations (*Beziehungslehre*), whereas Alfred Weber in Heidelberg practised *Kultursoziologie*. Nor was empirical research altogether neglected; important contributions were made to the sociology of the family (Albert Salomon), of social classes (Geiger) and of social psychology. Most German sociologists of the younger generation gravitated towards the left, but their political impact was virtually nil, partly because of the adverse climate prevailing in the universities, partly because of their own, sometimes excessive, caution. Above all their influence did not spread because, at a time of crisis, students looked for certainties rather than possibilities. A leading sociologist argued in later years, not without justice, that it was not really necessary for the Nazis to kill sociology in 1933; it had already reached a dead end.

Not all sociologists of the time were influenced by Marxism or, like Max Weber, engaged in a constant dialogue with it. Sombart had begun his career as a Marxist *tout court*, but in later years became the protagonist of a 'German Socialism'. Hans Freyer advocated a revolution from the right (the title of his best-known book) in which blood and race figured prominently. Tönnies's *Kulturpessimismus* made his views acceptable to the Nazis as well. But in Nazi eyes all sociology was *a priori* suspect. They dissolved the Sociological Association, and ignored the claims for the promotion of a specifically 'German sociology', even if, as some zealous advocates of the idea suggested, antisemitism was to be its main content.

*   *   *

In philosophy as in most other fields the main issues that agitated minds during the 1920s antedated the war. But the crisis of philosophy was incomparably deeper than the problems facing sociology. The sociologists quarrelled about a great many issues, including some fundamental ones, but they shared a common frame of reference. The philosophical schools, on the other hand, had moved so far apart that they no longer shared common concerns or even spoke a common language. There was no point in debating interpretations because there was no agreement on what questions philosophers should deal with.

The philosophies of the early twentieth century could in some respects be classified in terms of 'left' and 'right', with the protagonists of rationalism and enlightenment on one side and its critics on the other. Seen in this perspective, Neo-Kantianism would be in one camp and *Lebensphilosophie* in the other. But such a classification is of doubtful value, for the categories of philosophy are not those of politics. There were Hegelians at both extremes of the political spectrum; some existentialists found themselves drawn to Hitler, others, later on, to Stalin.

The most influential school at the time was that of the pheno-menologists. Husserl, its founder, wanted initially to establish a rigorous, strictly scientific theory of explanation, which would do away both with psychology (as it had been previously understood) and with empiricism:

> Phenomenology denotes a new, descriptive, philosophical method, which since the concluding years of the last century has established (1) an *a priori* psychological discipline, able to provide the only secure basis on which a strong empirical psychology can be built, and (2) a universal philosophy which can supply an organum for the methodical revision of all the sciences. . . . Thus the antique conception of philo-sophy as the universal science, philosophy in the Platonic, philosophy in the Cartesian sense, that shall embrace all knowledge, is once more justly restored.

Phenomenology maintained that the essential content of reality (*das Wesen*) was in the phenomena, in consciousness, and could therefore be investigated and understood by looking at the essence of consciousness (*Wesensschau*). But such analysis was of necessity impressionistic and intuitive; and since it was impos-sible to gain apodictic, *a priori* knowledge by way of intuition, Husserl was led into a never-ending search for the 'things', while many of his pupils moved farther and farther away from the quest for scientific explanation. Husserl continued to believe up to the end of his long life (he died in 1937) in the overriding importance of a rational philosophy, whereas the existentialists, his erstwhile pupils, much to his dismay gave up any claim to philosophy as a science.

Phenomenology exerted a considerable influence on psy-chology, and to a lesser extent on sociology; it paved the way for existentialism through its emphasis on 'being', which gradu-ally became a 'science of being'. For existentialism man, not his

ideas, was the centre of philosophical investigation; it dealt with
the relationship between man and his world. From Nietzsche it
took the idea of history as a repetition of things that had already
happened, from Kierkegaard the pessimistic-tragic element
(discarding religion in the process), the idea of 'life unto death'
and the preoccupation with *Angst* as a negative solution for
existence. While much of previous German philosophy had
been largely concerned with the problem of man in history and
the idea of freedom, for German existentialists there remained
very little freedom of choice for man, at most an advocacy of
heroic behaviour in a world that was essentially without meaning or purpose. Such scepticism led to the insight that in life
everything is possible and nothing is possible, and that real
freedom begins only with death. A philosophy of this kind,
devoid of constant values and certainties, was heady wine for
young students, who listened in their hundreds to Heidegger's
Freiburg lectures (his *Sein und Zeit* was published in 1927). In
many ways this message – or the assertion that there could be
no message – was more attractive, more in line with the general
intellectual climate than the quest for truth as practised by
other, more old-fashioned philosophers. But once Heidegger
and other philosophers had reached the conclusion that the
real and only subject of philosophy was the human condition,
the borderline between philosophy and other intellectual
concerns – such as poetry and theology – was effectively elimi-
nated, because they too shared the preoccupation with the
human condition. Heidegger did not deny this, frequently
pointing to the close relationship between philosophy and
poetry, for about being, he conceded, one could learn more
from the poets than from most philosophers. At this point the
end of philosophy as traditionally understood and pursued was
in sight, and some Marxists were not slow to contend that the
poverty of philosophy was merely the reflection of the bankruptcy of bourgeois society and its impending doom. *Lebensphilosophie*, Georg Lukács claimed, was the ruling ideology of
Imperial Germany; Scheler he considered the philosopher of
'relative stabilization', whereas Heidegger and Jaspers, who
continued this tradition, represented the Ash Wednesday of
'parasitic subjectivism', mirroring the chaos and impotence of
bourgeois society at the end of its tether. Such claims need

hardly be taken literally, for Scheler outlined his ideas well before stabilization set in, and Heidegger's main work was published well before the depression.

But perhaps the philosophers were seers with a heightened awareness of the shape of things to come? This is to attribute to the existentialist philosophers a measure of foresight which they clearly lacked. Heidegger was attracted by Nazism, at least for a while; Jaspers was a liberal of sorts subject to violent political aberrations (especially after 1945) which had nothing whatever to do with existentialism. Even the argument that German existential philosophy paved the way for fascist irrationalism contains no more than a small grain of truth. Nazism, like all other totalitarian movements, had no use for negative nihilistic philosophy; it needed positive, optimistic, 'heroic' ideas. Nazi ideology, in so far as there was such a thing, was based on belief and certainty, whereas existentialism rested precisely on unbelief and uncertainty. Heidegger greatly influenced young students of philosophy at a time of crisis by generating a great deal of excitement and by promising (as one critic put it) to accomplish what Western philosophy since Aristotle had been unable to achieve: to penetrate to the heart of Being. Of course he could not fulfil his promise; his main work remained a fragment, the second part of *Sein und Zeit* was never published: 'The fascination of his lectures and his books is due in no small measure to the way in which he manages to keep alive the hope that in just a few more pages, or surely before the course is over, he may see something that even now reduces any other enterprise to insignificance' (Walter Kaufmann).

Generalizations about existentialism are bound to be inaccurate and to a certain extent unfair, for there were (and are) different varieties of existentialism. In fact both Jaspers and Heidegger, in later years at any rate, refused to consider themselves 'existentialists', a term which had been coined in 1929 by Fritz Heinemann, who did not himself belong to that school.

Heidegger and Jaspers were for a time on friendly terms but broke off relations later on. Despite the similarity of their ideas, they hardly ever referred to each other in their published works. While their style is equally obscure, Heidegger was a teacher of genius whereas Jaspers, plagued by ill-health all his life, devoted more time to writing than to teaching. Existentialism, to summarize, was a reaction against a mechanistic interpretation of the world. It led to a highly individualistic philosophy which expressed itself in a highly abstruse language and had no hope to offer mankind. From such a philosophy, naturally, the Kantians were bound to dissent; some of them countered by presenting 'neo-humanism' as an alternative to existentialism. The Hegelians, too, were in disagreement. Some younger neo-Hegelians such as Herbert Marcuse tried for a while to provide a synthesis of Marx and Heidegger, something which Sartre later tried to achieve with equal lack of success. Lastly, there was a new trend emerging, logical positivism; the attitudes and preoccupations of its followers (such as the analysis of language) were as remote from the pursuits of traditional philosophy as existentialism itself.

The confusion prevailing in German philosophy towards the end of the Weimar era is neatly reflected in a little book, *Die Philosophie der Gegenwart in Deutschland*, written by August Messer, the holder of the chair of philosophy in Giessen. This was the most widely-read short survey; by 1934 some forty thousand copies had been published. Of its 120-odd pages, fewer than half were devoted to 'scientific philosophy' – including Spengler (who got three pages) and Cassirer (who got half a line). The rest of the book deals with theology as well as such 'philosophers' as Walther Rathenau and Hermann Graf Keyserling, with theosophy and spiritualism (ten pages) and, of course, Adolf Hitler (four pages). The philosophical scene towards the end of the Weimar Republic resembled the building of the Tower of Babel, with a great deal of commotion but no visible progress. The great counter-movement against positivism and historicism which had started several decades earlier had ended in a blind alley, but it was still the most popular and widespread school, and the philosophers who did not subscribe to this doctrine were on the whole on the defensive. The neo-Kantians had a certain impact on those specializing in the history of philosophy (Cassirer), the philosophy of law (Kelsen and others) and education (Natorp). Leonard Nelson, professor in Göttingen, had his neo-Kantian school and a faithful following among students, some of whom were to establish a radical socialist group in the 1930s (ISK). Towards the end of the decade there were signs that the pendulum was slowly swinging away again from irrationalism and the preoccupation with metaphysics. In 1929 the Vienna Circle published its first manifesto, proclaiming that the so-called problems with which their German colleagues were concerned were the product of semantic confusion and that a totally new philosophy was needed for specific purposes such as the clarification of methodology in the different sciences. During the early days most members of the Vienna Circle tended to the left, but not too much should be made of this fact for it was in all probability a coincidence unconnected with their philosophy. Hegelianism also experienced a revival at the time, manifesting itself in the establishment in 1930 of a World Hegel Association; there was a Hegel congress in Berlin in 1931 and again in Bonn in 1933. In general, however, German philosophy was showing signs of exhaustion; the age of the great systems was long past; the heritage of classical philosophy had been put to good use, but by and large it no longer seemed relevant to contemporary preoccupations.

*   *   *

It is not easy to think of any major new ideas in the field of political science and economics which emanated from Germany during the Weimar period; cynics may well argue that considering the state of German politics and the German economy at the time, this was no mere coincidence. There were not a few distinguished German economists but there was no specific 'German school' such as there had been fifty years earlier. Of those teaching at German universities at the time, Schumpeter was probably the most enterprising and original spirit. But he was a product of Vienna, which as a centre of economic thought far surpassed Germany, and he moved on to America even before Hitler came to power.

The systematic study of politics was not yet established as an academic discipline, even though a Hochschule für Politik had been founded in 1920, and three years later in Hamburg an institute devoted to the study of international relations came into existence. The Hochschule was an altogether admirable enterprise: while preserving strict neutrality it was, for once, a neutrality which fully accepted the republican order. Alone among institutes of higher learning, it opened its gates to students who had not graduated from high school, and so attracted young trade union officials and other students who would not otherwise have found their way to a German university. Among its lecturers and graduates there were not a few who became well-known political scientists and historians in later years (including Arnold Wolfert, Arnold Bergsträsser, Hajo Holborn, Sigmund and Franz Neumann). Significantly, many of them emigrated after 1933. With all this, it is not possible to identify any revolutionary contribution to knowledge made by the Hochschule; its main importance was that of a successful educational institution rather than an important centre of advanced study.

The conservative academics who were suspicious of sociology were naturally even more opposed to giving politics the status of a fully-fledged academic discipline; it could be argued in retrospect that their misgivings were not altogether misplaced. The first systematic exposition of 'theoretical politics' in Germany was provided not by a professor but by a journalist, Adolf Grabowski, who was also the editor of the journal of the early Politologists. Karl Haushofer in Munich, who introduced politics into the university by way of political geography (*Geopolitik*), had fewer obstacles to overcome; he had been a general before he became a professor and the orientation of his new school was *bien-pensant*, safely right of centre.

* * *

In recent times theological disputes have been of little if any interest to the non-specialist, unless they impinged directly on politics. German Protestantism in the 1920s was an exception, for in no other church were established beliefs and practices more radically challenged. Catholicism was conservative, unyielding in its outlook; its spiritual leaders did not see the need for a Catholic philosophy except perhaps as a polemical instrument against Protestantism. 'Modernism' in all its forms had been condemned in the encyclical *Pascendi Dominici gregis* (1907) which left independent Catholic thinkers little if any freedom of thought and action. They reacted by turning their attention to topics other than religion; if they persevered, their books were put on the Index (Hermann Schall); in extreme cases they were excommunicated (Josef Wittig).

Protestant thinkers were much freer to express their views, since there was no central authority to condemn heretics. The discussion was sparked off in 1918 with the publication of *Der Römerbrief* by Karl Barth, at that time a little-known Swiss pastor. It was a book not easy to read, full of philosophical and literary allusions, of negations and paradoxical statements. Some of the early critics regarded it as no more than a mani-festation of Expressionism in theology, a fashionable reversion to irrationalism, a reflection of the general climate of crisis. But Barth's book, and his subsequent writings, while influenced no doubt by the war and the postwar despair, was much more than an intellectual fashion. It inaugurated a relentless attack on scientific theology as practised for almost a century, an on-slaught on the liberal Protestantism which had tried to build bridges between science and religion, between reason and revelation, between ethics and God. The new dialectical theology (or 'theology of crisis') was fundamentalist in char-acter; it put all the emphasis on faith, on the imperfection of human beings, on the abyss between God and man which could be crossed only by revelation, not by reason; by God but never by man. Human endeavours, even the most noble and praise-worthy, even man's highest cultural achievements, were sinful, afflicted by God's wrath and malediction. There was hope for mankind only through God's Grace. This approach would have taken Protestantism back to its origins, to Luther, which was indeed Barth's intention. But there was one decisive differ-ence: while Luther had preached submission to established authority in worldly affairs, Barth, like Kierkegaard before him, denounced in the sharpest possible terms the Protestant Church's corruption, the consequence of its having become too worldly in character. This orientation towards otherworldliness was of paramount importance: paradoxically it involved Barth in politics. He sympathized with socialism and in 1933, in contrast to some other leading theologians, took a determined stand against Nazism and all it stood for.

Barth had written the *Römerbrief*, as he made known in later years, because as a clergyman he had felt quite helpless. Having to deliver sermons he faced acute perplexity, for in the univer-sities he and the men of his generation had merely been taught to respect history; they had not heard about God's revelation.

But history did not provide light and comfort in troubled times, and thus he came to reject the traditional liberal theology based on the historical-critical exegesis of the Bible. He attributed little importance to the various cultural activities of the church and preached a return to absolute, unbroken faith. This message was rejected, not surprisingly, by the older generation of theologians, which was shocked by its extreme subjective character and feared that it would have fateful consequences for the church. Von Harnack, the chief exponent of the liberal school, wrote Barth that if his approach were to be accepted, no one would bother to read the Gospels; the inspirational preachers would have a field day, everyone interpreting God's word as he saw fit.

Among his contemporaries and the younger theologians, on the other hand, Barth had many supporters, of whom Gogarten, Emil Brunner and Bultmann were the most important. Later on their ways parted, as Bultmann became more and more convinced that the message of the gospel (the *Kerygma*) should be de-mythologized, freed of its historical, mythological elements to make it acceptable to modern man. However this dispute belongs to a later period; during the 1920s there was to all intents and purposes a common front between Barth and Bultmann; their journal, *Zwischen den Zeiten*, published from 1923 to 1933, was the forum of the Protestant theological avant-garde. Barth became a professor in Germany, first in Göttingen, later in Münster and finally in Bonn; two years after Hitler's rise to power he returned to his native Switzerland. The multi-volume *Kirchliche Dogmatik* which he began to publish in 1932 became one of the basic works of modern Protestantism, the impact of which was felt well beyond Germany, even though among the younger generation of theologians the Bultmann school gained ground in later years at the expense of Barth.

The Protestant establishment was predominantly nationalist in its outlook, but Barth was by no means its only critic from the left. The religious socialists, best-known among them Paul Tillich, preached 'socialism derived from faith', attacking soulless capitalist society, the free market economy and the alienation of man in which it had resulted. They criticized the church establishment for condoning the iniquities of the world as it was. An even more radical group was Neuwerk, which established

two settlements whose members shared all their worldly posses-
sions as the early Christians had done. Originally a small group
of seven pioneers, members of the youth movement, they eventually numbered more than a thousand. After Hitler's rise to
power they were forced to leave Germany, settling first in
England, later in Paraguay and finally in the United States. It
was only a marginal group which did not develop a new
theology and had no influence outside its own ranks. *Verwirk-
lichen*, to carry out one's ideals, to translate them into reality,
was one of the fashionable key concepts of the time, but the
number of those who did something about it was in inverse
ratio to those who just discussed it and for this reason, if for no
other, Neuwerk has a claim to be remembered.

In close touch with the religious socialists was the Jewish
thinker Martin Buber, a man of great gifts, theologian, philosopher, sociologist and translator into German of the Bible.
Like Barth he wanted to revive the elemental religious forces,
but quite differently from the Protestant fundamentalist. His
way led him from the *Ecstatic Confessions* (1908) and a mysticism
which betrays the influence of Expressionism and of the seventeenth-century mystic, Jakob Böhme, to the rediscovery of
Hassidism, to a specific kind of religious existentialism culminating in the philosophy of 'I and Thou', the dialogue between man
and man, and man and God. In Buber's theology there are two
kinds of dialogues, the I-Thou dialogue (with God as the
eternal Thou), open and direct, in which both sides are equals,
and the I-It, which is not really a true dialogue but important
for the advance of objective knowledge and technical progress.
According to Buber there is a dialectical interaction between
these two dialogues, and in a dialectical fashion they again
become I-Thou on a higher level. In this philosophy, a revelation is a meeting with the Thou; it may take place at any time;
it is not (as orthodox Jews believe) something which occurred
at Mount Sinai, has become law and will not recur. Seen in this
light, the Bible is not a dead book but living speech. To understand Buber as well as other religious philosophers of the time,
a great deal of sympathy for the subject is needed. So far as
Judaism is concerned, he fell between two stools: to the non-
believer his ideas were words without meaning; to the Jewish
fundamentalists they were heresy. Thus his ideas were more

likely to appeal to some Protestant, even Catholic thinkers than to the rabbis, and in Israel Buber was to be remembered as a sociologist (*Paths in Utopia*) rather than a theologian – for which Jewish religion has little use.

* * *

The 1920s were not on the whole an age of introspection, and it is difficult to explain the sudden popularity of psychology at almost every level. Before 1914, broadly speaking, interest in psychology was limited to the philosophers, to some physicians and natural scientists. After the war it suddenly became fashionable. Scientists and writers alike tried to keep abreast of developments in a field which had been neglected for so long; and even if they did not always understand it, psychological terminology was widely and somewhat indiscriminately used, with expressions such as 'inferiority-complex' bandied about at the slightest provocation. Some of the most interesting developments in psychological research had hardly been noticed at first by non-specialists; it was to take many years before the full impact of *Gestaltpsychologie* was felt in the humanities. The origins of this new approach can be traced back to well before the First World War, but even by 1918 the general theory was not yet clearly formulated. All that was known at the time among psychologists was that Wertheimer of Frankfurt had undertaken interesting experiments on illusory movements and on the visual perception of shapes, that Wolfgang Köhler had spent the war years in the Canary Islands and Africa studying the behaviour of chimpanzees, and that Koffka had drawn some rather far-reaching conclusions from Wertheimer's research and from his own, directed against the prevailing atomistic trend in experimental psychology. The basic principle of Gestalt psychology was deceptively easy, for it just said that a whole is more than or different from the sum of its parts. In other words, an event, experience or action cannot be explained, described or accounted for by adding up the smaller events, actions or experiences of which it is composed. The Gestalt psychologists, in contrast to their colleagues and in deliberate disregard of traditional scientific practice, were interested in the overall structure of a perceived pattern rather than in the relationship between its parts. They were convinced that only in this way ('from above' rather than from below) could new light be shed on the function of each part. Their concern was with the relationship between the whole and its parts, as it affected perception, memory and thinking as well as social psychology. The striving towards a good Gestalt (or pattern, or structure) was in their view one of the basic laws of nature; for nature, as they saw it, was basically well organized. All one therefore had to do was to find the 'simplest, most regular, most symmetrical structure attainable in a given situation'.

Gestalt psychology was influenced by contemporary philosophical thought and in turn exerted considerable influence on the philosophers. But this and its impact on research in the natural sciences relates to a later period, namely the development of Gestalt psychology in the United States, where its leading practitioners found themselves after Hitler's rise to power. Suffice it to say that by the early 1930s it had become one of the dominant trends in modern psychology, and that it was thought to be an exciting and promising new attempt to extend the frontiers of knowledge.

Unlike Gestalt psychology, psychoanalysis provoked a violent commotion from the outset. It dealt with the unconscious, it put heavy emphasis on sexual taboos and it made far-reaching claims for its therapeutic approach. The overwhelming majority of German psychiatrists thought these claims preposterous and, as in Freud's native Austria, they were sufficiently influential to prevent the appointment of an analyst to a chair of psychiatry. Right-wing circles denounced psychoanalysis because it undermined national values, the Communists rejected it as a bourgeois idealist pseudo-science, and the churches were up in arms for reasons which need hardly be elaborated. Nevertheless, interest in psychoanalysis spread throughout the 1920s, and Berlin replaced Vienna and Budapest as the capital of the movement. Austria and Hungary had become backwaters after 1918, and though Freud and members of his inner circle still lived and practised there, many leading exponents of the second generation of analysts were either German or foreigners who had settled in Berlin.

The origins of the movement in Germany predate the First World War. The Berlin Psychoanalytical Society had been founded by Karl Abraham, a psychiatrist, in 1910. Abraham was one of Freud's close associates, the seven comrades in the quest for truth who had each been given a ring by the master as a token of their solidarity in this endeavour. Eitingon, a psychiatrist of Russian origin, was coopted to the inner circle later on and he too lived in Berlin. The importance of Abraham and Eitingon for the recognition of psychoanalysis can hardly be exaggerated; neither made a theoretical contribution of the first order (though Abraham did interesting work on war neuroses, drug-addiction and anal eroticism), but more than anyone else they helped to give the movement a sense of direction. They established the systematic training of analysts and were the first (in 1920) to set up a psychoanalytical clinic, which four years later became the Berlin Institute. Eitingon was the head of the publishing house of the world psychoanalytical association, while Sandor Rado, another Berlin-based analyst, acted as chief editor of the official journal of the movement. Many leading second and third-generation analysts who subsequently acquired world fame (such as Karen Horney, Theodor Reik, Helene Deutsch, Edward and James Strachey, Ernst Simmel and Rado) were analysed by Abraham. His early death in 1925 was a great blow to the movement, which lost in him a man of great tact and common-sense whose judgment in the movement's many internal disputes had often been superior to that of Freud himself. After Abraham's death Ernst Simmel became the president of the Berlin society; his chief interest was what would later be called 'psychosomatic disease' – the psychogenesis of organic disturbances.

Mention has already been made of Sandor Rado, who was one of the first to voice doubts about the excessive preoccupation of his colleagues with the early years of childhood; was not the study of present conflicts of equal importance to the patient? Rado was more concerned with therapy than with the theoretical understanding of the structure of personality. Hence he felt more acutely than his colleagues a problem that was of the greatest practical importance, and which was to cause no end of trouble to successive generations of analysts. If neurosis was a maladaptation, would the discovery of the origins of neurotic symptoms by itself help the patient to get rid of them? Franz Alexander and Karen Horney, who had also settled in Berlin, shared these misgivings. Alexander was the first student and graduate of the Berlin Institute but in later years moved away from the mainstream of orthodox psychoanalysis, favouring a shorter treatment and a more active role on the part of the analyst in helping the patient to gain insight into the roots of his affliction. Karen Horney was the daughter of a Norwegian sea captain, a somewhat unusual background for an early psychoanalyst; her deviation from orthodoxy in later years was in some respects similar to Alexander's, but there was in addition a specifically female ('anti-male chauvinist') aspect. She maintained that male analysts had committed serious mistakes because of their insufficient knowledge of female psychology, erroneously assuming that female sexuality arose from the desire to have a penis and thus overlooking the significance of what she defined as the basic vaginal urges. In her later writings Horney tended to regard infantile sexuality as of minor importance.

Some of the most gifted younger students of psychoanalysis in Germany had no medical background; this was true of Erich Fromm, Herbert Marcuse and Erik Erikson, but their books on the subject appeared only many years later, when they had become established in the United States. Marcuse and Fromm were men of the left, so was Ernst Simmel, the head of the Berlin socialist physicians' union. However, the most radical representative of left-wing ideas among the psychoanalysts was Wilhelm Reich, who had moved to Berlin from Vienna in 1930. Such political commitment on the part of many German students of psychoanalysis was certainly no mere accident; it can be explained in retrospect with reference to the the general Weimar climate. It was in strong contrast to the scepticism of Freud who, in *Civilization and its Discontents*, had stated why he had little faith in the possibility of radically improving the world by reform – let alone revolution.

Reich began his career as an orthodox analyst with a special interest in character analysis. In 1927 he published his book on the function of the orgasm and gradually came to regard this as the key to human psychology, and ultimately to the riddles of the universe. Freud took a dim view of such simplistic notions, and when Reich attempted to establish a synthesis between Marxism and psychoanalysis, denouncing the death-wish as a 'product of the capitalist system', he soon found himself outside the ranks of the movement. Reich's efforts to make psychoanalysis palatable to orthodox Marxism were bound to fail anyway, for Communists could not accept a theory according to which fascism was explained with reference to sexual repression and the authoritarian structure of the family (theories which, incidentally, may have influenced Fromm's work in later years). Reich was a fertile and original thinker, but even during his earlier years, before madness overtook him, he was always strongly inclined to exaggerate grossly the importance of his discoveries and to reduce complex phenomena to simple formulas.

Thus Berlin became the second capital of psychoanalysis but also the cradle of most deviations and heresies, until in 1933 this 'Jewish science' became one of the first victims of Germany's new masters. The Nazis, in so far as they understood what it was all about, regarded psychoanalysis as an abomination; the analysts had to leave Germany, their institutes and publications were closed down. Seen in retrospect, the German exodus gave a strong impetus to the spread of psychoanalysis, for in the United States the movement became eminently respectable and its practitioners were given academic honours. But it is also true that after 1933 the intellectual fountainhead, the inspiration of psychoanalysis, became institutionalized; there were few if any significant new developments. Perhaps the movement had run its course; perhaps the age of great discoveries and doctrine-building was over. And so, in retrospect, the years before 1933, despite the lack of official recognition, can be seen as the great creative period in the annals of psychoanalysis.

*　　*　　*

During the first third of the twentieth century Europe witnessed a revolution in scientific thought for which there is no precedent in recent centuries. In November 1895 Röntgen made the famous experiment in which he found that certain rays not only went through black paper (which he thought should have stopped them), but to his amazement even through wood and flesh. In 1900 Max Planck published a paper which showed by means of a mathematical formula that radiation was emitted by what he called quanta; 1905 saw the appearance of a paper of some twenty-odd pages entitled 'On the Electrodynamics of

Moving Bodies' in which the Special Theory of Relativity was first formulated by Einstein. In view of the tremendous importance of these breakthroughs and the subsequent scientific advances based on them, it may seem curious that an account, however summary, of cultural life in the Weimar period should place them at the end rather than the beginning. For was not progress in the natural sciences incomparably more important in its practical consequences than the debates of philosophers, theologians and historians, which generated much heat but shed little light? What proof was there that Husserl represented an advance over Dilthey, and that Heidegger's ideas were 'progress' compared with Husserl? All this is beyond dispute, and yet so far as the cultural history of Weimar is concerned, the natural sciences have to take a less central place than literature, the arts and the humanities, for the simple reason that they belong to all mankind rather than to one particular country. There was a German literature, a German theatre, German schools in the visual arts, even in history and philosophy. But only a fool or a fanatic would talk about German mathematics or German physics. The problem which Einstein solved (and to which Hermann Minkowski gave mathematical formality) had been posed by a Frenchman (Poincaré) and a Dutchman (Lorentz). In turn, the great advances in the study of matter and radiation based on the theories of Planck and Einstein were made by scientists from many countries: de Broglie, Rutherford, Niels Bohr on the one hand, and von Laue, Pauli, Schrödinger, Heisenberg on the other. There is however yet another reason why developments in natural science are in a category apart. It is easy to show the impact of the war and the postwar chaos on German literature and the visual arts, on historiography and on theology. The Weimar *Zeitgeist* clearly manifested itself in these fields as well as in many others. There was no Expressionism or Neue Sachlichkeit, no social protest or revanchism in scientific research; there was only good science and bad science, important breakthroughs and blind alleys.

The revolution in scientific thought had started around the turn of the century but its full implications were not immediately realized and there was also some resistance to it. Röntgen's discovery could be experimentally repeated without difficulty, but it took a fairly long time before quantum mechanics and the theory of relativity were generally accepted. They were not easy to understand; when Planck invited Einstein in 1911 to come to Berlin to be director of the Kaiser Wilhelm Institute of Physics, one of the main arguments was that, of the ten people who understood his theory, eight lived in the German capital. As for Planck's great discovery, which he had helped to develop further (photo-electric emission – moving quanta – photons), Einstein admitted that he never fully understood it. Some of the older generation of physicists contested the new theories because they undermined all conventional wisdom. It was typical of the prevailing political climate that Einstein's theories were attacked by some German scientists because he was a Jew, and by some foreign physicists because he was a German (in 1933 Rutherford was still opposed to giving Einstein shelter in Cambridge and even refused to attend a reception in honour of another refugee, Fritz Haber, a Nobel Prize-winner in chemistry). There was, of course, also professional jealousy. Why should the theory of relativity have become the major talking-point in salons and at cocktail parties? What had Einstein done to become the most famous resident of the German capital, while the names of other physicists, however distinguished, remained unknown?

The younger scientists were free from such feelings of envy. They realized that this (in the words of one of them) was the decade in which the most momentous discoveries were being made. Physicists and mathematicians from all over the globe flocked to Germany – young Hungarians like Johnny von Neumann, Leo Szilard, Eugen Wigner and Michael Polanyi; Americans like Oppenheimer, Rabi, Condon, Linus Pauling and many others. They went to Göttingen, which Courant, Hilbert, Weyl, Born and James Franck had made the mecca of mathematicians; to Leipzig; to Munich where Sommerfeld taught and, above all, to Berlin – the Berlin of Planck, Nernst, von Laue, Issai Schur and of course of Einstein's Thursday-afternoon seminar.

By the mid-1920s the cognoscenti were aware that a second revolution was imminent: Planck, Einstein and the other leaders of the older generation were no longer producing original work equal to their prewar research, the last decades of Einstein's life being devoted to a chimera, the chase after the unified field. The next giant steps in the development of the new physics were made in 1924–7 by younger men – some of them very young at the time, such as de Broglie's quantum theory, Schroedinger's wave mechanics, Heisenberg's uncertainty principle and Bohr's complementary principle. Einstein and other older scientists were reluctant to accept theories according to which statistical laws, not causal mechanisms, governed the universe – chance not determinism. 'God does not play dice with the world', Einstein said in a famous aside. Was this, as some argued, a clash of two different worldviews, the impact perhaps of Spengler and irrationalism? Such interpretations would be more convincing if the split had occurred on ideological lines, which it did not; they also assumed a high degree of dependence of physics on philosophy. Some physicists had an interest in philosophy, but even they did not look for guidance and inspiration outside their own field. Einstein found himself at odds with his old friends Born and Weyl in his opposition to indeterminism, whereas on this issue Lenard and Stark, the main spokesmen of the antisemitic anti-Einstein group, were in the same camp. Mathematics underwent a similar crisis with the appearance of the intuitionist school (Bouwert), challenging Hilbert's axiomatic method. For a time it seemed as if the idea of any logical foundation for the validity of principles had to be discarded. There was a new realignment in the natural sciences: nuclear physics, physics and chemistry moved much closer to each other than had been thought possible even a decade before. Nuclear physics and biochemistry provided the bridge between the organic and inorganic fields of study.

Advances in chemistry had been overshadowed for a long time by the revolutionary developments in physics, but the practical importance of the progress made in organic chemistry was of such magnitude that it was bound eventually to attract general attention. Germany had an impressive tradition in chemistry which went back to Justus von Liebig in the early nineteenth century. In the twentieth century Emil Fischer did pioneering work in biochemistry, as Nernst did in physical chemistry, while Paul Ehrlich established chemotherapy. Willstätter and Haber, James Franck and Wieland, Windaus and Staudinger continued this tradition, collecting Nobel Prizes on the way and making countless discoveries which were of immediate use in pharmacology and the manufacture of synthetic materials. To keep abreast of the latest advances in chemistry without a knowledge of German was almost impossible at the time.

With all their prestige and their spectacular discoveries, German scientists frequently found themselves short of money for their research. Gone were the days when great experiments had been carried out on a shoestring in little sheds. As research became more complicated, it also became vastly more expensive, and the help provided by the state – and in some cases by industry – was no longer sufficient. Commenting on the budget of the Association to aid German Scientists which had been established after the war, Fritz Haber said that one needed a magnifying-glass to study it. True, the deprivation felt by German scientists was relative; visiting their French colleagues, the Germans realized how well-equipped their own laboratories were. True also that some disciplines suffered less than others. Richard Goldschmidt, the distinguished zoologist and geneticist, relates in his memoirs that research laboratories again received the support they needed in the mid-1920s, and that the individual scholar again became an important member of society. The entertainment provided by the government for international scientific congresses, including sumptuous banquets and gala operas, was so lavish as to be almost embarrassing. But these were the years of prosperity; as the depression set in, stringent cuts affected scientific research. Young scientists, even the most gifted among them, could no longer be certain that they would find suitable employment. Since they, more than other academics, had connexions all over the world, they found it easier than their colleagues to settle abroad. A brain drain from Germany got under way during the late 1920s; the number of scientists who left the country was small, but it included some of the most promising among the younger generation. One of von Neumann's friends later wrote:

I remember Johnny telling me in 1930 that even though the number of existing and prospective vacancies in German universities was extremely small, most of the two or three score *Dozenten* counted on a professorship in the near future.

With his typical rational approach, Johnny computed that the expected number of professional appointments within three years was three, whereas the number of *Dozenten* was forty.

German science would have survived this brain drain, which was in some ways part of the general movement of young scientists from one country to another and had been going on in Europe for a long time, but the exodus after 1933 was a disaster of a different order. Even then the number of scientists involved was not that large, not more than a few hundred men and women. But these were the leaders in their respective fields and their most promising assistants and students. Thus within a few years Germany ceased to be one of the world's scientific centres. The German scientific tradition lived on abroad; it is one of the ironies of history that young scientists who had received their training in Germany were prominently involved in the great advances in nuclear physics, biochemistry and molecular biology (to mention but a few outstanding examples) which were made in the United States and Britain in the 1940s and 1950s.

*   *   *

Germany, to summarize, was in many fields of academic research among the two or three most important centres; in some its lead was undisputed. But this had been the case even before the First World War. In some respects the country was perhaps more open than others to new departures and to experimentation with new ideas. But the search for a common denominator would in the last resort be futile. Historians were on the whole conservative both in their politics and their professional approach, while most sociologists were not. Certain philosophical currents did no doubt reflect the general spiritual malaise of the age, but philosophy had long since lost its leading position and had become highly professionalized. A century earlier most educated people had been familiar, at least to some degree, with the writings of Kant, Hegel and Fichte. Twentieth-century philosophical thought reached a much smaller circle; there was no longer a common bond of interest, not even a common language, between educated people active in different disciplines. This is not to say that intellectual discourse had altogether ceased in the new age of progressive specialization. There was a certain amount of interaction and cross-fertilization between the various disciplines, even between the humanities and the natural sciences. But in the final analysis each field was subject to its own autonomous laws of growth. The more adventurous spirits would try to keep abreast of developments in other fields; theologians would follow with interest the activities of the philosophers but they would hardly venture much further afield, and the same applied to the academic community in general. Occasional intellectual fashions still attracted wider attention but their impact was neither deep nor lasting.

Academic life in Weimar Germany was still hierarchically structured. The professor reigned absolute, or very nearly so. The attempts by the Republic to make the universities more democratic in character both in their outlook and their structure were half-hearted and in the end not very successful. The university did change to a certain extent, not as the result of reforms imposed from outside but because over the years younger people rose on the academic ladder. There was no political interference on the part of the government; given the delicate balance of power, the Catholic Centre Party wielded some influence through the control of budgetary allocations for the universities, but the concessions made to appease the Centre Party (such as the appointment of a few philosophy professors teaching neo-Thomism) did not really constitute a serious infringement of academic freedom. If there was censorship, it came mainly from within the profession; a left-wing historian or Germanist did not stand much chance of being promoted. There were few of them anyway. Academic standards were on the whole high and if there was a great deal of distrust vis-à-vis new ideas and approaches, this was by no means a typically German phenomenon. In Britain, for example, academic recognition came to sociology much later than in German universities.

The Weimar experience shows yet again that there is no obvious correlation between a flourishing intellectual life on the one hand and political stability and economic prosperity on the other. When Kant and Hegel, Goethe and Schiller were alive,

Germany was a mere geographical term, or a dream, certainly not a powerful political reality. Weimar Germany was the sick man of Europe, whereas the Third Reich with its rampant anti-intellectualism became the leading power on the continent. Intellectual achievement does not make for contentment and security; but it would be a ridiculous oversimplification to conclude that instability and discontent are essential preconditions for an intense and fruitful intellectual life. The reality of Weimar culture was exceedingly contradictory. It was the best of times and the worst of times; it was the most depressing and the most exciting of times.

7
Berlin s'amuse

History is more than the sum total of the activities of kings, generals and statesmen; cultural history is not only the history of the avant-garde. Even the Weimar avant-garde did not spend all its waking hours pondering Marxism and psychoanalysis, reading Heidegger, admiring Brecht and Grosz. It was looking for entertainment, much to the horror of a later generation of earnest but uncomprehending historians, who now contend that trying to enjoy oneself with Hitler just around the corner was frivolous if not downright sinful. The intellectuals did not have the benefit of hindsight, hence they frequented their favourite coffee houses, missed few boxing matches and horse races, even went to cinemas, variety shows and other places of doubtful cultural value. Perhaps they should have known that they were dancing on the edge of a volcano, but they didn't. Had they known, it is doubtful whether they would have reacted any differently, for their tears would not have extinguished the flames. In their defence the intellectuals could have maintained that even Marx went for picnics on Hampstead Heath, that even Freud played cards once a week with friends. Whether such arguments would have the slightest impact on latterday moralists is not certain.

There was at any rate a light side to Weimar culture: Fritzi Massary and Richard Tauber, Marlene Dietrich and the *White Horse Inn*, the films and the hit songs of the time. It is just possible that an elderly philosopher living in semi-retirement in Erlangen or Greifswald would escape contamination. It is unlikely that a writer or artist, or indeed anyone living in a big city, could help being affected, regardless of whether he enjoyed or loathed it. The Weimar era gave birth to a popular culture which was *sui generis*, which left its mark on the whole period and has become part of its legacy.

After the end of the First World War Berlin became the entertainment capital of Europe. Truncated, impoverished, facing a permanent economic crisis and with little hope of a lasting improvement, Germany wanted to enjoy itself. Once the war was over a dance fever spread, the like of which had not been witnessed in Europe since the Middle Ages. According to the new *Zeitgeist*, sex, like justice, had to be seen to be done. The new sex wave ranged from the establishment of scientific (or pseudo-scientific) research institutes to nude shows and hard-core pornography. Periodicals called *Free Love*, *The Grass Widow*, *Woman Without Man*, tried to imitate with varying success *Rire* and *Vie Parisienne*, while the Admiralspalast and the Metropol-theater copied the Folies Bergères and the Casino de Paris. Those who wanted more substantial fare turned to the smaller establishments which mushroomed between 1919 and 1923, changing their names and their proprietors fairly often. A new genre of literature, hitherto traded, if at all, under the counter, made its appearance; it dealt, as the titles indicated, with nights in a harem, the white-slave traffic, women with whips, exotic methods of sexual intercourse; semi-factual or fictional, illustrated or not, this new venture in adult education attracted a great many students. On a different level there were the nude 'beauty dances' of Cilla de Rheidt, with her husband, an ex-Army officer, acting as impresario and master of ceremonies. She found a great many imitators for a few years, but eventually the public went back to the Admiralspalast. Sexual problems figured prominently in literature, in the cinema and in the theatre. Occasionally the censor would intervene but on the whole the climate was permissive, more so, at any rate, than in any other country at the time. The churches and the right protested about the spread of moral corruption but without much success. All in all, vice was not really as ubiquitous as the moralists would have it. The Tiller Girls who conquered Berlin in the late 1920s travelled with both a chaperone and a clergyman and they had to say their prayers every day.

For a time there was a flourishing trade in drugs; sniffing cocaine was the rage for a while, but this too passed. It was the age of experimentation, not of the relentless pursuit of virtue or vice. Trial marriage was discussed in literature and the *ménage à trois*, but there is no good reason to believe that the theory was more widely put into practice in Germany than elsewhere. Nevertheless Berlin acquired the reputation of a very wicked place indeed, whereas elsewhere in Germany there were narrow limits to temptation. Munich and Cologne had hardly anything to offer – even Frankfurt had only three nightclubs. Prostitutes figured prominently in literature and even more in the cinema, but there were not more of them in Germany than in other European countries. Venereal disease spread, as it does during and after any war, but after 1923 there was a steady decrease, and the number of patients treated in hospitals was actually smaller in 1925 than in 1913. There was, in brief, no more *dolce vita* in Berlin than in other capital cities, only more publicity, and this sufficed to attract the provincials and the foreign tourists. If they had any standards of comparison they returned home sadder and wiser men. The Tauentzienstrasse was not really superior to Pigalle.

Berlin had the edge on Paris so far as the *leichtgeschürzte Musen* of popular entertainment were concerned; the cabarets, the farces, the hit songs, the cinema. This was quite unexpected, not at all in accordance with German tradition, for frivolity and wantonness had always been thought to be the Frenchman's preserve. It is easy to think of many tragedies in the annals of the German theatre and opera; the comedies which have survived can be counted on the fingers of one hand. There was no German operetta, not a single composer who could even remotely be compared to Johann Strauss or Offenbach, to Milloecker or Gilbert and Sullivan. Yet precisely at the time when the operetta was on the decline elsewhere it enjoyed a triumphant revival in Berlin. The world premiere of Lehar's *Zarevich* took place in the German capital in 1927; *Friederike* was performed for the first time, also in Berlin, in 1928, and *Land des Lächelns* in 1929. All of Lehar's former operettas had opened in his native Vienna, and the move to Berlin was significant in more ways than one. 1930 was the year of the *White Horse Inn* and in 1931 Paul Abraham's *Blume von Hawai* was first performed. Little need be said about the content of these operettas; they all take place in the good old days before 1914.

Much of the talent and many of the ideas which made German showbusiness what it was came from outside Germany. Lehar, of course, was Viennese, the main stars in his operettas, Richard Tauber and Gitta Alpar, were Austrian and Hungarian respectively. So were Ralph Benatzky and Paul Abraham, the kings of the operetta after Lehar. Of the great cinema directors, Fritz Lang and G. W. Pabst were of Austrian origin, so were Joe May and Josef von Sternberg. German jazz would have been unthinkable without the talent lately imported from Poland, Hungary and Rumania. Specifically German were Claire Waldorf in Berlin, Karl Valentin and Liesl Karstadt in Munich – great characters, great actors, reciting and singing in dialect, untranslatable, inimitable. But these were the exceptions; the great world of show-business had become cosmopolitan; there was a constant coming and going between the capitals of the world. Just as Germany attracted the talent from east and south-east Europe, leading German producers and stars sooner or later found themselves on the road to Hollywood, some for a few years, others for good. Among them were the producers Billy Wilder, Robert Siodmak, Ernst Lubitsch and F. W. Murnau, Erich von Stroheim, and of course countless actors and actresses from Pola Negri to Marlene Dietrich.

Avant-garde and mass culture met in the coffee houses such as the Romanische Café, at the corner of Tauentzien and Budapester Strasse, a stone's throw from the Gedächtniskirche; there you could see writers and critics, painters and actresses and quite a few original characters who never published a book, drew a line or composed a sonata, but nevertheless had some influence on contemporary literature, music and painting. The painters had their own little table with Slevogt as unofficial chairman; so had the Dadaists during their heyday. When Karl Kraus came to Berlin his admirers met him in a *chambre séparée* in the nearby Schwanecke restaurant, because they were on bad terms with almost everyone in the Romanische Café. The elegant *Salonkommunisten* went there – Leonhard Frank, George Grosz (dressed up *à l'anglaise* with a homburg) and Rudolf Leonhard – complete with monocle, silk shirt, and a cane of rhinoceros hide to combat capitalism more effectively. Paul Cohen Portheim, a shy man, painter, writer, author of excellent monographs on Paris and London and the *arbiter elegantiarum* of the Romanische Café, was a regular guest. He lived in Berlin but his heart was in Paris. Every evening he would get his private weather bulletin from the French capital and would dress accordingly, rain or shine. There were the young *femmes fatales* of Berlin such as Anita Berber, the dancer, always with a host of admirers, always between hysterical outbursts or breakdowns. Like some other actresses and dancers of that circle she was to die young. Hermann Kesten, one of the regulars, has provided an excellent portrait of the place. In the Romanische Café, he wrote, a great many people were to be seen dressed up as poets with strangely growing beards, crazy ties and long manes. They exhibited their girl-friends, who were either writers or painters and who had formed themselves into a kind of *Gesamtkunstwerk* in the Wagnerian sense. One had done her hair to make herself look like Judith about to kill Holofernes, but without being able to make one forget that she came from Moabit; another, like Lucrezia Borgia, showed a full bosom (but without a dagger); a third had made herself up in a most sinister way, but in the end she looked even more philistine than her widowed aunt from Neu Stettin. It was a literary caravanserai: people took their inspiration from east and west, and in their turn inspired half the world. For what was discussed in the Berlin literary cafés in the evening was repeated two days later in New York, London, Paris and even Rio de Janeiro. School reformers were sitting there next to all kinds of fanatics, revolutionaries next to pickpockets, people on drugs next to apostles of health-food and vegetarianism. Such a mixture caused a great deal of confusion, but it also acted as a strong stimulant.

The journalists went to the Café Jaenicke in the Motzstrasse near the editorial offices of Ullstein, Mosse and Scherl. The stars of the cinema had their permanent rendezvous at Weiss Czarda, Anne Menz and the popular Russian tearooms and restaurants, Medved, Alverdi, of which there were a great many. They would sit there and drink and talk till late at night. Around midnight, after a premiere, messengers would be sent to get copies of the early editions of the morning papers. The reviews were fairly predictable: Kerr would damn most young playwrights with a pen dipped in acid. Ihering would defend Brecht, Bronnen and their contemporaries with warm if somewhat uncritical sympathy. The German capital had the most knowledgeable theatre public. What Berlin approves has stood the test, said Pirandello, while Zuckmayer wrote, 'This town devoured talent and human energy more than any other in order to digest it quickly, grind it small and spit it out again.' But in his innermost heart everyone saw in Berlin the realization of his dreams. It attracted a great many charlatans and impostors dabbling in finance as well as culture. But it also attracted much talent and created an ambiance such as existed nowhere else. Berlin was the epitome of New Times, whatever that meant; it was by far the most cosmopolitan of the big cities. The *Literarische Welt* was the best literary review of the time, the *Querschnitt* the most snobbish. There were first-rate satirical journals, cartoons and hit songs of real merit, or at any rate of lasting success. There had been, it appeared, a sudden infusion of *esprit* into the stolid German beef tea.

In later years some patrons of the Romanische Café were to reminisce with much bitterness about the 'so-called freedom and flowering of the arts'. It was a cauldron coming to the boil, George Grosz wrote in his memoirs; foreigners were too easily misled by the apparently carefree, merry whirl, whereas in actual fact it was a wholly negative world with a lot of gaily-coloured froth on the surface. Others saw in escapism the most pronounced feature of the period, for what was the hectic *Betrieb*, the activity for activity's sake, if not a form of escapism? In later years there was never a more implacable foe of everything German, past and present, than Ilya Ehrenburg; but at the time he was singing the praises of Berlin, its pulsating life and vigour, in almost ecstatic terms. The sweeping condemnation after Hitler had come to power betrays a personal disappointment. It had been no ordinary period, it had raised a great many expectations and precisely for that reason there was a tendency in later years to judge it too harshly and to forget what it had been really like at the time. In 1928 hardly anyone, except perhaps a few Nazis, would have argued that it was a wholly negative world. There were signs of recovery in most respects, the gaiety was not artificial, the energy was real, not secondhand. Every period has its form of escapism; that of the Weimar era was certainly no worse than that of others.

In some respects it was better. The German cinema of the time produced a great deal of rubbish but it also inspired the whole world with new techniques, new approaches and some superior works of art. The development of the German film is of importance in this context not just as a mirror of contemporary hopes, fears and illusions, but above all because it was of intrinsic interest. Even in its childhood and adolescence the new art opened up possibilities and ultimately reached a far wider public than any other medium.

By 1914 there were already some two thousand cinemas throughout Germany and another thousand in Austria-Hungary, all of them in need of fresh fare every week. But the very early film catered only for the simplest tastes. Several well-known artists half-heartedly tried their hand at the new medium, and so at one time did Max Reinhardt, but it was only with *Der Student von Prag* (1913), a variation on the Peter Schlemihl theme, that, in the words of a contemporary commentator, 'dramatic art first appeared on the screen'. *Der Student von Prag* was an expensive film by the standards of those days; it cost five thousand dollars to produce, and it was the first German film of which notice was taken abroad. However Germany was not an exporter but a consumer of foreign films at that time; most came from France and it was only when this source dried up with the outbreak of war that a powerful impetus was given to the development of a native film industry. There were 11 film companies in 1911; by 1915 their number had risen to 36; it rose further to 131 in 1918 and to 360 in 1922. This mushrooming was largely a by-product of inflation and the great majority of the companies were bound to collapse. But the basic assumption of the investors was not far wrong; the cinema was indeed a growth industry. The number of movie theatres rose steadily from 2,000 before the war, 3,700 in 1920, to over 5,000 in 1929. Whereas the pre-war cinema had more often than not been a shed or at best a small converted restaurant, the cinemas of the 1920s and 1930s were, as their names sometimes announced, little palaces. The number of films produced annually rose to a fantastic 646 in 1922, but then fell steeply to 241 in 1927 and to 175 in 1929. It continued to decrease, to 151 in 1930, 121 in 1932, and in 1935, under the Nazis, to 94. Even so Germany produced more films during the 1920s and early 1930s than all other European countries put together. The steady decrease in numbers was not surprising because the films of the 1930s were lengthy, incomparably more expensive to produce than the short reels of the early years. As the movie industry became big business only a few substantial firms such as UFA survived, having the capital necessary to engage in costly ventures. A similar process took place in the United States, but whereas the American cinema prospered during the 1920s, the post-inflationary period was a time of grave crisis for the German film industry. UFA was bought up by the right-wing Scherl group of publications which belonged to Alfred Hugenberg; the newsreels, too, passed under the control of right-wing companies. But there was little direct political interference; the big concerns were in the market to make money, not to peddle ideas.

The film world was surprisingly neutral; it was attacked by the extreme left for its sham objectivity, but the Nazis were even more violent in their denunciations of the 'Jewish industry'. During all these years only one communist film (*Kuhle Wampe*) was produced, and not a single one openly Nazi; there were no known Nazis in the film industry, except perhaps a few in subordinate positions. On the other hand quite a few patriotic films dealing with heroic episodes of Prussian or German history were produced. Von Czerèpy's *Fridericus Rex*, perhaps the first major film of this genre, was done so crudely, with such a total lack of humour, that it was acclaimed outside Germany on the mistaken assumption that it was anti-German propaganda. Censorship was less strict in Germany than in other countries; neither *The Blue Angel* nor *The Threepenny Opera* could be shown in France at the time; *Die freudlose Gasse* was banned in Britain and many a sequence would not have passed the American board of censors had it been submitted in the first place. The anti-left bias became more pronounced only during the last years of the Republic.

The majority of German film-makers were unpolitical men with vague left-of-centre sympathies. They did engage in social criticism but the message was usually muted and sometimes difficult to discover at all. *The Threepenny Opera, Berlin Alexander-platz* and *Blue Angel* were all tamer on the screen than their originals, and the same was true of the patriotic films; the anti-radicalism was in the nature of the medium. Books were written for a few thousand readers and could afford to be outspoken, extreme, even perverse and splenetic. But films were designed to reach a public of hundreds of thousands, if not millions, and moreover to please them. This meant catering for the broadest common denominator and avoiding so far as possible 'controversial issues'. If there was political bias it had to be subtly hidden, and for that reason, if for no other, it was not particularly effective. Siegfried Kracauer noted sadly that while the French understood the wider significance of *Dr Caligari*, the Germans did not. Whether this was really so is open to doubt, for the French were notoriously ill-equipped to understand anything about Germany – apart from the fact that they did not like the country and its inhabitants.

What then was the specific character of the German film? Strictly speaking there was no 'German film' only German film-makers, and because these were highly individual in character it is almost impossible to generalize about a 'German school'. Pabst has entered film history as the great realist and Fritz Lang as an expressionist. Lubitsch was called the 'Griffith of Europe'. But Pabst's films vary tremendously in approach and subject, and so do Lang's; if it is difficult to find a common denominator for the films put out by each of these distinguished producers, it is virtually impossible to detect features common to all of them. Certain favourite symbols, motifs and subjects can be found in the German cinema; the German avant-garde was introspective rather than extrovert. But the same applies, of course, to the avant-garde everywhere. According to Kracauer's well-known study of the German cinema, the introvert tendency had its origin in powerful collective desires. Shaken by convulsions, the German mind avoided or obstructed all external revolutionary possibilities, withdrew into itself, conducted an interior monologue, 'revealing developments in almost inaccessible layers of the German mind'. But as another critic has dryly commented, Herr Hinz and Fräulein Kunz would hardly have been aware of the existence of films revealing the mysteries of the German soul unless they strayed by accident into a West

End cinema of the few big cities. The highbrow films with the
hidden message are of interest as historical documents, open
sometimes to different interpretations; they certainly had no
major political impact at the time.

The Germans were not the first to produce films that were
generally recognized as works of art; the Swedish producer
Sjöstrom and others had preceded them. But it is certainly true
that during the 1920s the Germans produced a whole series of
films which were in their way pioneering and which exerted an
influence far beyond the country's borders. Pabst's technique
of shooting and editing, his fragmentation of the scenes, says
an American historian of the cinema, deeply influenced film-
makers everywhere. Perhaps the most important breakthrough
was Murnau's *Der letzte Mann* (1924). Previously, German film-
makers hardly ever left their studios; they could thus give close
attention to detail, but their scope was narrowly limited (though
admittedly they had in Neu Babelsberg the most modern
studios in the world). Murnau was not the first to use a moving
camera, but no one before him had thought of shooting with
an almost continuously moving camera. By this totally 'subjective' use of the camera it became an actor in its own right,
making it possible to view events through the eyes of the main
character (Emil Jannings in this case).

This was perhaps Jannings's greatest role: the old doorman
of a great hotel, immensely proud of his status and uniform,
who has become too old to do his job competently. Out of con-
sideration he is offered the job of lavatory attendant. Formerly
a person of great consequence in the eyes of his family and the
neighbours, he suddenly becomes the butt of mockery and
insults. His self-respect gradually disappears as he turns, literally, into *der letzte Mann*. There is a postscript – a parody on the
conventional happy ending: a millionaire dies in his arms and
leaves the attendant all his money. *Der letzte Mann* had no
captions – it needed none. It made a profound impression on
cinemagoers everywhere; contemporary critics compared it to
the Book of Job and Beethoven's Ninth Symphony. *Der letzte
Mann*, it was said at the time, pointed the way in which the
cinema was to advance.

There had been no such unanimity a few years earlier when
another film of comparable importance was first shown. It

concerned Dr Caligari, the hypnotist who engages in murder through a medium, a somnambulist. When pursued, he takes refuge as a patient in a lunatic asylum. The investigators track him down and finally find the proof they need to arrest him for his crimes. But then it suddenly emerges that master criminal, patient and the head of the clinic are one and the same. This is how the authors wanted to end their story, but the producer provided a different twist: in the end it appears that the man who tells the story is himself mad and has to be confined to the asylum, whereas the director is perfectly sane. Having heard the patient's story, he feels convinced that he will be able to cure him.

There are many versions of the origins of *Dr Caligari* and even more interpretations; Caligari, one of the authors wrote, was the omnipotent authority, the state which had lately been instrumental in murdering millions of people. But it is also known that the idea for the film had first occurred to its two young authors well before the war, and that the father of one of them, and of Robert Wiene, the producer, were afflicted by mental illness. Be that as it may, *Caligari* was the apex of Expressionism in the German cinema. It owed its success to many factors: the bizarre, gripping story, the decor with its fantastically stylized, distorted settings, the use of light and shade well in advance of contemporary techniques, the acting of Werner Krauss as the malignant Caligari and of Conrad Veidt as the somnambulist. *Caligari* depicted a topsy-turvy world, unreal, full of fear and terror, and thus perfectly reflected one aspect of the *Zeitgeist*. Although one of the greatest films of all time, its effect was much more limited than that of *Der letzte Mann*. It led nowhere, unless one considers it as a forerunner of later horror films – a kind of highbrow *King Kong*. It revealed many of the features peculiar to Expressionism, yet at the same time it was (to quote René Clair) 'cerebral cinema'. The finished product was somehow too perfect, based on too many stage effects to be altogether convincing. It was a great film but no school or tradition could be based on it.

The postwar audience had a weakness for horror films, usually with an exotic background. The story was almost always completely ludicrous but the films were well-produced and exceedingly well acted. In *Die Mumie Ma* (Lubitsch) the hero, a German painter, kidnaps an Egyptian temple dancer and is persecuted by the high priest of the cult. In Lupu Pick's *Mr Wu* the villain, a Chinese landowner, executes his own daughter for having fallen in love with a young European, and then tries to poison him and his mother. In *Die Pest in Florenz* just about no one remains alive after a series of involved matrimonial intrigues. In Fritz Lang's *Die Spinnen* an American sportsman tries to get possession of a Yucatan treasure but is pursued by a secret organization from San Francisco's Chinatown to the Falkland Isles. In *Das indische Grabmal*, directed by by Joe May in collaboration with Fritz Lang, the hero is thrown into a tiger's cage, but this is by no means his most perilous adventure. Strong meat was needed to attract the public after the horrors of the war. Joe May's *Herrin der Welt* is about young and pretty Maud Gregaard who has refused to marry Baron Murphy, who then decides to ruin her. First he drives her father to suicide and her mother to madness. Maud is now an orphan, but she still refuses to give in. She searches for and finds the treasure of the Queen of Sheba, but the young man whom she loves dies soon after. She returns to her homeland and avenges herself on Murphy. This was the first of a long series; it was shown in eight instalments with titles such as *The Benefactress of Mankind*, *The Rabbi of Kuan-Fu*, *Ophir, City of the Past* and *The Tragedy of Vengeance*. One could safely miss one or two and still share the excitement and enjoy the flavour.

Among the most popular themes at the time were the *Doppelgänger* and the robot. The German Romantics had experimented with these ideas and Meyrink had popularized the Golem. Caligari was a classical *Doppelgänger*, so was Dr Mabuse, the schizophrenic super-criminal who prepares his crimes scientifically and runs his own gang, a fantastic assortment of cretins, by way of hypnotism and terror. Forging money is his main business but he also engages as a sideline in many other unspeakable crimes. Dr Mabuse is a diabolically clever impersonator, but in the end, after many a climax and anti-climax, the police get him, a raving madman, in his subterranean cave. Fritz Lang later wrote that he had been directly influenced by the atmosphere of inflation, the street fighting, the murder of Rathenau, the exploits of Al Capone. First shown in 1922, it was a typical product of that period; the backers made a great deal of money from this film and ten years later Lang was asked to produce a sequel, *The Testament of Dr Mabuse*. The doctor is now in a Berlin asylum headed by Dr Baum, who has fallen under the master criminal's spell. In his cell he prepares a manual on how to destroy mankind by a wave of unspeakable acts of terror – attacks on railways, factories, the currency system. The two head a giant gang, out to destroy the social order. Mabuse dies but Baum, his reincarnation, continues his work until in the end the forces of order unmask him and he ends up in the cell of Mabuse, raving mad like his guru and predecessor. Lang later said that it was meant as an allegory of Hitler and Nazism, a somewhat unlikely story since the scenario was written in collaboration with his then wife, Thea von Harbou, a member of the Nazi Party. Nevertheless, some critics saw in it an anti-fascist film, albeit a pale one: 'As so often with Lang, the law triumphs and the lawless glitters', says Kracauer. The Nazis banned the film in Germany but probably because they regarded it as 'degenerate art' rather than for its political message. But even this was not the end of Dr Mabuse; well after the Second World War he was disinterred once again – with no success whatsoever.

Before the first Mabuse film Lang had produced *Der müde Tod*, the story of a young girl who, in order to save her lover from the Angel of Death, enters into a covenant which in the end she cannot keep. Only in death does she find herself re-united with her lover. In between, the viewer is taken to a fantasy Moslem city, to Renaissance Venice (with some fine photography of its bridges during the carnival, reminding some critics of Reinhardt at his best), and lastly to an allegorical Chinese town. In 1924 Lang produced the two-part *Nibelungen*, dedicating it 'to the German people'. This monumental and powerful film followed the old epic rather than Richard Wagner. The approach is far simpler and less artificial than in *Caligari*; good use is again made of shadows and halftones and there are some wonderful landscapes. The leitmotif of the film is vengeance: every misdeed has to be atoned for. Hagen and Kriemhild are not exactly gentle characters, but as the action moves on to the country of Attila and the Huns, standards of behaviour become very deplorable indeed. It ends in a great orgy of mutual extermination, 'the most extraordinary hecatomb seen so far on the screen', in the words of one critic. The *Nibelungen* was followed in 1926 by *Metropolis*, one of Lang's most famous films, about a factory town of the future. Reduced to a slave existence, the workers want to revolt but Maria, a pure girl, keeps them back because she knows that they will be massacred if they rebel. The boss's son is in love with Maria and joins the cause of the workers. At this point there is a startling dénouement. Rotwang, a nihilist inventor, creates a robot which, resembling Maria, will incite the workers to revolt. (The idea of the dictator inciting the people against his own rule had been previously used in *Homunculus,* a wartime film.) But against all expectation there is a happy ending, for Maria and the Boss's son get married, the 'heart mediating between hand and brain'. Imagery and decor dominate this film, which took a year to make and had a mixed reception. Goebbels liked it, H. G. Wells said it was rubbish. Two years later *Spies* was produced, the story of a mysterious but very powerful spy network (among its leaders the inscrutable oriental Matsumoto) which has infiltrated even the police. The chief female agent is given the assignment of seducing 'No. 326', the leading detective. But the two fall in love and manage to escape various assassination attempts, including a harrowing railway accident in a tunnel. Apart from a great deal of suspense the film has little to recommend it. Lastly *M* should be mentioned, Lang's first sound film. This is the story of a sadistic child murder, screened at a time when several such cases had shaken Germany. Disturbed by a sudden fit of police activity the local gangsters, helped by the beggars' union, undertake an investigation of their own. They find the murderer and their court sentences him to death. The police arrive on the scene, a deserted factory, as usual at the very last moment. With *M* Lang had finally moved from his early expressionism to something which the critics chose to call 'magic realism'. The world of *M* reminds one in some respects of the atmosphere of *The Threepenny Opera*. But the comic scenes are mere interludes, the prevailing atmosphere is one of suspicion, stark terror, of sadism and murderous instincts.

Having related the background of some of Fritz Lang's major films the question of their meaning arises. Critics have called the *Nibelungen* and *Metropolis* proto-fascist films, whereas *M* as well as *The Testament of Dr Mabuse* were thought to contain an anti-Nazi message. These interpretations are far-fetched; like the theatre director in the prologue to *Faust*, Lang wanted tó offer something for everyone. He shared with other producers of the era a definite penchant for such themes as suicide, inexorable fate, madness, death. He was fascinated by the idea of the Golem, the man-machine, as were Rippert (*Homunculus*) and Paul Wegener before him, Richard Oswald (*Alraune*, 1931) or Pabst in his first film (*Der Schatz*, 1923). The chaotic world of the postwar years was reflected in the multitude of monsters and vampires and other horrors in the cinema from *Nosferatu*, Murnau's version of *Dracula*, to *Svengali*, produced in 1927. These were rooted in the nightmares of the war generation, but they also incorporated an admixture of science fiction. In Lang's *Frau im Mond* several people are carried to the moon by rockets, with Professor Oberth, the pioneer of space travel, acting as scientific adviser. Between yesterday's catastrophes and the perils of the new technical civilization there was not much room for optimism.

To the same world of horrors belongs the hero who has either lost his identity or, worse, sold his soul to the devil, from *Der Student von Prag* (1913 and a new version in 1926) to Murnau's *Faust* (1926). It was in these films that Expressionism celebrated its greatest triumphs; Expressionist poems and pictures may be forgotten but *Caligari* and several other films have survived as milestones in the history of the cinema, despite their technical imperfections. This refers to the acting and the staging of these films, and to a certain degree also to their content. It is doubtful whether one can go any further, as some critics have done, interpreting the early postwar films as signs of rebellion against authority, to be replaced in later years by a spirit of acquiescence and submission. Politics did of course have a certain impact on the cinema but more often than not in an indirect, roundabout way. One would look in vain in the German cinema for the father-son conflict which figured so prominently in the contemporary theatre. Perhaps the early cinema was not yet able to deal with complex psychological problems, and by the time it had become more sophisticated in its techniques the father-son conflict had gone out of fashion. One would have thought that the stabilization period would bring with it a decline in social commitment and interest, whereas the depression would have the opposite effect. But so far as the German cinema is concerned this was not so. Social criticism had its heyday before 1929, with films such as *Die freudlose Gasse, Dürfen wir schweigen, Die Unehelichen, Berlin – Symphonie einer Grossstadt, Die Weber, Asphalt, Dirnentragödie, Jenseits der Strasse, Mutter Krausens Fahrt ins Glück, Menschen am Sonntag*. The years after 1929, on the other hand, witnessed the boom of the escapist love-story and the extravagant operetta. The cinema was apparently subject to logic and laws of movement of its own.

The mid-1920s were a period of transition for German film-making. Paul Leni's *Das Wachsfigurenkabinett*, the last important Expressionist film, already betrayed unmistakable new influences. The story is of little importance; the owner of the wax-works looks for a writer to provide scenarios for some of the figures in his establishment. In the young writer's dream Ivan the Terrible (Conrad Veidt) makes his appearance, so do Haroun Al-Raschid (Emil Jannings) and Jack the Ripper (Werner Krauss). But this film, unlike *Caligari*, left no doubt that it was dealing with fantasy not the real world, and it made a further concession to conventional practice by having a happy ending.

A very influential film was Dupont's *Varieté*, a story of jealousy in the circus world. An acrobat (Emil Jannings) leaves his wife for a younger girl. When they attain success, the girl decides to team up with a younger trapeze artist who is already internationally famous. Jannings avenges himself on his rival by intentionally missing his grasp during a triple somersault. He then surrenders to the police. The producer tackled this story with great psychological subtlety, so that the spectators felt like participants in the unfolding action. The film was shot in the Berlin Wintergarten, where the space was exceedingly confined and, out of necessity, a new technique was born: the lying-on-the-stomach school of photography. So great was the impact of the film on Hollywood that those connected with its production were immediately offered irresistible contracts – Dupont, the producer, Freund, the chief camerman, Emil Jannings and Lya de Putti, the young *femme fatale*.

Geheimnisse einer Seele, produced by Pabst, attracted much attention for breaking new ground in another direction. A chemistry professor, afraid of touching knives (because he might kill his wife), has come to associate sexual intercourse with the act of murder and this in turn causes impotence. The case-history and the account of the subsequent cure are presented without any attempt to sensationalize or vulgarize a difficult and delicate subject. Karl Abraham and Hanns Sachs, leading psychoanalysts, acted as advisers to Pabst and helped him to make a convincing artistic whole out of the fragmented parts of a dream. *Geheimnisse einer Seele* could not be copied because 'psychoanalysis in action' did not necessarily make good cinema; but in an indirect way, through the use of sexual symbols, this film exerted a profound influence.

Perhaps most characteristic for the film of the 1920s was the 'street theme'; Karl Gruene's *Die Strasse*, produced in 1923, had paved the way and the topic was to preoccupy German film-makers one way or another for a whole decade. In Gruene's film the street is a place full of temptation and danger. Follow-ing a sudden impulse, a lowly office-worker breaks away from conventional life. He enters a night club, follows a prostitute and spends the night with her. The next morning he returns home, having realized that 'the street' is a cruel place, that it spells ruin and destruction, whereas home, however unexciting, means peace and safety. The preoccupation with the soulless, anonymous city is in the Expressionist tradition, as is the decor (provided by Ludwig Meidner). But the message of the film certainly points beyond Expressionism. The most famous 'street film' was the one which made Pabst internationally famous, *Die freudlose Gasse*, which takes place in postwar Vienna. It was one of the last films in which Asta Nielsen appeared and it made Greta Garbo famous. It portrays the social ravages wrought by inflation, as illustrated by the ruin of a middle-class family. Rumfort, a city councillor, and his wife lose their savings and face starvation; their daughter goes to work in a night club and is driven to prostitution. The film shows both the world of the *nouveaux riches*, their restaurants and night clubs, and the misery of the impoverished masses, the queues in front of the food shops. The butcher asks for payment in kind from the female customers he finds attractive, which naturally provoked em-phatic protests from the butchers' defence association. There is a most implausible happy ending; Romfort and his daughter are saved by an American Red Cross official, appearing as *deus ex machina*. *Die freudlose Gasse* coincided with the emergence of 'Neue Sachlichkeit' in painting and literature and its realism inaugurated a new era in the history of the cinema. The street as the home of the homeless remained the favourite theme of film-makers for many years to come. Pabst's film was followed by several others dealing with street crime and prostitution, such as *Dirnentragödie*, Metzner's *Überfall* and, most successfully, Joe May's *Asphalt*, the story of the police sergeant who falls in love with the girl whom he arrested. He is suspected of murder but her evidence proves his innocence. In *Asphalt* the motor-car plays a major role for the first time; in another film of that period, *Die letzte Droschke von Berlin*, it is the incarnation of all evil. For the spread of the taxicabs has made the hero, an old coachman, unemployed. His wife tells him that he is no longer of use to anyone and, to make his humiliation complete, his daughter marries a young taxi-driver. He tries to commit suicide by driving horse and carriage into the Spree, but is saved by his son-in-law. In the end an abode is found even for his horse, between two garages. Both coachman and horse reluctantly accept the spirit of modernity.

So long as producers and cameramen were confined to their studios, the street remained a remote object of mystery and horror. But once their equipment became more sophisticated they could go out to take pictures of the street as it really was. Not surprisingly, they found it full of excitement and pulsating with life. Criminals and prostitutes lose their monopoly of the street; children and old people, working men and housewives appear in the inchoate, aimless, yet impressive shots of Ruttmann's and Freund's *Berlin – Symphonie einer Grossstadt* (1927), and in *Menschen am Sonntag*, produced by Siodmak, Wilder, Zinnemann and Schuftan in 1929. Young white-collar workers (all played by amateur actors) are seen spending their weekends at a lake near Berlin. The film shows the boredom of big city life and the inadequacies of leisure, but there is nothing particularly desperate or vicious about it – it is just part of life. The idea of depicting city life was in the air: the same year films in a similar vein were produced in France (Marcel Carné) and the United States. *Berlin* was praised for its technical excellence and for Edmund Meisel's music; some critics deplored its lack of commitment: it neither condemned nor idealized the street, it had no message, nor did it show clearly enough the anarchy of capitalist society. But the intention of producers and cameramen had been deliberately modest – to present a more or less realistic picture of big city life from early morning to late at night. They had realized, perhaps somewhat belatedly, that the cinema alone among all the arts was capable of reflecting certain aspects of city life: 'Let the camera bear witness' was their motto.

Some of the new street films were committed, such as *Mutter Krausens Fahrt ins Glück* – the French title, significantly, was *L'Enfer des pauvres* – but it was not necessarily more convincing. This film was based on an idea of Heinrich Zille, the painter of proletarian Berlin: Mother Krause, an old newspaper vendor, has two children, Erna and Paul, both unemployed. Her subtenants are a prostitute and her ponce. Poverty drives Erna into prostitution while Paul, enticed by the ponce to commit a robbery, ends up in prison. Mother Krause commits suicide, taking with her the prostitute's little child; for what good can there be in store for a child in this horrible world? There is however a ray of hope, for Erna's boyfriend, a class-conscious worker, leads her back to a decent life and to political awareness and militancy. Phil Jutzi, the director, certainly succeeded in capturing the atmosphere of proletarian Berlin; he went out of his way to find the most horrible slums and the most wretched creatures inhabiting them.

By this time the public had become a little restless; it preferred to see films about 'people like you and me' rather than stark, unrelieved misery. For this reason *Kuhle Wampe* (1932). the widely discussed communist film, wisely presented neither crime nor prostitution nor the other horrors of capitalist society, but chose a constructive, optimistic approach. Its political effect was limited because it followed too closely the party line, which at that time saw the main enemy in Social Democracy rather than in Nazism. It shows life in a tent colony outside Berlin and concentrates on the activities of the Communist sports movement. The younger generation, which, it proclaims, will change the world, is glorified, whereas the petty-bourgeois conventions of the older people personified by Social Democratic workers, are derided. *Kuhle Wampe*, the first major film of Slatan Dudow, a young Bulgarian producer, was not likely to promote working-class unity and it more or less ignored the rising tide of Nazism.

The films mentioned so far were outstanding in as much as they tried to provide more than mere entertainment. The average cinemagoer was far more likely to watch Joe May's early Stuart Webb series and in later years the many films of Harry Piel, the German Douglas Fairbanks. Stuart Webb was a private detective fashioned after Sherlock Holmes, complete with pipe and deerstalker, who survives the most hair-raising adventures and thwarts the designs of the most dangerous criminals. He was the hero of countless early films and, like Harry Piel, was the great attraction for the majority of cinema-goers. The great master of entertainment was Ernst Lubitsch, who made his debut with *Madame Dubarry* 1919, the first such monumental film ever produced in Germany. It made Pola Negri, a Polish born actress, a world star and it also inaugurated Germany's return to the international film market. *Madame Dubarry* had a sad ending whereas Lubitsch's subsequent pictures were mostly comedies, such as *Die Austernprinzessin*. Other producers tried to copy Lubitsch but they lacked his magic touch, and after he went to Hollywood German film comedy fell on sad days.

It was only in the early 1930s that the German cinema managed to produce thrillers and comedies of some merit. This was the period of *Emil and the Detectives* and the emergence of Hans Albers as daredevil adventurer and irresistible lover, whether the issue at stake was to bomb Monte Carlo or to re-establish contact with the artificial platform in mid-Atlantic in order to prevent some cosmic disaster (*F.P. 1 antwortet nicht*). The absence during the 1920s of good comedies and adventure films helps to explain the tremendous popularity in Germany not only of Charlie Chaplin but also of Buster Keaton, Harold Lloyd and, later, of Jackie Coogan. There was, however, one genre in which the German cinema excelled – the *Kulturfilm*. These educational features dealt with the work of famous artists, life in foreign countries, the marvels of nature, new technical and scientific achievements. They were on the whole of a very high standard and were widely shown all over the world.

The mountain films of Arnold Fanck, culminating in *Die weisse Hölle von Piz Palü*, should also be mentioned in this context. This was the school from which Luis Trenker and Leni Riefenstahl graduated and it was subsequently denounced as proto-Nazi; but if they contained a political message it was carefully hidden. Kracauer claimed that 'immaturity and mountain climbing were one' and 'the idolatry of glaciers and rocks was symptomatic of an anti-rationalism on which the Nazis could capitalize'. It is true that mountaineering was not then one of the favourite sports of German intellectuals, but this did not necessarily make it a fascist activity. Those who saw these films at the time were impressed above all by breathtaking shots of wonderful landscapes and by the exploits of the daring men who set out to master the mountains.

German inventors had been among the pioneers of the sound film but it was not until the breakthrough, initiated by Warner Brothers, that the new medium conquered Germany a decade later. Once the new machinery had been installed and new films were shown, there was no looking back; the transition from silent to sound film was rapid. It was the end of a whole era; some actors and producers became much more famous than before, others failed to take the hurdle and were forgotten. While inevitable, the change was not without its drawbacks. Movie-makers were now inclined to stress the dialogue at the expense of the visual element, and there was a decline in the high standards of photography which had been attained towards the end of the silent film era. Thus in some ways the early sound film was more superficial than the silent film at its best. On the other hand it is difficult to imagine *The Blue Angel* as a silent film. Produced by Erich Pommer and Josef von Sternberg, who were recalled from Hollywood, this, one of the earliest German sound films, was a milestone in the history of the cinema. True, some critics argued that Professor Rath, the hero of Heinrich Mann's novel, had become a mere puppet in the film, one-dimensional and unconvincing. The political and social criticism which figured so prominently in the book had virtually disappeared; what remained was a study in sado-masochism, the story of a pathetic old bachelor reduced to total servitude by a sexy young actress with beautiful long legs (Lola Lola). He gives up his position as a respected teacher and joins

Lola's circus group. Mistreated by everyone, above all by his new wife, he tries to kill Lola backstage while crowing like a cock – his act in the circus. He returns to his old school, collapses and dies.

The Blue Angel was enormously successful in Germany and abroad, because it showed, perhaps for the first time, the great possibilities of the new medium. For the wider public, Marlene Dietrich's performance as the provocative tart overshadowed everything and everyone else; she became the new sex-symbol. The cult of film stars, not unknown in the era of the silent film, now reached new heights. *Blue Angel* was followed by several sound films conveying a message of social criticism such as *Threepenny Opera, Berlin Alexanderplatz* and *Cyankali*. It has been noted that the political message in the cinema usually had to be low-keyed, partly to evade censorship, partly because films catered for a wide public. But this by no means always spelt ruin for the film; Friedrich Wolf's film about abortion, while less outspoken, was more powerful than the play precisely because *Cyankali*'s producers tried to do more than simply preach to the converted. In the original version of the *Threepenny Opera*, Brecht makes the queen's messenger the *deus ex machina*, who saves Mackie Messer from certain death. Pabst, who did the film version, preferred a different ending, with Polly establishing a bank, together with Peachum, Tiger Brown and Mackie. Brecht was dissatisfied with these changes; it was a clash between two talents and temperaments, and it is by no means certain that Pabst's version is less effective than Brecht's. The most powerful of the pre-Hitler anti-authoritarian films was *Mädchen in Uniform*. Made by a small group of independent producers, it was unique in a number of ways: there was no male in the cast, and most of the young actresses were quite unknown at the time. The action takes place around 1925 in a Potsdam boarding school for officers' daughters, run on strictly disciplinarian lines. Emilia Unda, the head, moves around with a cane, a cross between Frederick the Great and a regimental sergeant major, awe-inspiring, repulsive, and slightly comic. Manuela von Meinhardis, a newcomer, finds the whole atmosphere suffocating and falls in love with a sympathetic young teacher (Melle von Bernburg), who in contrast to the head of the school is adored by all the girls. When she blurts out her feelings for the teacher, the headmistress gives orders that no one is to talk to Manuela. Driven to utter despair and feeling herself forsaken even by the one she loves Manuela tries to commit suicide, but her classmates pull her from the staircase from which she was about to jump. The headmistress arrives, met by the accusing stares of the girls. For once she is unable to cope with the situation, she has no orders to give, her authority is broken. *Mädchen in Uniform* was a powerful attack on an outdated and inhuman educational system. It was produced and first shown at a time (1931) when such attacks on authority were no longer the fashion and it dealt with a subject considered highly delicate by the standards of the day. Nevertheless it was almost universally acclaimed.

Patriotic films had been produced throughout the Weimar era; towards its end they became even more frequent. King Frederick the Great and the war against Napoleon were the favourite subjects. They showed the great king as a rebel against his narrow-minded and strict father, or alternatively as a man sacrificing his own feelings (friendship and love) because he felt a higher duty to the state. Naturally, he demanded the same from others. The king appears as a solitary figure, powerful, undaunted by defeat (*Der Choral von Leuthen*). He outwits Prussia's enemies and is a true father to his people. He is a man with a social conscience, the father of Prussian socialism, soaking the rich, caring for the poor. All the virtues of Prussianism, real and imaginary, are embodied in him.

The films about 1812–3 glorify individual acts of heroism, or alternatively deal with the conflict of loyalties which faced German patriots at the time (*York* and Luis Trenker's *Der Rebell*). Prussia has been defeated, the king has made peace with Napoleon – are they entitled to continue the struggle? Though profoundly conservative in inspiration, these films are not rabidly chauvinistic. The enemy is not, as in later years, an *Untermensch*; he is just a soldier doing his duty; war is neither good nor bad but a natural occurrence. While there were countless books which openly derided the Weimar Republic or were antisemitic in inspiration, there were no such films. Even the war films, of which there were not a few towards the end of the period, were as a rule by no means militaristic. Even if they extolled courage and other manly virtues there was no attempt to glorify war itself. This refers also to the very last such film produced during the Weimar era, *Morgenrot*, which was first shown after Hitler's rise to power and in his presence. Foreign observers who attended the first showing praised this film, which dealt with submarine warfare, for the absence of any chauvinistic tendency.

Westfront 1918 (1930) and Travas's *Niemandsland* (1931), depicting trench warfare during the last year of war, were clearly pacifist in inspiration. The first is the story of a small group of German soldiers in a forward outpost commanded by a tough young lieutenant who in the end goes mad. In addition there is a love affair between a student soldier and a French girl; while Karl, the hero of the film, home on leave, finds his wife in bed with another man. Above all it is a film of men dying, of mutilated bodies and an overwhelming sense of utter purposelessness. The German censor in his comment said that the film was 'one-sided' in as much as it did not show the heroic side of war, that it might weaken the willingness of the young generation to defend their country and that as a result its effect was profoundly defeatist. Yet although it was more outspokenly pacifist than *All Quiet on the Western Front*, which reached Germany at about the same time, it was not banned – perhaps because it did not attract Nazi demonstrators. Nor was *Niemandsland* banned in Germany, whereas in France it could not be shown. Produced by one of Fritz Lang's former assistants, it presents the story of five soldiers, each of a different nationality, who find themselves in a big foxhole in no-man's-land during the last days of the war. Former enemies come to respect each other and even become friendly. Despite its praiseworthy intentions *Niemandsland* was not a commercial success; the public had seen enough of the horrors of war, and the story was admittedly a little far-fetched.

The public wanted to be entertained rather than shocked, and what better means to that end than an operetta, if possible with a Viennese background? Escapism flourished precisely because the situation was desperate. Those who were hit by the depression, who had lost their money or became unemployed, needed no refresher-course in social criticism – they wanted to forget reality, at least for a few hours. Hence the phenomenal success of *Drei von der Tankstelle* (1930), of *Zwei Herzen im*

Dreivierteltakt, of *Walzerkrieg* and above all of Erik Charrell's *Der Kongress tanzt* (1931). This was the great era of Willy Fritzsch and Lilian Harvey, his permanent screen sweetheart, of Hans Albers, the irresistible adventurer, of brilliant tenors such as Richard Tauber, Jan Kiepura and Josef Schmidt. The sound film opened up possibilities which had not existed before and with songwriters of genius, such as Werner Richard Heymann (*Das gibt's nur einmal*), the sentimental musical comedy conquered the German cinema.

1933 witnessed the exodus of producers and actors of Jewish extraction but, compared with the other arts and the mass media, the continuity of the pre-Nazi German cinema beyond 1933, and even beyond 1945, is striking. The German press was thoroughly purged and the German radio, which had four and a half million listeners by the time Hitler came to power, was wholly reorganized; its former heads (Bredow, Flesch and Magnus) were arrested and put on trial. No such tragedies befell the producers and stars of the German cinema unless they had the misfortune to be Jewish. In January 1932 Axel Eggebrecht, an anti-fascist intellectual of the extreme left, wrote in the *Weltbühne* criticizing the lack of spirit among his colleagues: 'We are about to surrender. . . . All is over. . . . With folded arms we quietly await Hitler.' But Eggebrecht did not mount the barricades; in January 1933, like so many others, he found employment in the cinema as a scriptwriter for *Bel Ami* and other films. Fritz Lang was asked by Goebbels who had admired some of his work to reorganize the German film industry, but he had a Jewish mother and could not oblige. Pabst, the pacifist and social critic, who was abroad in 1933, later returned to Nazi Germany and produced two – admittedly wholly unpolitical – films. Carl Froelich, who had made the anti-authoritarian *Mädchen in Uniform*, became one of the most productive and prestigious film-makers during the Nazi era and continued his career after 1950. Hertha Thiele had been the sweet young innocent in *Mädchen in Uniform*, and later Annie, the heroine of the communist film *Kuhle Wampe*; she, too, appeared in a film on German youth, in a rather different spirit, after January 1933. Erich Engel, who had started his career with Piscator, did well in the Third Reich, and even better in East Germany after 1945. Helmuth Käutner had been a successful cabaret artist before 1933; his subsequent career resembles that of Engel and of countless others. None of them was a convinced Nazi.

There was even more surprising continuity in Nazi political films, some of them highly effective in putting their message across. The actors in these films included Heinrich George and Werner Krauss who had been among the great stars of the Weimar period, from *Caligari* to *Die freudlose Gasse* and *Berlin Alexanderplatz*. There were Theodor Loos (of *M* fame), Gustav Diesel, who had given a memorable performance as Karl in *Westfront 1918*, and Jacob Tiedtke (of *Berlin Alexanderplatz*).

Wolfgang Staudte, who filmed the exploits of the Luftwaffe during the war, produced after 1945 in East Germany the great anti-fascist film, *Die Mörder sind unter Uns*. Yet only a few years before he had appeared in *Jew Süss*, the most viciously anti-semitic film, joined by Theodor Loos. Otto Wernicke had played the police inspector in the anti-fascist *M*; two years later he was given the leading role in *SA-Mann Brandt*. Gustav Gründgens had been the chief gangster in *M*, was one of the greatest stars in the Third Reich and became even more famous after 1945. With the exception of Leni Riefenstahl not a single producer or actor came to lasting harm, and even her films were eventually shown again. Most of these producers and actors were genuinely unpolitical, able to serve any master. Most Weimar films were basically unpolitical too, and this, contrary to expectations, did not change under Hitler. Film-making in the Third Reich was relatively free from control. Thus neither 1933 nor 1945 marked a total break in the history of the German cinema. True, the Expressionist tradition disappeared after 1933, but then it had not been much in evidence anyway for a number of years. True, also, that after 1945 nationalist themes had to be dropped and in East Germany a socialist realism of sorts prevailed. But by and large there was surprising continuity. Producers and actors, like technicians and physicians, had become an indispensable part of modern civilization, without whom, it would appear, no society could function.

*　　*　　*

The 1920s were the age of the operetta as much as of the cinema – of Fritzi Massary and Richard Tauber, of gala performances which were social as well as musical events. But whereas the film was then in its beginnings, passing through various diseases of infancy, the great era of the operetta had already passed. The operetta flourished for less than a century; its history begins in 1858 with *Orpheus in the Underworld*, it ended shortly before the Second World War with the works of Nico Dostal and Fred Raymond. The golden years were the 1870s and 1880s; no subsequent work can stand comparison with *Fledermaus* (1874), *Bettelstudent* (1882), and *Zigeunerbaron* (1885). Around the turn of the century the operetta experienced a revival (Leo Fall, Oscar Straus and above all Lehar and Kalman), and outside the Continental tradition there were Gilbert and Sullivan and Jones (*The Geisha Girl*). By and large, the classic operetta was a Viennese affair with Hungarian flavouring. If Germany became the world capital of the operetta in the 1920s, those instrumental in the transfer – composers, musical directors and singers – had more often than not been imported from Vienna and Budapest.

However, Berlin had its own tradition of light music which goes back well before the First World War. Its most prominent representative was Paul Lincke, a handsome and dashing young band-leader who wrote his own music to the farces which were performed in the Apollo Theater. After he had become famous he moved to the Metropol where theatrical revues were presented. These were short sketches, variety acts, a little ballet and a great deal of the typical Berlin humour – pert and pungent, in remarkable contrast to Viennese sentimentality. Lincke's tunes were catchy and vigorous, many of them were immediate hits and some became classics of their kind. Together with two younger men, Jean Gilbert and Walter Kollo, Lincke established what came to be known as the Berlin operetta. Their overtures and songs appealed to the public of 1910, and even if the critics were at best disdainful, the public, high and low, loved them, quite often preferring them to the Viennese operetta with its stock characters and situations – the old emperor, the impoverished Polish nobleman, the gipsy adventurer, the *chambre séparée*, the Grinzing inn.

The revival of the operetta during the 1920s would have been unthinkable without the part played by two Austrians. Fritzi Massary had arrived in Berlin before 1914; she conquered the city with her charm, her inimitable grace and exquisite dresses,

and she made the ⟨...⟩ pr⟨...⟩ ⟨...⟩ high society. Queen
of the genre, sh⟨...⟩ ⟨...⟩ s⟨...⟩ almost three decades.
Richard Taube⟨...⟩ hi⟨...⟩ ⟨...⟩ conductor, and then
acquired some ⟨...⟩ ar⟨...⟩ *ieder* singer. In 1924 he
met Lehar an⟨...⟩ ⟨...⟩o⟨...⟩ ls; he became the chief
interpreter of ⟨...⟩ ⟨...⟩p⟨...⟩ *y Widow* and the darling
of the Berlir⟨...⟩ ⟨...⟩.

Occasion⟨...⟩ ⟨...⟩ ⟨...⟩ppeared and showed that
⟨...⟩ was ⟨...⟩ d not be neglected. Kün-
ne⟨...⟩ *V.* ⟨...⟩ an example; it successfully
integ⟨...⟩ rot, tango, one step and
boston⟩ into ⟨...⟩ ie pillars of the revival were
the newc⟨...⟩ ⟨...⟩ nd Budapest. When Paul
Abraham⟨...⟩ ⟨...⟩ius, arrived in the German
capital i⟨...⟩ thirties and totally unknown.
He ha⟨...⟩ and several string quartets of
whi⟨...⟩ with respect. Within a year
Vi⟨...⟩ im fame; this was followed by
I⟨...⟩ *voy.* More than other contem-
⟨...⟩ used modern dance rhythms;
⟨...⟩ melodies such as had not been
⟨...⟩ ung Lehar.

⟨...⟩ to Berlin a few years earlier. His
great succe⟨...⟩ *Inn,* the story of Leopold the head
waiter who is in love w⟨...⟩ his boss, Josepha Vogelhuber, the
pretty innkeeper. Unfortunately she prefers a lawyer; following
many misadventures and the personal intervention of no less a
person than the emperor, Leopold prevails over the lawyer.
White Horse Inn was in fact a rehash of a farce by Kadelburg
first performed fifty years earlier, and he had in turn plagiarised
Goldoni. But what did it matter? A producer of genius, Eric
Charrell, realized the possibilities of the old story. He transposed
it to Salzkammergut and found an excellent composer and
song-writer as well as first-rate actors. The farcical character of
the play and the wealth of melodies made it a resounding
success; there were 416 consecutive performances in Berlin and
651 in London. But, alas, Benatzky and Paul Abraham were the
last representatives of a great tradition. When Hitler came to
power Abraham had to leave Germany and a few years later
the history of the European operetta came to an end.

Mention ought to be made of jazz music not so much because the Germans made a significant contribution to its development as because they enjoyed it very much. Before 1914 ragtime had reached Central Europe but no one had ever heard original Dixieland jazz, and the war and the blockade prevented foreign records from reaching Germany. After 1918 the dance orchestras played the cake walk, the paso doble and the one step – and, if they were really up to date, the foxtrot and the shimmie. A daring saxophonist would improvise from time to time, whether because he was particularly gifted or because he was unable to read the music. But the orchestras of Marek Weber, of Dajos Bela and Bernhard Etté, the kings of dance music in the 1920s were essentially small symphony orchestras playing light music – one would look to them in vain for hot jazz. The situation changed with the visits to Berlin of the first foreign bands and soloists, including the Ohio band, Sam Wooding's band, Paul Whiteman, Sidney Bechet and others. Lud Gluskin played in Berlin from 1928 to 1930; he and the other visitors found imitators, some of them quite gifted. Others, less talented, thought that the essence of jazz was to play quickly, loudly and with a great deal of unnecessary clowning. At their best, German bands such as the Weintraub Syncopators (who appeared in *Blue Angel*), or the Comedian Harmonists (who were not, however, in the jazz tradition), introduced a fresh note. But with the beginning of the Great Depression many dance-halls closed, leading musicians went abroad and whole orchestras disintegrated. The opposition of the Nazis to jazz music was of long standing; they had always denounced it as the decadent outpourings of Negro *Untermenschen*. When Frick was put in charge of Thuringia, one of his first actions was to ban jazz altogether. Yet with all their ideological opposition to jazz, the bark of the Nazis was for once worse than their bite. British jazz bands continued to appear every year in Berlin up to the outbreak of the war. Arthur Lombard came to Hamburg fairly regularly, and German bands circumvented the ban simply by calling their music 'swing', which was not covered by the ban.

No mention has been made so far of the *chanson*, which flourished at the time in the Berlin cabarets. The librettists and composers such as Friedrich Holländer, Marcellus Schiffer and

Mischa Spoliansky were mostly Jews; their songs – often witty and impertinent, sometimes sentimental, not always in good taste – frequently referred to current events, not necessarily political. The cult of the *chanson* lasted for less than a decade; it was replaced by the pseudo-folk song such as 'Ich hab mein Herz in Heidelberg verloren' – the author of which, fittingly, was Viennese. There were some excellent comic artists such as Claire Waldorf in Berlin and Karl Valentin in Munich, but they too were facing an uphill task, for the climate of a dictatorship was inclement to satire, however good-humoured.

Weimar, in brief, was the age of Fritz Lang, of Marlene Dietrich and Richard Tauber as much as of its thinkers. In many ways the films of the period, the operettas and the hit songs, reflect the *Zeitgeist* as accurately as *The Magic Mountain* and *Demian*. In the cinema in particular the hopes and fears of the immediate postwar era, the trend towards objectivism during the stabilization period, the shock and the confusion of the Great Depression, are manifest. But it is also true that there was a constant desire to be entertained, to escape to far-away ages, to distant countries or to a better future. In the cinema the daydreams usually prevailed over the nightmares for the simple reason that the public wanted it that way. Thus it is dangerous to read too much into the content of the films of the period; whether they provide a key to the depths of the German soul, let alone to subsequent trends in German politics, is at best a moot point. Dr Caligari was followed after some delay by Hitler, but hindsight sometimes distorts the historian's view. Would not an analysis of the early Swedish film lead to some very disturbing prognostications – unnecessarily, as we now know? But even if the films and the *chansons* can be used only with great caution for an analysis in depth, even if the search for hidden meanings is strewn with pitfalls, they too were an integral part of the Weimar scene – and above all, at their best, they are still entertaining.

8
'An End with Horror'

Käthe Kollwitz, the painter of proletarian Germany, wrote in her diary on Easter Sunday, 1932, of 'the unspeakably difficult general situation. The general misery. People sliding into dark distress. The disgusting political incitement.' She could have added: The fear of proletarianization on the part of the middle classes. The fear of starvation on the part of the working classes. The loss of confidence on the part of the rulers of Germany. The masses of unemployed in front of the employment exchanges, the brutalization of public life, the greyness of the houses and the streets, which had never before been so strongly felt. The very same day the leader-writer of the *Frankfurter Zeitung* chose as a starting-point for his Easter message the words of Major Schill, the hero of the abortive revolt against Napoleon in 1809: 'Better an end with horror than horror without end.' Schill was executed by a French platoon and, the leader continued, 'the wild clamour of our own barbarous days means only the postponement of a tremendous emotional hangover which will be our lot sooner or later'.

The economic crisis and the explosive advance of National Socialism initiated the last phase of the Weimar Republic. There had been certain warning signs foreshadowing the coming storms; neither economic nor political stabilization was as deeply rooted as many had thought. But neither was the disaster as inevitable as it was to appear to later observers. The victory of Hitler's party in September 1930 came as a surprise not only to his enemies but to the Nazis themselves. They had at the time five daily newspapers in all, much fewer than any other major political party, and their membership in the whole of Germany was less than a hundred thousand. They had their greatest successes precisely in those districts of north and east Germany where their organization was weakest, or in some cases non-existent. The vote for Hitler and his party was at that stage essentially the expression of a mood, a demonstration against the existing state of affairs rather than in favour of any specific political programme. It was a vote which expressed the conviction that Germany was badly governed, that the established political parties and parliament were incompetent, that new men and ideas were needed to cope with the crisis. The growth of the Nazis on the one hand and the advance of the Communists on the other were directly connected with the economic crisis which had started in Wall Street on Black Friday (25 October 1929) and then quickly spread to Europe. While it affected all European countries, it had particularly grave consequences in Germany, which was suffering from an endemic agricultural crisis and, in view of the shocks of the early 1920s, was psychologically ill-prepared for further setbacks; moreover the banking houses were overextended and thus unable to weather even comparatively minor upsets. Industrial production declined within three years to little more than half of what it had been in 1928–9. There were six million unemployed. Wages fell substantially and unemployment benefits were cut or discontinued altogether. There was stark misery throughout the country and an all-pervasive atmosphere of hopelessness which engendered the breakdown first of parliamentary democracy and ultimately of the entire political system. And yet in the last resort there was nothing inevitable about the advance of the catastrophe; conditions during the years of inflation had been even worse without causing a general political breakdown. Other European countries and the United States did not succumb to fascism, which incidentally came to power only after the peak of the depression had passed. The downfall of the Weimar Republic was not the result of 'objective circumstances' beyond human control; it was to a large extent the outcome of loss of nerve, of political failure and economic error.

When the economic crisis broke, Germany was ruled by a

coalition, under Social Democratic leadership, which was torn apart by social conflict. The German People's Party (DVP) supported industry in its drive for higher prices and in its resistance to wage claims. The Social Democrats on the other hand were paralysed by internal disputes the trade unions and the left wing dissociating themselves from the more conciliatory stand taken by the SPD representatives in parliament. After the death of Stresemann, the undisputed leader of the DVP who had acted as a moderating influence, the disruptive forces in his party gained the upper hand; the coalition fell apart, and was succeeded by governments in which the Social Democrats were no longer represented, and on whose policy they had not the slightest influence. In the elections of 1930 the Social Democrats lost heavily; the DVP lost even more votes and ceased to be an effective political factor; in Berlin the Communists emerged for the first time as the strongest party. But the great surprise of the elections was of course the Nazi victory. From now on no government could count on a parliamentary majority and the country was ruled by emergency regulations (*Notverordnungen*). In so far as these were based on any consistent policy and were not just stop-gap measures, they were derived from a deeply erroneous conception of how to cope with the economic crisis. Brüning and his successors were firmly convinced that inflation was the greatest evil of all, that it had to be prevented at any cost, and consequently they pursued a deflationary policy, cut expenditure all along the line, refusing even to consider deficit spending. In their attempt to remedy the financial situation and to boost exports, they fixed lower wages and prices which paralysed large sections of the economy. These measures caused a further growth in unemployment and political radicalization, and eventually brought down the Brüning government together with the remnants of the democratic system. The Nazis were the principal beneficiaries of the crisis; they promised no more and no less than an immediate solution to all of Germany's problems and their assurances found willing ears. All other parties were more or less helpless. The centre parties, with the exception of the Catholic *Zentrum*, virtually melted away; the Social Democrats lacked political will; their appeals to reason and patience sounded hollow. The Communists polled more votes than ever before, but they were identified in the public mind with narrow class interests and the interests of a foreign power, and their electoral appeal was therefore limited to sections of the working class. At the time almost half of Germany's trade unionists were out of work and strike action was out of the question; as a paramilitary force, in the street fighting which became a daily feature of German politics in 1930–2, the Communists were vastly inferior to the Nazis. And so with all their confident slogans they were politically no more effective than the Social Democrats.

The dual crisis affected the German intelligentsia materially and psychologically. It had immediate and far-reaching repercussions on their stand during that last agonizing chapter of Weimar history. By 1932 there were about 60,000 'academic unemployed' out of a total of some 350,000–400,000. According to other statistics, every third *Akademiker* was unemployed by early 1933; but even those who still had jobs found their income shrinking. Each year some 25,000 students graduated from German universities; for many, perhaps most of them, there was no prospect of finding work in their professions in the foreseeable future. Various suggestions were made for tackling the problem of academic unemployment, including emigration, agricultural settlement, an earlier retirement age, voluntary labour service, one or more 'practical years' after graduation. None of these proposals evoked enthusiasm. All plans to expand higher education were shelved; on the contrary, measures to restrict it were discussed. Many theatres and opera houses, including those maintained by the state and the municipalities, closed down or had to merge, with the result that many actors were out of work. As cabarets and music halls closed down more musicians lost their jobs, for the cinema could offer employment to only a few of them. At one time it was estimated that about three-quarters of all musicians were unemployed. The public could no longer afford the price of theatre and opera tickets; one critic reported that already at the second performance of Gerhart Hauptmann's *Vor Sonnenuntergang* there were yawning gaps in the audience, and this although Hauptmann was Germany's leading playwright and the play had been hailed by the critics as one of his greatest. Special cheap tickets were provided by the cinemas for the unemployed, but even so about a hundred of them had to close down in Berlin alone. Publishing houses and writers also suffered from the depression; the number of books published was hardly affected, but their price had to be reduced and the income of the writers, including even bestselling authors, fell steeply. Allocations to scientific institutes were severely cut, support by industry for research to all intents and purposes ceased, state allocations fell from eight million marks in 1928 to five million in 1931; but even this reduced grant was largely fictitious, for the treasury declared itself incapable of providing the sums which had been promised. As a result, research in many fields was restricted or ceased altogether and young scientists had to be dismissed. Painters and sculptors found no buyers. It was a bad time for everyone, with the possible exception of those practising various occult sciences, who, not altogether surprisingly, found themselves in greater demand than ever before. Impoverishment made the intelligentsia politically more aware and also radicalized them, but did not make them more favourably disposed towards the left.

As the political pendulum was swinging to the right, the cultural climate too showed a marked change. The Brüning government and, to an even higher degree, its reactionary successors with their many urgent preoccupations, still found sufficient time and energy to combat *Kulturbolschewismus*. True, like everything else they did, the measures they applied were half-hearted; a few Communist editors and writers were prosecuted and sentenced to short prison terms, a few Communist plays were banned (or banned locally), and a handful of books were seized. But on the whole this kind of harassment did not do the Communists any serious harm. On the contrary, it attracted sympathy among sections of the liberal intelligentsia. (The corresponding measures applied against the Nazis were even less effective.) The one serious case of intimidation was the trial of Carl von Ossietzky, editor of the *Weltbühne*, who was sentenced to eighteen months imprisonment in 1931 on the strength of a prewar law. He was charged with having published two years earlier an article which provided details about the reconstruction of a German air force in contravention of the Versailles treaty. The trial was all the more scandalous because the Versailles treaty, hated or not, was part of the German constitution, and the data which allegedly constituted betrayal of military secrets had been mentioned in a Reichstag debate. But the whole case was symptomatic of the resentment of 'national circles' against the left wing and the pacifists and of their eagerness to teach them a lesson. More important than the legal chicanery were the Nazi demonstrations against individual intellectuals; while the brunt of the Nazi terror campaign was directed against the Social Democrats and the Communists, the left-wing intelligentsia and the academic opponents of Nazism also came in for their share. Mention has been made of the fact that small but highly militant Nazi groups had succeeded in seizing key positions in most German and Austrian universities even before the Nazi electoral victory of September 1930. During 1931–2 they made further progress and emerged as the strongest force in almost all of them; demonstrations against liberal, 'Marxist' and Jewish professors became routine occurrences. The university authorities more than once acceded to their demands, removing those (such as Professor Gumbel of Heidelberg) who had provoked the ire of the young stormtroopers. Sometimes the demonstrators chose to argue with the authorities. A Munich law professor had dared to suggest that the peace treaties of Brest-Litovsk and Bucharest imposed by Germany had been as unjust as Versailles. But towards the end of the period there was no longer any pretence of pointing to specific outrages. The dismissal of a particular professor was demanded simply because he was a liberal or a Jew.

If university riots became an almost daily occurrence, demonstrations in theatres and cinemas were on the whole an exception. But there were such incidents – for instance when *All Quiet on the Western Front* was shown or when in December 1931 Brecht and Weill's *Mahagonny* was first performed – and they did not fail to intimidate those concerned. Nazi journals published blacklists of scholars, writers and artists whose heads were to roll on the day of judgment. There had been such threats before, but in view of the growing power of the Nazis they could no longer be ignored. Books by left-wing or pacifist authors were on occasion removed from public libraries, and some observers thought that they could already hear the deathknell announcing the end of the freedom of the press and of expression. It is of course true that Germany was no longer democratically ruled, at the very latest after July 1932, when

Chancellor von Papen unconstitutionally deposed the Social Democratic government of Prussia. At the same time Nazism had by no means yet prevailed, and the misguided references of later historians to para-fascist structures only tend to obliterate important differences. If the authoritarian governments which ruled Germany in the transition period strongly disliked the liberal and left-wing culture and tried to counteract it, it is also true that their actions were not very effective. With the exception of the radio stations, which were state-controlled and thus subject to direct management and supervision, there was little outright intervention; and even in broadcasting, despite the appointment of some 'nationally minded officials' and even a few Nazis, the old pro-republican staff were by no means all dismissed. Despite censorship and trials, there was still as much freedom of expression in Germany in 1932 as in most other European countries. Authors of the extreme left published their novels and poems right up to the Nazi takeover, modernist composers' works were performed and exhibitions of avant-garde paintings arranged; no newspaper, periodical or publishing house was permanently closed for political reasons. If the Bauhaus ceased to exist in 1932 or the *Linkskurve* went out of business the same year, if Piscator failed yet again in Berlin in 1931, the reasons were mainly financial, though, in the case of the Bauhaus, vanishing sympathy on the part of those who had formerly supplied the subsidy did, of course, play a role.

Far more important than censorship or other forms of harassment was the general climate of uncertainty and fear which was rapidly spreading. Newspaper proprietors, publishers and theatre directors were influenced by the general swing to the right and they tried to a certain extent to adapt themselves. The liberal press continued to attack Nazism but became far more cautious in its attitude towards von Papen, Schleicher and their backers; self-censorship was incomparably more effective than open government intervention. Some Jewish and left-wing editors were dismissed – though few of prominence; Communists and fellow-travellers continued to write for the *Berliner Tageblatt* and the *Frankfurter Zeitung* right up to the end. The theatres which had been so eager to engage in experimentation, however radical, were now very reluctant to accept plays likely to provoke an uproar. Brecht had difficulties with his *St Joan*, although his other plays were still being staged. (But the state radio broadcast this play, which shows that even in 1932 it was by no means fully *gleichgeschaltet*.) Few members of the liberal and left-wing intelligentsia went over to the enemy with flying colours during those years; Arnolt Bronnen was a blatant exception. It is of course also true that few would have been welcomed by the Nazis.

It is easier to write about the attitudes of the Weimar intellectuals during the transition period than about their actions. But to blame them for their inactivity is pointless; their isolation was never more acutely felt than in those years. In one way or another most of them were involved with various anti-Nazi organizations; the trouble was that none of them was effective. The message of the intellectuals could be found in hundreds of manifestoes, but even if there had been thousands of them they would still have fallen on deaf ears. The real problem was, of course, the failure of the centre and the left, the unfortunate fact that the Nazis showed far more dynamism and purpose than their rivals and that their nationalist, anti-liberal and anti-semitic demagoguery made a far stronger appeal to the masses than the Social Democratic calls for discipline and order and the Communist appeals for a Soviet Germany.

To comment on the stand taken by the educated middle classes during the crisis is merely to repeat what has been said already on hostility to the Republic which, always latent, now received a fresh impetus. The willingness of the young to join tne march of the brown battalions was greater than the enthusiasm of the older generation. But since no alternative was offered by those who were frightened by the fanaticism of the extreme right, the political impact of the moderate right was minimal. They were at a loss to explain the rise of National Socialism, except as a belated reaction to Versailles and to the short-comings of the parliamentary system and the miseries of the Great Depression. They saw in it a great deal of 'unfermented idealism' which could be put to good use or to bad, according to the will of the leaders of the movement. Some, but only a few, saw in it the germs of a New Barbarism, but since they felt that there was nothing they could do to resist it they preferred to retire to their studies, having uttered their words of warning for the historical record.

The pro-republican forces and the left-wing intelligentsia looked to the political parties for leadership, but the Democratic Party virtually ceased to exist after 1930 and the Social Democrats were even less well equipped to cope with Nazism than they had been for the succession in 1918. Their leaders had received their political education in the Wilhelmian age; they knew how to organize trade unions and (less well) how to cope with parliamentary situations. They could, with difficulty, understand their rivals of the left, because these, after all, to a certain extent spoke the same language. But they were utterly bewildered by the onslaught of a movement which was quite unlike anything they had ever known, which concentrated its main activities not on parliament but in the streets, which appealed neither to reason nor to progress – as after all the Communists did – but to unbridled passion and national resentment. The Social Democrats, in other words, had learnt nothing from the Italian example. Even though the coalition had broken down they continued, while Brüning was in power, to regard themselves as one of the main pillars of the Republic, with all the responsibilities that entailed. After all, they argued, there were still many democratic positions to be defended. Unlike the Communists, they understood that 'fascism' was not yet in power. But what could be done to prevent its further progress? It is of course quite true that this could not have been achieved by traditional Social Democratic practices. On the other hand it was not foreordained that a leader, or a group of leaders, should not have risen to the occasion and have led their party effectively in the struggle against fascism. In the last resort the Social Democrats trusted that Hindenburg (whom they had supported against Hitler in the presidential elections of 1932), together with the Reichswehr, would not permit a Nazi seizure of power. The Communists relied neither on Brüning nor on Hindenburg, but this was about the only positive aspect of their policy during these decisive years. The main enemy as they saw it was 'Social Fascism', not the Nazi movement. While publishing occasional appeals against the fascist danger, they warned equally often against overrating this danger, for this meant 'objectively' playing into the hands of the real culprits, the Social Democrats. Ernst Thälmann, the Communist leader, declared in the Reichstag on 11 February

1930 that fascism was already in power in Germany – and this at a time when a Social Democrat headed the government.

Given the paralysis of social democracy and the suicidal policy of the Communists, the Weimar intelligentsia found themselves by and large outside any party framework. Yet their comments on current political problems do not on the whole reveal a greater astuteness than those made by the spokesmen of the parties, and this although the intellectuals kept silent not from a mistaken feeling of responsibility and loyalty (like the Social Democrats), nor because they were gagged by Comintern instructions (like the KPD). Both the *Weltbühne* and the *Tagebuch* suggested in editorials at one time or another that Hitler should be given power. For, once in power, the Nazis would soon *abwirtschaften*, reveal their utter incompetence. It is of interest that some writers with no claim to political expertise wrote in protest that once in power the Nazis would never voluntarily abdicate. The *Weltbühne* repeated many of the mistakes of the Communists – that Hitler was a lackey of heavy industry, that fascism was in power already – and it attacked the Social Democrats in 1930 for having campaigned against little Goebbels ('who does not exist at all'), rather than concentrating their efforts against Brüning, the real candidate for dictatorship. In the *Weltbühne* as well as other organs of the intellectual left, the Nazis were described as a party of effeminate cowards, a bunch of lunatics and criminals who, in the final analysis, had no chance of success. In 1923 the *Tagebuch* had assessed the motive forces activating Nazism more realistically; the passage of time had seemingly clouded the issues instead of clarifying them. The Communist *Linkskurve* decided that Nazism was altogether of no importance. In the words of its historian Werner T. Angress (*Central European History*, March 1968):

The last issues, from October through December 1932 contained hardly any commentary of note on the German situation. Instead, they contained such contributions as an account of the lot of a negro mother in the American South; a panegyric on Maxim Gorky; two scathing essays attacking respectively Gerhart Hauptmann and Heinrich Mann, a review article on Soviet literature during the past fifteen years; and an uncomplimentary assessment of contemporary social democratic lyric poetry. Nobody perusing these last issues now could possibly suspect from their contents that they were published at a time when the fate of the republic and the German proletariat hung in the balance.

Münzenberg's journal showed a slightly greater awareness of the danger; it devoted an entire issue to the financial help received by the Nazis from industry, as if other parties had not received much more money. As 1932 drew to its close, the *Weltbühne* renewed its appeals for unity of action between the two big left-wing parties. The editorials were still permeated with optimism but the journal had already made arrangements for publication in Vienna in case anything untoward should happen in Berlin, whereas the *Tagebuch* in summer 1932 actually transferred its editorial offices to Munich on the mistaken assumption that the Bavarian capital would provide more safety in case of emergency. The Nazi setback in the elections of November 1932 induced many observers on the left to believe that the worst was over – but not for long.

The intellectuals of the homeless left, in short, the professional pessimists alone excepted, were no more far-sighted than anyone else. Hence the charges against them by a subsequent generation of historians that they became aware of the dangers facing them too late, that they failed to join the big political parties which were resisting Hitler.* There were feelings of remorse even among the writers themselves; Heinrich Mann wrote that he should have done more than he did. But, to repeat, given the constitution of the left-wing intelligentsia and the lack of moral and political authority of intellectuals in Germany in general, their sins of omission were of no consequence. It would not have made the slightest difference if they had acted from within a major political party; *qua* writers and artists they had no special standing in the political struggle. Admittedly they had no inkling of the coming horrors of Nazi rule, but who else had,

*Thus, a German historian of the literary emigration has noted recently with evident indignation that Feuchtwanger, Brecht and Heinrich Mann bought houses or apartments in or near Berlin during the two years before Hitler's accession to power. At the same time he criticizes them for being insufficiently militant and for not making preparations for their emigration in time. (Hans Albert Walter, *Deutsche Exilliteratur, 1933–50*, I, 1972.)

with the exception of a few eccentrics such as George Grosz, whom no one took seriously as a political figure? In conversation with Thomas Mann, Grosz predicted in 1933 that Hitler would last not six months but six or ten years, that the Germans who had elected him deserved him, that both Nazism and Communism were based on terror and slavery and that within a few years there would be an alliance between Hitler and Stalin.

The years 1930–3 were among the less creative ones in the annals of Weimar culture, and the reasons were not only political and economic. A feeling of exhaustion could be detected in the arts. Neue Sachlichkeit had had its day but there was nothing to replace it. The *Zeitstück* in the theatre was on the way out, but no new genre or trend had taken its place. The great theatrical events of 1932 were the performances in commemoration of the Goethe centenary and the celebration of Gerhart Hauptmann's seventieth birthday. *Vor Sonnenuntergang* was the last great drama of the Republic; it would have been a fitting title for the end of a whole era, except that it referred not to the 'sunset' of German freedom but to the love affair between a young girl and a man old enough to be her grandfather. Some novels on unemployment and social conditions appeared in the bookshops, interesting as sociological documents but hardly great literature. Neither the years of crisis nor the rise of Hitler inspired a single German novel or a play which was to last. As Karl Kraus, the Viennese writer, commented, *Mir fällt zu Hitler nichts ein.*

It was a time of exhaustion and yet it was exaggerated to claim, as among others Ernst Robert Curtius did, that 'everything was finished' by 1932 (*Deutscher Geist in Gefahr*), and that Weimar culture collapsed from within. It was a period of weariness but, given a little more political stability and gradual economic recovery, there is little doubt that there would have been a cultural revival too, though not necessarily in the tradition of 'high Weimar'. The riots in the universities would have died down and the cultural pendulum would have swung back, away from irrationalism and contempt for the old humanist values. It was not to be, but this had nothing to do with the 'exhaustion of ideas'.

Thus we approach 30 January 1933. What happened during

the following weeks belongs to another and sadder chapter in the history of German culture. By the time Hitler came to power, some of the leading exponents of the Weimar spirit had already left Germany. A few had taken up residence abroad, others were outside Germany by mere chance. Among them were Tucholsky, George Grosz, Remarque, Fritz von Unruh, Piscator, Herwarth Walden, Georg Lukács, Ehrenstein, Rudolf Leonhard and Carl Sternheim. Thomas Mann, Feuchtwanger and Arnold Zweig left within the first two months after Hitler's rise to power. Others, such as Ossietzky, Erich Mühsam and Ludwig Renn, were arrested almost at once, and only the last of these emerged alive a few years later. In late March local Nazi youth and student organizations began to organize the burning of books, apparently as a partisan initiative. This practice spread from smaller places to Berlin, where it found its apogée in early May in the presence of Goebbels, who quoted Ulrich von Hutten – 'Oh century, oh sciences, it is a joy to be alive!' – as the books were consigned to the flames, though it was not readily obvious in what way the destruction of books would help to promote science.

The dismantling of Weimar culture proceeded much more sporadically and took longer than might have been expected after the first violent beginnings. The most renowned exponents of the 'system' were, of course, arrested or expelled. George Grosz, not surprisingly, was the first to lose his German citizenship (on 8 March 1933). The first list of emigrés who lost their citizenship was published in August 1933 and included Feuchtwanger, Helmut von Gerlach, Kerr, Heinrich Mann, Tucholsky, Toller and Münzenberg. Becher, Einstein, and Plievier were on the next list in March 1934. Bredel, Frank, Herzfelde, Klaus Mann and Piscator followed in November 1934; Friedrich Wolf, Brecht, Hiller and Mehring in 1935; Paul Bekker, Arnold Zweig and Thomas Mann in 1936.

In practice censorship was erratic. Max Brod's books were banned – but not his *Tycho Brahe*; Döblin's (but not his *Wallenstein*), Leonhard Frank's (but not the *Räuberbande*), Renn's (but not *Krieg*), Kästner's (but not *Emil and the Detectives*), Werfel's (but not *Verdi*). Some of the more esoteric theoretical writers of the extreme left were not to be banned for a long time; probably the Nazis had never managed to read them. Within the

Nazi hierarchy various authorities were competing for the right to carry out the cultural spring-cleaning, and frequently they did not see eye to eye. That Jews had to be removed from the cultural scene was of course taken for granted, and the same general ban applied to leading Communists and the most prominent enemies of Nazism in literature, journalism and the universities. These fields were hardest hit by the purge and the Nazis were not particularly eager to make converts there. On the contrary, turncoats such as Benn came under fire from Nazi purists. Elsewhere the purge was less rigorous; few non-Jewish professors were compelled to leave Germany. There was hardly a painter or sculptor among the emigrés, apart from Klee who returned to his native Switzerland and Kandinsky who went on to Paris, and this although many of them had been bitterly attacked. If they kept out of the limelight they usually had no great difficulty in finding a new job, sometimes not far from their old profession.

If the Nazi campaign against the spirit of Weimar was relentless, some individuals suffered more than others. The benevolent attitude towards film-makers and actors has been noted, and the threats against the exponents of jazz were not always followed up. Of the *Kulturbolschewisten* in the visual arts, none was imprisoned, though many museum directors were pensioned off and some painters and sculptors were forbidden to pursue their work in the Third Reich.

In Nuremberg in 1935 Streicher opened an exhibition of 'degenerate art'; the idea was taken up on a larger scale in the famous Munich exhibition of 1937. German museums were subjected to a second and third purge; as a result those lucky enough to be in Lucerne in June 1939 and able to dispose of a little money could acquire a Van Gogh self-portrait for twenty thousand dollars, famous pictures by Gauguin for some eight thousand, while the Picasso absinthe drinker did not even find a buyer. On the other hand Käthe Kollwitz and Paula Modersohn-Becker were permitted to exhibit for a while in Germany after 1933. The North German Expressionists such as Nolde, Barlach and Christian Rohlfs were bitterly attacked in the Nazi press, but they also found their defenders; it was not till the late 1930s that their pictures and sculptures had to be withdrawn. Hindemith's works were performed in 1934 and so were

Stravinsky's; eventually Hindemith had to leave Germany although powerful supporters such as Furtwängler – not exactly a modernist himself – had spoken up in his support. Erich Kästner and other writers continued to publish their un-political books; Mies van der Rohe could have remained in Germany and found work; Ihering and Otto Flake, Ehm Welk and Gerhard Pohl, Walter Karsch and Walter Kiaulehn, to mention but a few well-known contributors to left-wing and liberal periodicals, stayed and most of them continued to publish. Ernst Glaeser and Georg Pabst returned to Germany from exile, so did Ernst Rowohlt, the one-time (and future) leading publisher. Nazism had grandiose ambitions as a move-ment of cultural revival, but only a very few of its leaders had any real cultural interests. A specific Nazi culture, properly speaking, never came into being, and there were no doubt good reasons for this. As a result, the cultural scene in Nazi Germany was considerably more checkered than it should have been if the Nazi programme had been followed, and certain remnants of Weimar were not totally eradicated during the twelve years of Hitler's rule.

Among the intellectual emigrés the majority were Jewish, because they were doubly exposed to Nazi threats. German historians have since observed that but for the racial persecution it is doubtful whether many of them would have left the country. There is no way of proving or disproving this thesis; the only fact beyond dispute is that relatively few non-Jewish intellectuals emigrated, however much they disapproved of the regime, and that of these a few later returned to Nazi Germany. Of the emigré writers most congregated in Paris or in the South of France. Vienna was not a secure haven; Prague served mainly as a transit station; Moscow provided shelter only for a few, and of these some were later executed as Trotskyites or German spies; nor was London very congenial at the time. For writers and artists America became the desirable destination only in later years; for the academics it had been the main centre of absorption all along.

The story of Weimar-in-exile is beyond the purview of this account. Of the well-known writers few 'made it' in exile, whereas conductors and musicians were in much greater demand. But in addition to the senior established figures there were quite a few young men and women, who had just about graduated from university in Germany or had entered their first teaching or research posts, who were to rise to fame in their new countries. This happened in the case of scientists such as Hans Bethe and Ernst Chain, Konrad Bloch, Hans Krebs and Fritz Lipmann, of psychologists, political philosophers, sociologists and literary critics such as Erich Auerbach, Franz Neumann, Erik Erikson, Erich Fromm, Hans Morgenthau, Leo Strauss, Herbert Marcuse and others. They too belong at least to some extent to the Weimar tradition, even though most of their work was done after 1933 and outside Germany. They provided fresh stimulus to the development of new fields of study and their exodus caused irreparable harm to German cultural life well beyond the Nazi period. As has been repeatedly shown, the beginnings of Weimar culture predate the birth of the Republic: but the end coincides to the very day. The torchlight parade along Unter den Linden and the burning of books in the Opera Square were more than a symbolic act; they were the inauguration of a new epoch.

9
Weimar in Perspective

Less than five decades have passed since the heyday of the
Weimar Republic, hardly a sufficient time-span to warrant a
final judgment with any degree of assurance on the place of its
culture in history. Yet during these fifty years attitudes towards
this period have already undergone marked changes more than
once, and an interim balance-sheet is clearly possible.

The Nazi era, needless to say, was the antithesis to everything Weimar stood for. The reception of German emigré
intellectuals abroad, even when polite and helpful, seldom
revealed intellectual curiosity. The view then prevailing among
anti-Nazi circles in Britain, France and the United States was
that these unfortunate men and women were deserving of help
and that some of them could certainly make a useful contribution in their country of exile. But essentially they were social
cases: what Einstein and Thomas Mann did or said was news,
about the others no one greatly cared. This lack of interest in
the refugees, beyond a general feeling of compassion and solidarity, reflected the cultural provincialism of Europe in the
1930s. Among the emigrés themselves the feeling of failure was
fairly widespread – failure not only in the political sense. It was
reflected in the suicides of Tucholsky, Toller and Stefan Zweig;
it was given perhaps its most eloquent expression in Tucholsky's last, deeply pessimistic letters. The conviction was fairly
widespread that Weimar culture was irrevocably finished, that
it would be of little interest to anyone but those who had been
personally involved, and that it would be studied by future

generations as the prelude to Nazism rather than in its own right. This much was common to emigrés in West and East even if the reasons for resignation stemmed from different motives. When in 1935 the Moscow-based German-language magazine *Das Wort* inaugurated a debate on Expressionism it was denounced in retrospect by orthodox party stalwarts (Kurella) and cautious revisionists (Lukács) alike as a tragic mistake in German cultural history. Expressionism in this context stood for modernism, for experimentation, for all that had made Weimar *sui generis*.

With the end of the Second World War it seemed as if this pessimistic appraisal of the Weimar heritage was only too justified. When Alfred Döblin returned in French uniform to establish a cultural magazine for occupied West Germany, his endeavour, mainly devoted to the writers of the 1920s, found little response, his failure was in some ways typical of the lack of communication. The cataclysmic events of the intervening years made the Weimar period appear in retrospect irrelevant, if not frivolous. Some of its leading writers were republished in West Germany almost immediately after the war but they were not widely read; they appeared to belong to another age. It seemed as if many more years than a mere dozen had passed since these books had been burned. These were the years of hunger, with political responsibility in the hands of the occupying powers; it was by no means certain whether an independent Germany would ever re-emerge and, if it did, in what form. It was clearly the time for rethinking the course of German history, for finding out what had gone wrong before looking for roots and links in the recent past. So soon after the horrors of the war, the problems and the preoccupations of the Weimar intelligentsia seemed remote, if not altogether incomprehensible.

If there was to be a renewal of Weimar culture it seemed far more likely at the time that it would take place in East Germany. It was not just that many emigrés congregated there during the early postwar years; the East German government made a deliberate effort to help them and those other Weimar figures who had spent the war years in Germany but who had re-emerged with their reputation intact. In contrast to the West, East Germany had a cultural policy and it seemed that it was resolved to make good use of the Weimar tradition in the reconstruction of the new state. This applied to Brecht's theatre as well as to leading writers of the period such as Heinrich Mann, Feuchtwanger, Arnold Zweig – most of them not Communists or fellow-travellers but 'progressives', men of good will, prepared to give a hand in the building of a new democratic Germany. Even the *Weltbühne* was revived in 1948 in the same format, the same red cover, the same type. Only the contents were quite different – straight party propaganda. The failure of the new *Weltbühne*, too, was not accidental; it symbolized the fact that the Weimar revival was a false blossoming. For the year was 1948, and by that time cultural controls had become more and more stringent; within a year or two East German culture was effectively Stalinized. The critical spirit and the tolerant climate of the Weimar period were in stark contrast to the atmosphere of unquestioning belief and obedience that was now the order of the day. True, *Sergeant Grischa* and the novels of Feuchtwanger and Heinrich Mann were still published, and Brecht kept his theatre at Schiffbauerdamm, though from time to time he ran into trouble with the authorities. But the avant-garde art and the music of the 1920s (let alone psychoanalysis) were anathema, and so were the ideas of the Western Marxists which were first developed during that period. This reaction was only natural, for the political regime, and the society which came into being in the eastern part of Germany, differed totally in all essential respects from the first Republic. The spirit of alienation and contradiction prevalent among the Weimar left-wing intellectuals made them highly undesirable as cultural heroes for a regime eager to inculcate very different values and traditions in its intelligentsia. So far as this regime was concerned, the best that could be said about the Weimar intelligentsia – excepting only a handful of party members and sympathizers – was that some of them had played a progressive role in the struggle against the bourgeois-fascist regimes of the day. But since they lacked close contact with the working class few of them had been able to escape the ideological confusion of the 1920s, and to advance from a petty-bourgeois, half-hearted affirmation of humanist values to a full, wholehearted identification with Marxism-Leninism.

The years that followed were lean years so far as the heritage of Weimar was concerned. In the DDR the attempts to revive the tradition had been given up; in West Germany they had not yet got under way. It was only towards the end of the decade, but particularly after 1960, that interest in the 1920s was gradually reawakened in the West. It started with vague feelings of nostalgia and led eventually to a wholesale and somewhat indiscriminate revival. The first impulses came apparently from the cinemagoers and the devotees of light music: memories of the pre-Hitler movies and the hit songs still lingered on; there was an increasing demand for records of the 'golden twenties'. At the same time there was renewed interest in German modernism; the works of the artists of the Blaue Reiter and Brücke were eagerly sought by directors of museums and private art-collectors, the price of their pictures and sculptures shot up. In the universities dissertations were written about prominent writers and artists of the 1920s, and those still alive basked in the glow of renewed recognition. Some authors and playwrights became more famous than ever; every line of Brecht and Tucholsky was republished. The typical representatives of the 1920s novel on the other hand – Heinrich Mann for instance, or Arnold Zweig, Feuchtwanger, Leonhard Frank – were less fortunate, and some of the most popular and representative writers such as Wassermann were forgotten altogether. The Weimar revival reached its apogée in the late 1960s with the rise of the New Left, which saw in some of the intellectuals of the first Republic kindred spirits. Almost the entire Marxist literature of the 1920s, including for instance the complete *Linkskurve*, was reprinted. This was the period which witnessed the rediscovery of the Frankfurt School and all who had been connected with it, including some, like Walter Benjamin, whose names had previously been known only to a few cognoscenti. Lukács's early writings had a new vogue, as had Karl Korsch, Siegfried Kracauer, the early debates on psychoanalysis and Marxism, discussions on Marxist aesthetics, the writings of Wilhelm Reich and Hodann, the pictures of George Grosz. Thus the focus of rediscovery was narrowly limited by ideological considerations; no one would have thought of reprinting the volumes of Hilferding's *Die Gesellschaft*, though its theoretical level was vastly superior to the primitive and sectarian reprints which swamped the bookshops.

Independently of these political fashions the Expressionist boom continued, as did the demand for Expressionist painters; the Bauhaus celebrated a revival and became (like the Blaue Reiter) the subject of a large and widely admired exhibition. Even the lesser lights of screen and stage had their records reissued.

There were manifold reasons for this reawakened interest. The Third Reich had been a cultural desert, and it was only natural that once cultural concerns came to the fore again in West Germany attempts should be made to establish links with the period that had preceded it. As under Adenauer political stabilization and economic prosperity set in, the spirit of opposition grew among the postwar intelligentsia, thus providing a parallel with the 1920s. There were few if any outstanding writers or playwrights, artists or composers, in West Germany in the 1960s, and this too contributed towards the cult of the 1920s, which in retrospect seemed an age of giants, an incomparably richer period. In stark contrast to the 1960s, the spirit of irony had been one of its most significant features. The earnest young men and women of the later period admired the satirists of Weimar, but they themselves had nothing of remotely similar quality. So far as Marxist theory was concerned the 1960s were also largely a repeat performance. They discovered, somewhat to their consternation, that by and large the important issues had been discussed well before Hitler. The most significant difference was that in the 1920s the Marxists had been a small and usually isolated and embattled minority, whereas in the 1960s they were far more influential and in some universities became the dominant force.

Thus left-wing intellectuals of the 1960s felt a strong affinity with the 1920s; yet at the same time they wanted to apply their critical method to the period from which they drew their inspiration. The political and cultural history of the age was rewritten with a great deal of loving care, and an even greater measure of political passion, hindsight and self-righteousness. From these writings it emerged beyond doubt what political mistakes had been committed, and theories were advanced about how they could have been avoided. The authors were fully prepared for action if by any chance a situation similar to that of 1919 or 1925 or 1932 should recur. According to this school of thought even the liberal Weimar intellectuals were found wanting because they had been insufficiently committed at a time when political action in the framework of the militant working-class organizations was called for. But since the Communist Party had not been quite blameless, to put it mildly, such criticism was not very helpful even in hindsight. The writings of the 1960s included a great many references to monopoly capitalism and to pre-fascist structures, but it was doubtful whether this contributed towards an understanding of the quality of cultural life in the Weimar Republic – any more than the economic history of the late eighteenth and early nineteenth centuries can help to explain the uniqueness of Goethe and Schiller, Kant and Hegel, Mozart and Beethoven. Strictly speaking, the critique was not really new: to maintain that there is no basic difference in 'late capitalism' between a liberal-democratic regime and fascist rule, that fascism can be explained with reference to the primacy of socio-economic factors over political forces, was something the Communists had asserted all along. The fact that these theories acquired a new lease of life revealed more about the mood of the 1960s than about the realities of the 1920s.

It was one of the peculiarities of the post-1945 scene in Germany that the right had disappeared as an effective force on the intellectual stage. Those who did not accept the New Left reappraisal of the 1920s viewed with some concern the selective and uncritical revival; it was perhaps significant that there were not a few survivors of the Weimar period among those who protested against the resulting distortions at a conference in Munich in 1960. Golo Mann maintained that while the Piscator theatre and its public, the *Salonkommunisten*, had talent, it was in the last analysis unserious; Walter Mehring declared on the same occasion that *The Threepenny Opera* for all its charm was not an apotheosis of the ideals of 1918 but an anachronism devised by epigones who unconsciously and innocently were abetting Nazi propaganda. The report on this conference, echoing Musil's famous novel, was entitled *Time without Qualities*. It was also argued that there was a tendency to overrate the importance of the conflict between the generations, and to exaggerate the influence of the left-wing intelligentsia in general.

Gradually it became clear that there was a growing discrepancy between the real Weimar and the myth of Weimar as cultivated by a later generation. Some reputations were inflated out of all proportion; writers, playwrights and artists were praised not because of their innate qualities, but because they had had the good fortune either to survive in the right place, or because good friends were pushing their cause. Others were less fortunate, as their work did not suit the fashions of the 1960s. One could decry and deplore such judgments, but without much hope of immediate redress, for history has never been an incorruptible court of justice. Furthermore, there always remained the comfort that time, the great leveller, would do its work and that future generations might well quarry different heroes from the rich mine of the 1920s.

It was also during the 1960s that the cult of Weimar spread to places as far afield as Tokyo and Paris, London and New York. German poets and novelists benefitted only in rare cases. Hermann Hesse was probably the outstanding exception, and he, after all, was no more typical of 'Weimar' than Kafka or Musil. But modern German painting was discovered, the surviving members of the Bauhaus were lionized, and Brecht became the magic name in world theatre. The contribution of German refugee intellectuals in transplanting part of their culture abroad was recognized. Lukács and Korsch, Walter Benjamin and Wilhelm Reich, became names to conjure with in New Left circles all over the world; they and other minor thinkers were widely translated and discussed – to mention only those whose most important work had been done before they left Germany. In the United States the similarities with Weimar were debated: the general political situation, the polarization of forces, reminded some of Weimar, and the disaffection of large sections of the intelligentsia seemed to constitute an obvious parallel. In some circles the 'Tucholsky syndrome' was rapidly spreading: the rejection of America, its way of life, the aspirations of most of its citizens, with an emphasis that recalled Tucholsky's *Deutschland, Deutschland über alles*. There was the same conviction that fascism had already triumphed, and that the situation could not deteriorate any further. There was the same opposition not just to American foreign policy but to patriotism, national symbols, traditional values and the legacy of the past. But the parallel, like all historical parallels, was at best of limited value. It was true in the very general sense that all unhappy historical periods, like all unhappy marriages, have certain features in common. But in most other respects America in the 1960s was totally unlike Germany in 1930; the economy was expanding, there was no fascist force on the horizon, certainly not from the right; the intellectuals, furthermore, were far more numerous and politically powerful. On the other hand there was not even remotely the same abundance of talent, of new impulses, of real cultural innovations and breakthroughs, as there had been in Weimar Germany. Instead there were rapidly changing fads and fashions, of which parts of the Weimar heritage were but one.

To repeat, five decades are hardly sufficient to establish what of this heritage will last. As one of the main cradles of cultural modernism its place in history is certain. It was an age of experimentation, not of fundamental discoveries; a restless, extrovert age, not one given to that calm introspection which is usually associated with true greatness; an age of conflict not of synthesis; rich in talent, wanting in true genius. It was fascinating, pulsating with life, but with all its openness to foreign influences it was in some respects very German in character; and for this reason, in the last resort only of limited interest to other cultures and traditions. In so far as its appeal was universal, the Weimar heritage has already become firmly embedded in the general cultural tradition of our time. But a third Weimar, like a third Rome, is unlikely to arise.

Gottfried Benn, the poet who had little good to say about the Republic and its culture while it lasted, wrote to a friend in 1955, looking back on the period: 'The most wonderful years of Germany and Berlin, its Parisian years, full of talent and art – it won't come again.'

Bibliography

INTRODUCTORY NOTE

A detailed comprehensive history of Weimar Germany remains to be written; there are many hundreds of specialized monographs. The fullest bibliography is still *From Weimar to Hitler: Germany 1918–1933* (Wiener Library, 2nd ed., London 1964). Among the shorter political histories, the books by Arthur Rosenberg, Helmut Heiber, Albert Schwarz, G. Scheele, William S. Halperin and Georges Castellan should be mentioned. Erich Eyck, *A History of the Weimar Republic*, is the most detailed account but it deals exclusively with political matters and is now partly out of date; Wolfgang Ruge's *Deutschland 1917–1933* (1967) and Gilbert Badia's *Histoire de l'Allemagne contemporaine 1917–1962*, I (1962) present the communist approach. For the later years of the Republic Karl Dietrich Bracher's *Die Auflösung der Weimarer Republik* is the standard work. There is not so far a comprehensive socio-economic history of the Weimar Republic; the works of H. Bechtel, G. Stolper, and Dieter Petzina cover a larger period of German history.

The following bibliography is necessarily highly selective; thus the section on literature lists some of the significant novels and poetry of the 1920s, but omits others which could no doubt have been included with equal justification. The bibliographical notes on academic life are for obvious reasons even more selective; they cover studies of German universities during the 1920s, some biographies and a few representative writings by leading German academics. The biographical section – to provide another example – is almost entirely confined to books by men and women who were part of the cultural scene; political memoirs, however important, have not as a rule been listed. Nor have articles published in periodicals been included.

Chapter Two

LEFT-WING INTELLECTUALS

Albrecht, Friedrich, *Deutsche Schriftsteller in der Entscheidung* (1970).
Albrecht, Friedrich, et al., *Aktionen – Bekenntnisse – Perspektiven* (1966).
Angress, Werner T., *Stillborn Revolution: The Communist Bid for Power in Germany, 1921–1923* (1963).
Benjamin, Walter, *Schriften*, 2 vols (1955).
————————, *Briefe*, 2 vols (1965).
————————, *Gesammelte Schriften* (1972–).
Bloch, Ernst, *Geist der Utopie* (1918).
————————, *Das Prinzip Hoffnung*, 3 vols (1954–9).
————————, *Gesamtausgabe*, 16 vols (1962–).
————————, *Vom Hasard zur Katastrophe: Politische Aufsätze aus den Jahren 1934–1939* (1972).
Deak, Istvan, *Weimar Germany's Leftwing Intellectuals* (1968).
Dreschler, Hanno, *Die Sozialistische Arbeiterpartei Deutschlands* (1965).
Eckert, H., *Zur Bedeutung der proletarisch-revolutionären Literatur in Deutschland 1927–1933* (1958).
Esseling, Alf, *Die Weltbühne* (1962).
Fähnders, Walter, and Rector, Martin, eds., *Literatur im Klassenkampf* (1971).
Fischer, Ruth, *Stalin and German Communism* (1948).
Flechtheim, Osip K., *Die KPD in der Weimarer Republik* (1948).
Frei, Bruno, *Carl von Ossietzky* (1966).
Gallas, Helga, *Marxistische Literaturtheorie: Kontroversen im Bund proletarisch-revolutionärer Schriftsteller* (1971).
von Gerlach, Hellmut, *Von Rechts nach Links* (1937).
Gross, Babette, *Willi Münzenberg* (1967).
Grossmann, Kurt R., *Ossietzky – Ein deutscher Patriot* (1963).
Grosz, George, *Das Gesicht der herrschenden Klasse* (1921).
Gumbel, Emil, *Verräter verfallen der Feme* (1929).
Hannover, Heinrich and Elisabeth, *Politische Justiz 1918–1933* (1966).
Herzfelde, Wieland, *Der Malik Verlag, 1916–1947* (1967).
————————, *Unterwegs* (1961).

Hiller, Kurt, *Köpfe und Tröpfe* (1950).
Horkheimer, Max, and Adorno, T. W., *Dialektik der Aufklärung* (1947).
Hunt, Richard N., *German Social Democracy 1918–1933* (1964).
Ihlau, Olaf, *Die roten Kämpfer* (1969).
Jay, Martin, *The Dialectical Imagination* (1972).
Kantorowicz, Alfred, *Porträts. Deutsche Schicksale* (1947).
————, *Deutsches Tagebuch*, 2 vols (1959).
Korsch, Karl, *Marxismus und Philosophie* (1923).
Link, Werner, *Die Geschichte des Internationalen Jugendbundes (IJB) und des Internationalen Sozialistischen Kampfbundes (ISK)* (1964).
Lukács, Georg, *Geschichte und Klassenbewusstsein* (1923).
————, *Lenin* (1924).
————, *Gesamtausgabe*, 15 vols (1963–).
Mühsam, Erich, *Werke in Einzelausgaben* (1961)
Pollatschek, Walter, *Friedrich Wolf* (1963).
Poor, Harold L., *Kurt Tucholsky and the Ordeal of Germany 1914–35* (1968).
Prager, Eugen, *Geschichte der USPD* (1921).
Ludwig Renn zum 70.Geburtstag (1959).
Rohe, Karl, *Das Reichsbanner Schwarz-Rot-Gold* (1966).
Rudolph, Johanna, *Der Humanist Arnold Zweig* (1955).
Rühle, Jürgen, *Literature and Revolution* (1969).
Schade, Franz, *Kurt Eisner und die bayrische Sozialdemokratie* (1961).
Schmidt, Konrad, ed., *Feuilleton der roten Presse 1918–1933* (1960).
Schwarzschild, Leopold, *Die letzten Jahre vor Hitler* (1966).
Sternberg, Fritz, *Der Imperialismus* (1926).
————, *Der Niedergang des deutschen Kapitalismus* (1932).
Tucholsky, Kurt, *Deutschland, Deutschland über alles* (1929).
————, *Gesammelte Werke*, 3 vols (1960–7).
Walter, Hans-Albert, *Deutsche Exilliteratur*, I : *Bedrohung und Verfolgung bis 1933* (1972).
Weber, Hermann, *Die Wandlung des deutschen Kommunismus* 2 vols (1969).
Weinert, Erich, *Gesammelte Werke in Einzelausgaben* (1955–).
Wilde, Harry, *Theodor Plievier* (1965).

Chapter Three

RIGHT-WING INTELLIGENTSIA

Alter, Junius, *Nationalisten* (1930).
Benn, Gottfried, *Der neue Staat und die Intellektuellen* (1933).

Beumelburg, Werner, *Sperrfeuer um Deutschland* (1928).
Bronnen, Arnolt, *Rossbach* (1930).
Boehm, Max Hildebert, *Ruf der Jungen* (1920).
——————, *Das eigenständige Volk* (1930).
Eschmann, E. W., *Wo steht die junge Generation?* (1931).
Freyer, Hans, *Revolution von Rechts* (1931).
Fried, Ferdinand, *Das Ende des Kapitalismus* (1931).
Gerhart, Walter, *Um des Reiches Zukunft* (1932).
Greiffenhagen, Martin, *Das Dilemma des Konservativismus in Deutschland* (1971).
Grimm, Hans, *Volk ohne Raum* (1926).
——————, *Der Schriftsteller und seine Zeit* (1931).
Gründel, E. G., *Die Sendung der jungen Generation* (1932).
Hesse, Max René, *Partenau* (1929).
Hielscher, Friedrich, *Das Reich* (1931).
Hock, W., *Deutscher Antikapitalismus* (1960).
Jung, Edgar, *Die Herrschaft der Minderwertigen*, 2 vols (1928–30).
Jünger, Ernst, *Der Kampf als inneres Erlebnis* (1922).
——————, *Der Arbeiter* (1932).
Jünger, F. G., ed., *Aufmarsch des Nationalismus* (1926).
Klages, Ludwig, *Der Geist als Widersacher der Seele*, 3 vols (1929).
von Klemperer, Klemens, *Germany's New Conservatism* (1957).
Kolnai, Aurel, *The War against the West* (1938).
Krockow, Karl, *Die Entscheidung* (1958).
Lebovics, Herman, *Social Conservatism and the Middle Class in Germany 1914–1939* (1969).
Mariaux, Franz, *Der Schutthaufen* (1931).
Moeller van den Bruck, *Das Recht der jungen Völker* (1919).
——————, *Das dritte Reich* (1923).
——————, *Der politische Mensch* (1933).
Mohler, Armin, *Die konservative Revolution in Deutschland 1918–1932* (1950).
Mosse, G. L., *The Crisis of German Ideology* (1966).
Neurohr, Jean, *Der Mythos vom dritten Reich* (1958).
Niekisch, Ernst, *Entscheidung* (1930).
Paetel, Karl Otto, *Versuchung oder Chance* (1965).
Rosenberg, Alfred, *Der Mythus des 20. Jahrhunderts* (1928).
zu Reventlow, Ernst, *Deutscher Sozialismus* (1930).
Schauwecker, Franz, *Aufbruch der Nation* (1929).
Schmitt, Carl, *Politische Romantik* (1919).
——————, *Politische Theologie* (1922).
——————, *Die geistesgeschichtliche Lage des heutigen Parlamentarismus* (1923).

Schmitt, Carl, *Legalität und Legitimität* (1932)
Schüddekopf, O. E., *Linke Leute von Rechts* (1960).
Schulze-Naumburg, Paul, *Kunst und Rasse* (1928).
Schwarz, H. P., *Der konservative Anarchist. Politik und Zeitkritik Ernst Jüngers* (1962).
Schwierskott, H. J., *Arthur Moeller van den Bruck* (1962).
Sombart, Werner, *Deutscher Sozialismus* (1934).
Sontheimer, Kurt, *Antidemokratisches Denken in der Weimarer Republik* (1968).
Spengler, Oswald, *Der Untergang des Abendlandes* 2 vols (1918–22).
——————, *Jahre der Entscheidung* (1933).
——————, *Politische Schriften* (1933).
Stapel, Wilhelm, *Literatenwäsche* (1930).
——————, *Der christliche Staatsmann* (1932).
Stern, Fritz, *The Politics of Cultural Despair* (1961).
Ullmann, H., *Das werdende Volk* (1929).
——————, *Durchbruch zur Nation* (1933).
Winnig, August, *Vom Proletariat zum Arbeitertum* (1930).
Witkop, Philip, ed., *Kriegsbriefe gefallener deutscher Studenten* (1928).

Chapter Four

LITERATURE: TEXTS

Becher, Johannes R., *Verfall und Triumph* (1914).
——————, *Roter Marsch* (1925).
Benn, Gottfried, *Morgue* (1912).
Borchardt, Rudolf, *Vermischte Gedichte* (1924).
Brecht, Bertolt, *Dreigroschenroman* (1934).
Bronnen, Arnolt, *O.S.* (1929).
Däubler, Theodor, *Nordlicht* (1910).
Döblin, Alfred, *Die drei Sprünge des Wang-lun* (1915).
——————, *Wallenstein* (1920).
——————, *Berlin Alexanderplatz* (1929).
Fallada, Hans, *Kleiner Mann, was nun?* (1932).
——————, *Bauern, Bonzen, Bomben* (1933).
Feuchtwanger, Lion, *Jud Süss* (1925).
——————, *Erfolg* (1930).
Flake, Otto, *Ruland* (1922).
Frank, Bruno, *Trenck* (1926).
——————, *Politische Novelle* (1928).
Frank, Leonhard, *Die Räuberbande* (1914).
——————, *Der Mensch ist gut* (1917).

Frank, Leonhard, *Von drei Millionen Drei* (1932).
George, Stefan, *Das Neue Reich* (1928).
Hesse, Hermann, *Demian* (1919).
——————, *Zarathustras Wiederkehr* (1919).
——————, *Klingsors letzter Sommer* (1920).
——————, *Der Steppenwolf* (1927).
——————, *Siddhartha* (1930).
Heym, Georg, *Dichtungen* (1922).
Jahnn, Hans Henny, *Perrudja*, 2 vols (1929).
Jünger, Ernst, *In Stahlgewittern* (1920).
——————, *Das Wäldchen 125* (1925).
Kästner, Erich, *Emil und die Detektive* (1928).
——————, *Fabian* (1931).
Kolb Annette, *Das Exemplar* (1913).
Mann, Heinrich, *Professor Unrat* (1905).
——————, *Der Untertan* (1914).
——————, *Macht und Mensch* (1919).
——————, *Diktatur der Vernunft* (1923).
Mann, Thomas, *Friedrich und die grosse Koalition* (1915).
——————, *Betrachtungen eines Unpolitischen* (1918).
——————, *Der Zauberberg* (1924).
——————, *Deutsche Ansprache: Ein Appell an die Vernunft* (1930).
Pinthus, Kurt, ed., *Menschheitsdämmerung* (1920).
Remarque, Erich Maria, *Im Westen nichts Neues* (1929).
Renn, Ludwig, *Der Krieg* (1928).
Roth, Joseph, *Radetzkymarsch* (1932).
Schickele, René, *Symphonie für Jazz* (1929).
Seghers, Anna, *Der Aufstand der Fischer von St Barbara* (1930).
Seidel, Ina, *Das Wunschkind* (1930).
Stadler, Ernst, *Aufbruch* (1914).
Stehr, Hermann, *Heiligenhof* (1918).
Stramm, August, *Gesammelte Dichtungen*, 2 vols (1919).
Trakl, Georg, *Sebastian im Traum* (1915).
——————, *Die Dichtungen* (1917).
Wassermann, Jakob, *Der Fall Maurizius* (1928).
——————, *Etzel Andergast* (1931).
Zech, Paul, *Der feurige Busch* (1917).
Zweig, Arnold, *Der Streit um den Sergeanten Grischa* (1927).
——————, *Junge Frau von 1914* (1931).

LITERATURE: CRITICISM

Arnold, A., *Die Literatur des Expressionismus* (1966).
——————, *Prosa des Expressionismus* (1972).

Arnold, H. L., ed., *Heinrich Mann* (1971).
Bahr, Hermann, *Expressionismus* (1918).
Ball, Hugo, *Flucht aus der Zeit* (1927).
Banuls, A., *Heinrich Mann* (1970).
Blei, Franz, *Das grosse Bestiarium der modernen Literatur* (1924).
Bode, D., ed., *Gedichte des Expressionismus* (1967).
Cysarz, H., *Zur Geistesgeschichte des Weltkrieges* (1931).
David, Claude, *Von Richard Wagner zu Bertolt Brecht* (1964).
——————, *Stefan George: Sein dichterisches Werk* (1967).
Diesel, Eugen, *Der Weg durchs Wirrsal* (1926).
Duwe, W., *Deutsche Dichtung des 20. Jahrhunderts*, 2 vols (1962).
Edschmid, Kasimir, ed., *Über den Expressionismus in der Literatur und die neue Dichtung* (1919).
——————————, *Frühe Manifeste* (1957).
Friedmann, Hermann, and Mann, Otto, *Expressionismus* (1956).
Gray, Ronald, *The German Tradition in Literature 1871–1945* (1965).
Haas, Willy, *Die literarische Welt* (1957).
——————, *Gestalten* (1962).
Heller, Erich, *The Ironic German: A Study of Thomas Mann* (1958).
Jens, Inge, *Dichter zwischen rechts und links* (1971).
Jens, W., *Statt einer Literaturgeschichte* (1962).
Huelsenbeck, Richard, ed., *Dada* (1964).
Kesten, Hermann, *Meine Freunde die Poeten* (1959).
Kliemann, Helga, *Die Novembergruppe* (1970).
Klein, Alfred, et al., *Literatur der Arbeiterklasse* (1971).
Killy, W., *Über Georg Trakl* (1960).
Kunisch, Hermann, ed., *Handbuch deutscher Gegenwartsliteratur* (1965).
Landmann, Georg Peter, ed., *Der George-Kreis* (1965).
Lethen, Helmuth, *Neue Sachlichkeit* (1970).
Lukács, Georg, *Theorie des Romans* (1920).
Mahrholz, Werner, *Deutsche Literatur der Gegenwart* (1930).
Mayer, Hans, *Zur deutschen Literatur der Zeit* (1967).
Mehring, Walter, *Berlin, Dada* (1959).
de Mendelssohn, Peter, *S. Fischer und sein Verlag* (1970).
Muschg, Walter, *Die Zerstörung der deutschen Literatur* (1958).
——————, *Von Trakl zu Brecht: Dichter des Expressionismus* (1961).
Naumann, Hans, *Die deutsche Dichtung der Gegenwart* (1931).
Pörtner, P., ed., *Literatur-Revolution 1910–1925*, 3 vols (1960–).
Raabe, Paul, ed., *Die Zeitschriften und Sammlungen des literarischen Expressionismus* (1964).
——————, *Expressionismus: Aufzeichnungen und Erinnerungen der Zeitgenossen* (1965).

Rothe, Wolfgang, ed., *Expressionismus als Literatur* (1969).
Salin, Edgar, *Um Stefan George: Erinnerungen und Zeugnisse* (1964).
Samuel, R., and Hinton Thomas, R., *Expressionism in German Life, Literature and the Theatre 1910–24* (1939).
Schäfer, Wilhelm, *Die dreizehn Bücher der deutschen Seele* (1922).
Soergel, A., and Hohoff, C., *Dichtung und Dichter der Zeit*, 2 vols (1963).
Sokel, Walter H., *The Writer in Extremis: Expressionism in Twentieth-Century German Literature* (1959).
Sontheimer, Kurt, *Thomas Mann und die Deutschen* (1961).
Steffen, Hans, ed., *Der deutsche Expressionismus* (1965).
Walden, N., and Schreyer, L., *Der Sturm* (1954).
von Wiese, B., ed., *Deutsche Dichter der Moderne* (1965).

STAGE

Bab, Julius, *Kränze der Mimen* (1954).
Barlach, Ernst, *Das dichterische Werk*, 3 vols (1956–9).
Berger, Ludwig, *Theatermenschen* (1962).
Bernauer, Rudolf, *Das Theater meines Lebens: Erinnerungen* (1955).
Braulich, Heinrich, *Max Reinhardt* (1969).
Brecht, Bertolt, *Gesammelte Werke* (1967).
Bronnen, Arnolt, *Vatermord* (1920).
——————————, *Katalaunische Schlacht* (1924).
Bruckner, Ferdinand, *Krankheit der Jugend* (1926).
——————————, *Elisabeth von England* (1930).
Denkler, Horst, *Drama des Expressionismus* (1967).
Eisenlohr, F., *Carl Sternheim* (1926).
Esslin, Martin, *Brecht: The Man and his Work* (1959).
Fechter, Paul, *Ernst Barlach* (1957).
Fehling, Jürgen, *Die Magie des Theaters* (1965)
Frank, Bruno, *Zwölftausend* (1927).
Garten, H. F., *Gerhart Hauptmann* (1954).
——————————, *Modern German Drama* (1958).
Goering, Reinhard, *Seeschlacht* (1918).
Hasenclever, Walter, *Der Sohn* (1914).
——————————, *Die Menschen* (1918).
Hauptmann, Gerhart, *Vor Sonnenuntergang* (1932).
Herald, Heinz, *Max Reinhardt* (1953).
Hoffmann, Ludwig, and Hoffmann-Ostwald, Daniel, eds., *Deutsches Arbeitertheater 1918–1933* (1961).
von Horváth, Ödön, *Geschichten aus dem Wienerwald* (1931).
Ihering, Herbert, *Emil Jannings* (1941).
——————————, *Die zwanziger Jahre* (1948).

Ihering, Herbert, *Von Reinhardt zu Brecht*, 3 vols (1958).
Kaiser, Georg, *Von Morgens bis Mitternachts* (1912).
——————, *Die Bürger von Calais* (1912).
——————, *Die Koralle* (1917).
——————, *Gas* (1918–9).
Karasek, Helmuth, *Carl Sternheim* (1965).
Kändler, Klaus, *Drama und Klassenkampf* (1970).
Kenworthy, B. J., *Georg Kaiser* (1957).
Kerr, Alfred, *Die Welt im Drama* (1954).
Knellessen, F. W., *Agitation auf der Bühne* (1970).
Krauss, Werner, *Das Schauspiel meines Lebens* (1958).
Lampel, Peter Martin, *Revolte im Erziehungshaus* (1928).
Lacis, Asja, *Revolutionär im Beruf* (1971).
Luft, Friedrich, *Gustav Gründgens* (1958).
Mann, Heinrich, *Madame Legros* (1913).
Mehring, Walter, *Der Kaufmann von Berlin* (1929).
Piscator, Erwin, *Das politische Theater* (1929).
Paquet, Alfons, *Fahnen* (1924).
——————, *Sturmflut* (1926).
Rühle, Günther, ed., *Theater für die Republik, 1917–1933* (1967).
Sternheim, Carl, *1913* (1915).
——————, *Tabula Rasa* (1916).
Sorge, R. J., *Der Bettler* (1917).
Toller, Ernst, *Die Wandlung* (1919).
——————, *Masse Mensch* (1920).
——————, *Die Maschinenstürmer* (1922).
von Unruh, Fritz, *Ein Geschlecht* (1918).
Willett, John, *The Theatre of Bertolt Brecht* (1959).
Wolf, Friedrich, *Cyankali* (1928).
——————, *Die Matrosen von Cattaro* (1930).
Zuckmayer, Carl, *Der fröhliche Weinberg* (1925).
——————, *Der Hauptmann von Köpenick* (1931).

Chapter Five

MUSIC

Austin, William W., *Music in the 20th Century* (1966).
Adorno, T. W., *Philosophie der neuen Musik* (1949).
Böhmer, K., *Zwischen Reihe und Pop* (1970).
Brockhaus, H. A., *Hanns Eisler* (1961).
Busch, Fritz, *Pages from a Musician's Life* (1953).
Del Mar, Norman, *Richard Strauss* 3 vols (1962–72).

Dent, Edward J., *Ferrucio Busoni* (1933).
Furtwängler, Wilhelm, *Ton und Wort* (1966).
Geissmar, Berta, *Musik im Schatten der Politik* (1948).
Heinsheimer, Hans, *Best Regards to Aida* (1968).
Klemperer, Otto, *Minor Recollections* (1964).
Kotschenreuter, Helmuth, *Kurt Weill* (1962).
Krenek, Ernst, *Über neue Musik* (1937).
Leibowitz, René, *Schönberg et son école* (1947).
Mersmann, Hans, *Deutsche Musik des XX. Jahrhunderts im Spiegel des Weltgeschehens* (1958).
Panofsky, Walter, *Richard Strauss* (1965).
Pfitzner, H. E., *Gesammelte Schriften*, 3 vols (1926).
Piatigorsky, Gregor, *Mein Cello und ich* (1972).
Redlich, H. F., *Alban Berg* (1957).
Reich, Willi, *Alban Berg* (1963).
Rufer, Josef, ed., *The Works of Arnold Schoenberg* (1963).
Rutz, Hans, *Hans Pfitzner* (1949).
Rognoni, L., *Espressionismo e dodecaphonia* (1954).
Schnabel, Arthur, *My Life and Music* (1961).
Strauss, Richard, *Betrachtungen und Erinnerungen* (1954).
Strobel, Heinrich, *Paul Hindemith* (1948).
Stuckenschmidt, H. H., *Neue Musik* (1951).
——————————, *Arnold Schönberg* (1953).
——————————, *Schöpfer der neuen Musik* (1958).
Vlad, Roman, *Storia della dodecaphonia* (1958).
Walter, Bruno, *Thema und Variationen* (1960).
Wellesz, Egon, *Arnold Schönberg* (1921).
Westphal, Kurt, *Die moderne Musik* (1928).

THE VISUAL ARTS

Apollonio, U., *Die Brücke e la cultura dell' espressionismo* (1953).
Bayer, H., Gropius, I., and Gropius, W., eds., *Bauhaus 1919–1928* (1959).
Beckmann, Max, *Tagebücher* (1955).
Bildersturm nach 25 Jahren (1962).
Breuer, Marcel, *Sun and Shadow* (1956).
Brion, M., *Kandinsky* (1961).
Buchheim, Lothar-Günther, *Deutscher Expressionismus* (1956).
——————————, *Die Künstlergemeinschaft Brücke* (1957).
——————————, *Der Blaue Reiter* (1959).
——————————, *The Graphic Art of Expressionism* (1960).
Bultmann, B., *Oskar Kokoschka* (1959).
Conzelmann, Otto, ed., *Otto Dix* (n.d.).

Drexler, Arthur, *Ludwig Mies van der Rohe* (1960).
Dube-Heynig, A., *Kirchner* (1966).
von Eckardt, Wolf, *Erich Mendelsohn* (1960).
Einstein, Carl, *Die Kunst des 20. Jahrhunderts* (1926).
Fehr, Hans, *Emil Nolde* (1957).
Fitch, James, *Walter Gropius* (1960).
Giedion, Siegfried, *Walter Gropius* (1954).
Gordon, D. E., *E. L. Kirchner* (1968).
Grohmann, Will, *Bildende Kunst und Architektur zwischen zwei Welt-kriegen* (1958).
——————, *Wassily Kandinsky: Life and Work* (1959).
——————, *Ernst Ludwig Kirchner* (1961).
——————, *Oskar Schlemmer* (1965).
Gropius, Walter, *The New Architecture and the Bauhaus* (1965).
Grote, Ludwig, *Der Blaue Reiter. München und die Kunst des 20. Jahrhunderts* (1949).
——————, *Die Maler am Bauhaus* (1950).
——————, *Oskar Kokoschka* (1950).
Haftmann, Werner, *The Mind and Work of Paul Klee* (1954).
——————, *Emil Nolde* (1959).
Hartlaub, F. G., *Die Graphik des Expressionismus in Deutschland* (1947).
Hausenstein, Wilhelm, and Reifenberg, B., *Max Beckmann* (1949).
Hess, Hans, *Lyonel Feininger* (1961).
Hofer, Karl, *Aus Leben und Kunst* (1952).
——————, *Erinnerungen eines Malers* (1953).
Hodin, J. P., *Oskar Kokoschka: The Artist and his Time* (1960).
Jödicke, J., *Geschichte der modernen Architektur* (1961).
Kandinsky, Wassily, *Über das Geistige in der Kunst* (1912).
Kandinsky, W., and Marc, F., eds., *Der Blaue Reiter* (1912).
Klee, Paul, *Pädagogisches Skizzenbuch* (1925).
——————, *On Modern Art* (1948).
——————, *The Thinking Eye* (1961).
Köhn, H., ed., *Erich Heckel* (1959).
Kokoschka, Oskar, *Schriften 1907–1935* (1956).
Kollwitz, Käthe, *Briefe der Freundschaft* (1966).
Kuhn, Charles L., *German Expressionism and Abstract Art* (1957). *Supplement* (1967).
Lane, Barbara Miller, *Architecture and Politics in Germany 1918–1945* (1970).
Lankheit, Klaus, *Franz Marc* (1950).
Lemmer, K., *Max Pechstein und der Beginn des Expressionismus* (1949).
Lewis, Beth Irwin, *George Grosz. Art and Politics in the Weimar Republic* (1971).

Löffler, F., *Otto Dix* (1960).
Miesel, Victor, ed., *Voices of German Expressionism* (1968).
Moholy-Nagy, Sibyl, *Moholy-Nagy, a Biography* (1950).
Motherwell, Robert, ed., *The Dada Painters and Poets* (1951).
Myers, Bernard S., *The German Expressionists* (1963).
Nolde, Emil, *Jahre der Kämpfe* (1957).
Plaut, J. S., *Kokoschka* (1948).
Rathenau, E., *Karl Schmidt-Rottluff* (1964).
Richter, Hans, *Dada* (1965).
Roh, Franz, *Nach-Expressionismus, Magischer Realismus* (1925).
—————, *German Painting in the Twentieth Century* (1968).
Röthel, Hans Konrad, *Moderne Deutsche Malerei* (1957).
Roters, Eberhard, *The Painters of the Bauhaus* (1968).
Rubin, William S., *Dada, Surrealism and their Heritage* (1968).
Sauerlandt, Max, *Die Kunst der letzten 30 Jahre* (1948).
Schlemmer, Oskar, *Briefe und Tagebücher* (1958).
Schmied, Wieland, *Neue Sachlichkeit und magischer Realismus in Deutschland* (1970).
Schreyer, Lothar, *Erinnerungen an Sturm und Bauhaus* (1956).
Selz, Peter, *German Expressionist Painting* (1957).
—————, *Emil Nolde* (1963).
—————, *Max Beckmann* (1964).
Taut, Bruno, *Die Auflösung der Städte* (1920).
Verkauf, W., Janco, M., and Bollinger, H., eds., *Dada, Monographie einer Bewegung* (1958).
Willett, John, *Expressionism* (1971).
Wingler, Hans M., ed., *Das Bauhaus, 1919–1933* (1962).
Worringer, Wilhelm, *Problematik der Gegenwartskunst* (1948).

Chapter Six

THE ACADEMIC SCENE

Alexander, Franz, *The Western Mind in Transition* (1960).
Aron, Raymond, *German Sociology* (1964).
Barth, Karl, *Der Römerbrief* (1919).
—————, *Theologische Existenz Heute* (1933).
Baumgarten, O., *Die Not der akademischen Berufe nach Friedensschluss* (1919).
Bavink, E., *Ergebnisse und Probleme der Naturwissenschaften* (1954).
Becker, C. H., *Gedanken zur Hochschulreform* (1919).
—————, *Vom Wesen der deutschen Universität* (1925).
Bleuel, H. P., and Kinnert, E., *Deutsche Studenten auf dem Weg ins dritte Reich* (1967).

Bleuel, H. P., *Deutschlands Bekenner* (1968).
Born, Max, *Physik im Wandel meiner Zeit* (1957).
———— *Albert Einstein: Briefwechsel* (1969).
Brentano, Lujo, *Mein Leben* (1931).
Buber, Martin, *Ich und Du* (1923).
Bultmann, Rudolf, *Theologie des Neuen Testaments*, 2 vols (1953).
Curtius, Ernst Robert, *Deutscher Geist in Gefahr* (1932).
Cassirer, Ernst, *Philosophie der symbolischen Formen*, 3 vols (1923–9).
Clark, Ronald W., *Einstein, the Life and Times* (1971).
Das akademische Deutschland, 4 vols (1930).
Diemer, A., *Edmund Husserl* (1965).
Goetz, Walter, *Historiker in meiner Zeit* (1957).
Gogarten, Friedrich, *Politische Ethik* (1932).
Hahn, Otto, *My Life* (1970).
Haenisch, Konrad, *Staat und Hochschule* (1920).
Hartmann, H., *Max Planck als Mensch und Denker* (1953).
Heidegger, Martin, *Sein und Zeit* (1927).
Heisenberg W., *Das Naturbild der heutigen Physik* (1954).
Herbert, K., *Zur Frage der Entmythologisierung* (1951).
Jäckh, Ernst, ed., *Politik als Wissenschaft* (1931).
Jaspers, Karl, *Die geistige Situation der Zeit* (1931).
————, *Existenzphilosophie* (1938).
Jonas, F., *Geschichte der Soziologie*, 2 vols (1968–9).
Jones, Ernest, *Sigmund Freud, Life and Work*, 3 vols (1953–7).
Kafka, G., *Geschichte der Philosophie in Einzeldarstellungen*, 37 vols (1921–33).
Katz, D., *Gestaltpsychologie* (1948).
Klages, H., *Geschichte der Soziologie* (1969).
Klose, W., *Freiheit schreibt auf ihre Fahnen* (1967).
Koffka, K., *Principles of Gestaltpsychology* (1935).
Lilge, Frederic, *The Abuse of Learning: The Failure of the German University* (1948).
Litt, Theodor, *Wissenschaft, Bildung und Weltanschauung* (1928).
Mannheim, Karl, *Ideology and Utopia* (1955).
Meinecke, Friedrich, *Republik, Bürgertum und Jugend* (1925).
————————, *The German Catastrophe* (1950).
Messer, A., *Der Fall Lessing* (1926).
Oncken, Hermann, *Nach zehn Jahren* (1929).
Partington, J. R., *A History of Chemistry*, 4 vols (1961–7).
Planck, Max, *Das Weltbild der modernen Physik* (1925).
Pongratz, L. J., ed., *Psychologie in Selbstdarstellungen* (1972).
Reich, Ilse, *Wilhelm Reich* (1969).
Reich, Wilhelm, *Die Massenpsychologie des Faschismus* (1933).

Ringer, Fritz K., *The Decline of the German Mandarins* (1969).
v. Rinteln, F. J., *Contemporary German Philosophy* (1970).
Robinson, P. A., *The Freudian Left* (1969).
Scheler, Max, *Gesammelte Werke*, 13 vols (1954–66).
Schneider, E., *J. A. Schumpeter* (1970).
Schwarz, Jürgen, *Studenten in der Weimarer Republik* (1971).
Spiegelberg, H., *The Phenomenological Movement*, 2 vols (1960).
Steinberg, S., *Die Geschichtswissenschaft der Gegenwart in Selbstdarstellungen*, 2 vols (1925–6).
Töpner, Kurt, *Die Revolution von 1918 im Urteil deutscher Hochschullehrer* (1970).
Volkmann, Helmuth, *Die deutsche Studentenschaft in ihrer Entwicklung seit 1919* (1925).
Weber, Alfred, *Die Not der geistigen Arbeiter* (1923).
Weber, Max, *Wissenschaft als Beruf* (1921).
————————, *Gesammelte politische Schriften* (1958).
Wende, Erich, *C. H. Becker, Mensch und Politiker* (1959).
Willstätter, Richard, *Aus meinem Leben* (1949).
Wyss, D., *Die tiefenpsychologischen Schulen von den Anfängen bis zur Gegenwart* (1970).

Chapter Seven

CINEMA

Amengual, B., *G. W. Pabst* (1966).
Borde, R., Buache, F., and Courtade, F., *Le Cinéma réaliste allemand* (1965).
Buache, F., *G. W. Pabst* (1965).
Courtade, F., *F. Lang* (1963).
Dickens, H., *The Films of Marlene Dietrich* (1968).
Eisner, Lotte, *The Haunted Screen* (1969).
————————, *Murnau* (1973).
Fantastique et réalisme dans le cinéma allemand 1912–1933 (1969).
Fraenkel, H., *Unsterblicher Film*, 2 vols (1955–7).
Hempel, Rolf, *Carl Meyer* (1968).
Jameux, Charles, *Murnau* (1962).
Jensen, Paul, *The Cinema of Fritz Lang* (1969).
Kaul, Walter, *Caligari und Caligarismus* (1970).
Knietzsch, Horst, *Film Gestern und Heute* (1963).
Kracauer, Siegfried, *From Caligari to Hitler* (1947).
Kurtz, Rudolf, *Expressionismus im Film* (1925).
Lamprecht, Gerhard, *Deutsche Stummfilme 1923–1926* (1968).

Manvell, Roger, and Fraenkel, Heinrich, *The German Cinema* (1971).
Riess, Curt, *Das gab's nur einmal* (1956).
Rotha, Paul, *The Film Till Now* (1949).
Sadoul, Georges, *Histoire générale du cinéma*, I-III (1947–51).
Verdone, Marc, *Lubitsch* (1964).
Weinberg, H. G., *Joseph von Sternberg* (1967).
———————, *The Lubitsch Touch* (1968).
von Zglinicki, F., *Der Weg des Films* (1956).

LIGHT MUSIC AND JAZZ

Berendt, I. E., *Der Jazz* (1950).
Czech, St., *Das Operettenbuch* (1960).
Greul, Heinz, *Bretter die die Zeit bedeuten* (1967).
Grun, Bernhard, *Kulturgeschichte der Operette* (1961).
Holländer, Friedrich, *Von Kopf bis Fuss* (1965).
Imbert, Ch., *Geschichte des Chansons und der Operette* (1967).
Kaubisch, Herbert, *Operette* (1955).
Lange, Horst, H., *Jazz in Deutschland* (1966).
Napier-Tauber, Diana, *Richard Tauber* (1949).
Nick, Edmund, *Paul Lincke* (1951).
Schaeffers, Willi, *Tingeltangel* (1959).
Waldorf, Claire, *Weeste noch . . .!* (1953).
Westermeyer, W., *Die Operette im Wandel des Zeitgeistes* (1931).

Chapter Eight

Born, Karl Erich, *Die deutsche Bankenkrise 1931* (1967).
Bracher, Karl Dietrich, *Die Auflösung der Weimarer Republik* (1960).
Jasper, Gotthard, ed., *Von Weimar zu Hitler* (1968).
Matthias, Erich, and Morsey, Rudolf, *Das Ende der Parteien 1933* (1960).
Raupach, Hans, et al., *Die Staats- und Wirtschaftskrise des deutschen Reiches 1929–1933* (1967).
Treue, Wilhelm, ed., *Deutschland in der Weltwirtschaftskrise in Augenzeugenberichten* (1962).

Other Works

WEIMAR CULTURE (GENERAL)

Behr, Hermann, *Die goldenen Zwanziger Jahre* (1964).
Gay, Peter, *Weimar Culture* (1969).
Koch, Thilo, *Die goldenen Zwanziger Jahre* (1970).

Reinisch, Leonhard, *Die Zeit ohne Eigenschaften* (1960).
Schoeps, H. J., ed., *Zeitgeist der Weimarer Republik* (1968).
Social Research, Germany 1919–1932. The Weimar Culture (Summer 1972).
Werner, Bruno E., *Die Zwanziger Jahre* (1962).

SOCIAL REPORTAGE, MASS CULTURE, ENTERTAINMENT

Ermann, Hans, *Bei Kempinski* (1967).
Friedrich, Otto, *Before the Deluge. A Portrait of Berlin in the 1920s* (1972).
Goldschmidt, Alfons, *Deutschland Heute* (1928).
Hass, Hermann, *Sitte und Kultur im Nachkriegsdeutschland* (1932).
Kiaulehn, Walter, *Berlin – Schicksal einer Weltstadt* (1958).
Ostwald, Hans, *Sittengeschichte der Inflation* (1931).
Pfeiffer, Herbert, *Berlin, Zwanziger Jahre* (1961).
Zievier, Georg, *Das Romanische Café* (1965).

YOUTH MOVEMENTS

Engelhardt, V., *Die deutsche Jugendbewegung als Kulturhistorisches Phaenomen* (1923).
Frobenius, Else, *Mit uns zieht die neue Zeit* (1927).
Kindt, Werner, *Grundschriften der deutschen Jugendbewegung* (1963).
Laqueur, Walter, *Young Germany* (1962).
Raabe, F., *Die bündische Jugend* (1961).

AUTOBIOGRAPHIES

d'Abernon, Viscount, *The Diary of the Ambassador* (1930).
Baum, Vicki, *Es war alles ganz anders* (1962).
Bäumer, Gertrud, *Lebensweg durch eine Zeitwende* (1933).
Brecht, Arnold, *Aus nächster Nähe* (1966).
Bronnen, Arnolt, *Gibt zu Protokoll* (1954).
Cowley, Malcolm, *Exile's Return* (1951).
Domela, Harry, *Der falsche Prinz* (1927).
Durieux, Tilla, *Eine Tür steht offen* (1954).
Feder, Ernst, *Heute sprach ich mit . . .* (1971).
Feuchtwanger, Lion, *Moskau 1937* (1937).
Flake, Otto, *Es wird Abend* (1960).
Flesch, Janos, *Janos erzählt von Berlin* (1958).
Frank, Leonhard, *Heart on the Left* (1954).
Graf, O. M., *Wir sind Gefangene* (1927).
————, *Gelächter von Aussen* (1966).
Grosz, George, *A Little Yes and a Big No* (1946).

Gumpert, Martin, *Hölle im Paradies* (1939).
Herzog, Wilhelm, *Menschen denen ich begegnete* (1959).
Heuss, Theodor, *Erinnerungen 1905–1933* (1963).
Hiller, Kurt, *Leben gegen die Zeit*, 2 vols (1969–73).
Hoelz, Max, *Vom Weissen Kreuz zur Roten Fahne* (1929).
Jäckh, Ernst, *Weltsaat, Erlebtes und Erstrebtes* (1960).
Jameson, Egon, *Berlin so wie es war* (1969).
Jung, Franz, *Weg nach Unten* (1961).
Kessler, Count Harry, *In the Twenties* (1971).
Koestler, Arthur, *Arrow in the Blue* (1952).
Kortner, Fritz, *Aller Tage Abend* (1959).
Krell, Max, *Das Alles gab es einmal* (1961).
Lania, Leo, *Today we are brothers* (1952)
Loerke, Oskar, *Tagebücher 1903–39* (1955).
Mann, Klaus, *The Turning Point* (1942).
Mann, Viktor, *Wir waren unser fünf: Bildnis der Familie Mann* (1949).
Marcuse, Ludwig, *Mein Zwanzigstes Jahrhundert* (1960).
Mayer, Gustav, *Erinnerungen* (1949).
Mehring, Walter, *Die verlorene Bibliothek* (1964).
Niekisch, Ernst, *Gewagtes Leben* (1958).
Osborn, Max, *Der bunte Spiegel* (1945).
PEM (Paul Erich Marcus), *Heimweh nach dem Kurfürstendamm* (1952).
Piper, Reinhard, *Mein Leben als Verleger* (1964).
Schoenberner, Franz, *Confessions of a European Intellectual* (1946).
—————————————, *The Inside Story of an Outsider* (1949).
Stolper, Toni, *Ein Leben im Brennpunkt unserer Zeit* (1960).
Tau, Max, *Das Land das ich verlassen musste* (1961).
Toller, Ernst, *Eine Jugend in Deutschland* (1933).
Victor, Walther, *Kehre wieder über die Berge* (1945).
Viertel, Salka, *The Kindness of Strangers* (1969).
Ullstein, Heinz, *Spielplatz meines Lebens* (1961).
Wolff, Kurt, *Autoren, Bücher, Abenteuer: Betrachtungen und Erinnerungen eines Verlegers* (1965).
Zuckmayer, Carl, *Als wär's ein Stück von mir* (1966).

MASS MEDIA

Bausch, Hans, *Der Rundfunk im politischen Kräftespiel der Weimarer Republik 1923–33* (1956).
Ermann, Hans, *August Scherl* (1954).
Koszyk, Kurt, *Zwischen Kaiserreich und Diktatur. Die sozialdemokratische Presse von 1914–1933* (1958).
—————————————, *Deutsche Presse*, III (1972).
Lerg, W. B., *Die Entstehung des Rundfunk in Deutschland* (1965).

de Mendelssohn, Peter, *Zeitungsstadt Berlin* (1959).
Osborn, Max, *50 Jahre Ullstein* (1927).
Pechel, Rudolf, *Die Deutsche Rundschau* (1961).
Pross, Harry, *Literatur und Politik* (1963).
Reichert, H. U., *Der Kampf um die Autonomie des deutschen Rundfunk* (1955).
Schlawe, Fritz , *Literarische Zeitschriften*, II; *1910–1933* (1962).

PERIODICALS

Die Aktion
Bücherkarren
Deutsche Republik
Deutsche Rundschau
Deutsches Volkstum
Der Gegner
Gesellschaft
Das Gewissen
Hilfe
Historische Zeitschrift
Hochland
Kölner Viertelsjahreshefte für Sozialwissenschaften
Kunstblatt
Kunstwart
Linkskurve
Literarische Welt
Melos
Neue Blätter für den Sozialismus
Neuer Merkur
Neue Rundschau
Preussische Jahrbücher
Querschnitt
Der Rote Aufbau
Schöne Literatur
Stimmen der Zeit
Der Sturm
Süddeutsche Monatshefte
Tagebuch
Tat
Die Weissen Blätter
Weltbühne
Zeitschrift für Politik
Zeitschrift für Sozialforschung
Zeitwende

Index

DATE DUE

OC 11 77			
OC 25 77			
AP 25 '84			
GAYLORD			PRINTED IN U.S.A.